Additional Praise for *Declining by Degrees*:

"Contributors do an excellent job . . . Because of its broad focus, the book will interest a wide range of readers, from educators and policy makers to parents concerned about their children's education."

—*Publishers Weekly*

"[B]efore your next child begins visiting campuses, we suggest studying *Declining by Degrees* . . . This single volume is an expansive reality check . . ."

—*Northeast Breeze*

"Anyone who cares deeply about American higher education will read this book and feel enlightened and enraged, delighted and despondent, encouraged and in despair. A 'must read' for those interested in both good news and bad, from higher education's influential insiders and jaded outsiders."

—Lee S. Shulman, President, The Carnegie Foundation for the Advancement of Teaching

"The decline of our once-proud colleges and universities—well documented in this book—is the bitter fruit of our ever-more ineffective K-12 education. This book makes it clear that our nation is still at risk."

—E. D. Hirsch, Jr., author of *Cultural Literacy and The Schools We Need*

Declining by Degrees: Higher Education at Risk

Edited by
Richard H. Hersh and John Merrow

Foreword by
Tom Wolfe

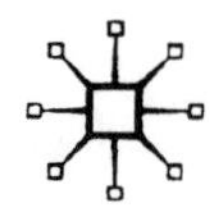

DECLINING BY DEGREES

First published in hardcover in 2005 by Palgrave Macmillan
First PALGRAVE MACMILLAN™ paperback edition: May 2006
175 Fifth Avenue, New York, N.Y. 10010 and
Houndmills, Basingstoke, Hampshire, England RG21 6XS.
Companies and representatives throughout the world.

PALGRAVE MACMILLAN is the global academic imprint of the Palgrave Macmillan division of St. Martin's Press, LLC and of Palgrave Macmillan Ltd. Macmillan® is a registered trademark in the United States, United Kingdom and other countries. Palgrave is a registered trademark in the European Union and other countries.

ISBN 1–4039–7316–4

Library of Congress Cataloging-in-Publication Data

Declining by degrees : higher education at risk / edited by Richard Hersh and John Merrow ; foreword by Tom Wolfe.
p. cm.
Includes index.
ISBN hardback 1–4039–6921–3
ISBN paperback 1–4039–7316–4
1. Education, Higher—United States. I. Hersh, Richard H., 1942– II. Merrow, John.

LA227.4.D45 2005
378.73—dc22 2005043024

A catalogue record for this book is available from the British Library.

Design by Newgen Imaging Systems (P) Ltd., Chennai, India.

First PALGRAVE MACMILLAN paperback edition: May 2006

10 9 8 7 6 5 4 3 2 1

Printed in the United States of America.

Contents

Acknowledgments

The book you are holding in your hand and the companion PBS documentary began quite innocently, when the distinguished documentarian Robert Frye, a mutual friend, introduced us. We discovered that both of us were curious and concerned about the state of American higher education. We knew that higher education was generally seen as the crown jewel of our system of education, but that compliment, it occurred to us, was a classic case of damning with faint praise, given the state of K–12 schooling.

That sense of faint praise gave us a question to try to answer. However, we might not have moved beyond our conversations over coffee had it not been for the support of dozens of key individuals and six foundations. First among our tutors was the late Frank Newman, who gave freely of his time and energy and provided what amounted to an ongoing tutorial for our production team. We dedicate this effort to his memory.

Others provided valuable insights and perspectives: Franklyn L. Rogers, Patricia Albjerg Graham, Russ Edgerton, Lee Shulman, Pat Hutchings, and Ray Bacchetti of the Carnegie Foundation for the Advancement of Teaching, which provided a home for one of us during this project, Kay McClenney, Byron McClenney, Steven Brint, Gordon Winston, Sister Joel Read, Pat Callan, George Kuh, Derek Bok, Vince Tinto, Clara Lovett, Margaret Miller, William Tierney, Sandy Shugart, George Boggs, Carol Twigg, Richard Lapchick, James Duderstadt, Diane Halpern, Rachel Toor, Katherine Cohen, Carole Gitnik, Larry Faulkner, Tom Kane, Tom Bailey, Robert Zemsky, Yolanda Moses, Andrea Leskes, Katie Haycock, Cliff Adelman, Burton Clark, Sandy Astin, and Kevin Kruger.

The Spencer Foundation was the first to give us a vote of confidence in the form of a grant. Other foundations followed suit, most notably the Lumina Foundation for Education. Our program officer at Lumina, Susan Conner, thoughtfully provided part of the grant in the form of a challenge, a tactic that helped persuade other foundations, including the W. K. Kellogg Foundation, the Bill and Melinda Gates Foundation, the Park Foundation, the Christian A. Johnson Endeavor Foundation, and the William and Flora Hewlett Foundation, to support the endeavor.

Our essayists received a small check for their efforts, insufficient payment for their brilliance. We hope that this public expression of our deep gratitude will begin to reduce our debt to them. We also are indebted to our editor, Amanda Johnson, who did not even receive a small check from us but worked tirelessly to make this book a reality.

Our colleagues at Learning Matters, our television production company, worked long and hard to produce the PBS documentary. Kudos to Carrie Glasser, David Wald, John Heus, Hillary Kolos, and Shae Isaacs.

In a very real sense, neither the documentary nor the book would have come to pass had it not been for the generosity and openness of the four college presidents, Tony Marx of Amherst, Christine Johnson of Community College of Denver, Peter Likins of the University of Arizona, and Gary Ransdell of Western Kentucky University. Although all four leaders knew that we would be digging deeply and, at least occasionally, asking embarrassing questions, their commitment to truth did not waver. We salute them.

Most important, a special acknowledgment for the women in our lives, Judith Meyers and Joan Lonergan, who graciously put up with the usual time and authorial demands on Richard and John respectively. But more than that, each provided wise guidance throughout the writing and editing process in ways that only have improved the final product. We, of course, absolve them of any responsibility for whatever mistakes that may be contained herein.

Foreword

Tom Wolfe

In the spring of 1988, not long after publishing a book called *The Bonfire of the Vanities*, which among other things had to do with the *Gelt*rush of Yale and Harvard graduates to Wall Street investment banking firms to lay hands on the stupendous incomes suddenly available to even the newest hirelings, I was invited to Harvard to speak to a group of seniors. Quite a large group, as it turned out. I have no memory of what my message was that day, and I don't entertain the delusion that they do, either. But there is one thing I will never forget; namely, what they looked like . . . as they sat before me . . . row after row of the very flowers of American undergraduate education. They were all dressed like nine-year-olds.

Flip-flops, shorts, jeans, creaseless khakis, Heavy Metal *in medias mosh* T-shirts, sweatshirts, sweatshirts with hoods, hooded windbreakers, sneakers, elf boots, platypus-toed sandals, baseball caps, baseball caps worn backwards, baseball caps worn sideways, crunchy-crafted home-strung necklaces with as-found stone pendants polished smooth by waves, tectonic plate shifts or other environmental forces, the occasional collared shirt—always worn with the shirt-tails flopping out over the pants, gaudy cheap cotton bandanas rolled up and worn as headbands, surfer-girl hair hanging down below the shoulder blades, clotted unwashed never-parted rumpus-weed Huck Finn hair that made one think of dirt behind the ears, wristbands plaited out of string . . . which is to say, as I was to learn later, they looked like practically every other assemblage of undergraduates in the United States.

This was no small matter, not to me. I have been accused of being obsessed, in writing as well as in life, with clothes. Well, Balzac was accused of having an obsession with furniture. The best-known French critic of the nineteenth century, Saint Beuve, once wrote, "If this man

Balzac is so obsessed with furniture, why doesn't he open up a furniture shop and spare us all these novels that crush one under the sheer accumulation of Recamier sofas and tables of English oak and Bourbon Louis bergeres and what-not?" But Balzac knew that the furniture one chose for the interior decoration of her salon was a door that opened upon her secrets concerning who she thought she was and where she hoped to be on the social ladder.

And here they were before me, Harvard seniors dressed like nine-year-olds. My daughter was eight that year, and my son was three. Both of them and their little friends were dressed in a more grown-up fashion than these offsprings of Mother Harvard—who were no doubt about to go forth and get the aforementioned jobs on Wall Street or go to law school and medical school and, in general, have their pick of whatever was available for college students graduating in the year 1988. As I approached the lectern, I couldn't help but ask myself, "Do their parents have any idea of what's happened to them?"

But that wasn't the way I put it as I reached the microphone and had their attention. Instead, I said, "You know, I come from a town, New York City, where families are rated according to whether or not their children get into Harvard. But I have never met a single parent—not one—who has ever shown the slightest curiosity about what happens to them once they get here or what they may have become by the time they graduate. So I am delighted by this opportunity to meet you. Perhaps I'll find out for myself."

Getting into Harvard! The pandemic known as college mania had just begun to show its true virulence that year. Parents in large cities and many smaller ones had begun succumbing in droves to the mad compulsion to cover their families with glory by getting their children into the very best colleges as rated each fall by *U.S. News & World Report*.

The matter of how this third-rate news magazine, forever swallowing the dust from the feet of *Time* and *Newsweek*, managed to jack itself up to the eminence of ringmaster of American college education, forcing both parents and college administrators to jump through their hoops and rings of fire, is a long and perfectly ludicrous story that would inevitably reduce one to helpless laughter and distract us from the matter at hand. In any event, the result was that parents caught up in the madness of it all—and, as I say, it had become, and remains, a pandemic—were utterly consumed by a single passion: *getting in* . . . getting their children into a college whose name would go *bingo!* in every listener's head . . . preferably Harvard, or, if not Harvard, Yale; or, if not Yale, Princeton; or, if not Harvard, Yale, or Princeton, then. . . .

On and on raged the fever. *Getting in!* Getting in became the be-all and the end-all. All else—education, character (a word that had become as anachronistic at colleges as cohabitation), conceptual thinking, work discipline, God, Freedom, and Immortality (Kant's trinity)—all else was a mopping up operation. Get your puppy *in*! That was the main idea. Pay literally tens of thousands of dollars to tutors who promise (and deliver) an additional hundred points, at least, to the child's SAT score! Nag friends of college trustees to jimmy letters of recommendation out of them! (Does no good.) Dangle vast prospective donations before the administrators! (Seldom works unless the offer is in units, "unit" being Texas talk for a hundred million dollars. . . .) Turn your children into public service freaks in their junior year of high school! (Effect: marginal to nil.) Hire coaches to work one on one with the kid to turn him into a fabulous athlete in some minor sport! (The problem: he actually has to wind up fabulous. . . .)

What parent had any energy or perseverance left to be concerned about the aftermath, namely, the ensuing four years of "education"? I have never heard a single parent speculate about what value might be added by those four undergraduate years, other than the bachelor's degree itself, which is an essential punch on the ticket for starting off in any upscale career.

The book before you is, to my knowledge, the first to confront the question head-on. All those boys and girls . . . do parents—does anybody—have any idea what happens to them in college?

Dedicated to
Frank Newman (1922–2004)
Friend and Mentor

Introduction

Richard H. Hersh and John Merrow

Higher education, long viewed as the crown jewel of American education, is tarnished. As the thoughtful essays in this book make clear, the many problems are complex, but they can be solved.

This book is not alone in sounding an alarm, of course. Numerous reports in the last decade have pointed to a decline in the quality of undergraduate education. The National Association of Alumni and Trustees condemned a lack of any reasonable set of college requirements, especially in history, literature, math, science, and writing. The Association of American Colleges and Universities (AAC&U), representing more than one thousand institutions, recently concluded a three-year study on the quality of college education and found that undergraduate education in this country is significantly underperforming.

What makes this volume different, and perhaps unique, is the variety of perspectives. We invited a variety of well-informed men and women, most of them from outside the academy, to examine higher education from their particular vantage point. Thus we have journalists, a pollster, a novelist, social scientists, college presidents, professors, and foundation officers reflecting on what may be our most essential enterprise.

American higher education consists of about 3,400 institutions, but it will never be confused with a "system." Higher education in this country, unlike in Europe, for example, is not one unified entity—indeed autonomy is prized. About 1,200 of these are two-year institutions. At this writing, nearly 15 million students are enrolled in colleges and universities, some full time, some part time, some living in dorms, and others living in their own homes or apartments. About 45 percent are of "traditional" age (eighteen to twenty-two), but today the median age is twenty-nine. Higher education is both democratic and elite; some institutions accept any applicant who is over the age of fifteen, while a handful of colleges rejects eight out of every ten applicants. Every year about 2 million degrees are granted, and more than 80 percent of graduates immediately enter the workplace. Higher education is also big business. It employs about 3 million people, including 575,000 full-time faculty members and untold numbers of part-time teachers. In all, it is about a $250 billion enterprise.

Its history is a proud one. Bill Gates and a few others may have succeeded without completing college, but they are exceptions, not the rule. Our colleges and universities have educated most of the country's national leaders and technical, managerial, and professional workforce. Its capacity for basic research has given the world such inventions and developments as the Internet and molecular biology constructs that inform new miracle drug formulations. Without our crown jewel, the United States would never have achieved and maintained economic and technological preeminence.

But that preeminence is in question. Other countries no longer send their "best and brightest" to be educated here. If they do, they may insist that the graduates return to the homeland. In recent years, athletic scandals, increasing abuse of alcohol and other drugs, grade inflation, escalating costs, and dissatisfaction with the competence of college graduates have tarnished higher education's reputation. Scandals aside, we sought to ask a deeper and more important question about learning: What, we wanted to know, actually happens between admission and graduation? How much "deep learning" occurs? And when it does not, who should be held responsible?

As we began our early planning for the documentary and book project in the year 2000, we met with dozens of thoughtful observers and asked their help in identifying the most salient issues facing higher education. From those conversations we developed a potential list of authors for this volume. Later as we crisscrossed the country filming on campuses, it became increasingly clear that something in undergraduate education was seriously amiss. We found an insidious erosion of quality that we now believe places this nation at risk. The threat, it seems to us, is more serious today than it was in 1983, when the famous "A Nation at Risk" report warned that our schools were "drowning in a rising tide of mediocrity." Our K–12 system, although somewhat improved from that time, continues to wallow in mediocrity, and now higher education is suffering from the same condition. The tide continues to rise, the rot is creeping upward, and time is running out.

Readers of this volume may, of course, read essays in the order of their choosing. We have arranged them in a way that introduces readers to the issues via a wide-angle lens and then zooms in on a variety of essential issues. But the volume now belongs to you.

At our request, Gene Maeroff, former national education correspondent for the *New York Times*, and Deborah Wadsworth, former president of the public opinion research organization, Public Agenda, wrote analyses of public perceptions of higher education and media coverage. These chapters appear first in this volume because they provide sweeping views. The media has given higher education a "free pass," as Maeroff explains in chapter 1. In chapter 2, Wadsworth notes how the public seems concerned only about costs but otherwise has also given higher education a free pass. By virtue of much turnover and lack of training, most reporters simply do not pay attention to this beat.

Jim Fallows of the *Atlantic Monthly* and Jay Mathews of the *Washington Post*, however, are two journalists who have followed the education story for years. Fallows, in chapter 3, and Mathews, in chapter 4, dig deeply into particular aspects of the academy: admissions and curriculum. What they report may surprise readers.

If media myopia is widespread, what stories are not being reported? College rankings and ratings like those found in *U.S. News & World Report* and myriad guidebooks have lulled most into a comforting belief that all is well on college campuses. Yet there are few reliable measures of what students actually learn or are able to do *because* they attended a particular college or university. Relatively naïve conjecture fills the vacuum.

In chapter 5, Carol Schneider, president of AAC&U, frames the issue of quality: Given the heightened importance of higher education to our nation, we ought to be asking fundamental questions about quality and equity. Because we do not debate the ends and means of higher education, suggests Schneider, we are "slip-sliding" into a conception of education that is too narrow in scope. We are defining education as job preparation and nothing more. In chapter 6, Vartan Gregorian, former president of Brown University and current president of Carnegie Corporation of New York, eloquently criticizes our mass higher education system for taking a "Home Depot" approach that fails to differentiate between consumption and digestion, or between information and learning.

Money, and the lure of money, attracts the attention of several essayists. As he states in chapter 7, Howard Gardner, Harvard professor of education, believes that colleges and universities have become cross-eyed, with one eye focused on the financial status of the institution and the other on the *desires* of the student. Such vision pushes out of sight what should be the primary goal of the academy: authentic education. David Kirp, professor of public policy at University of California, Berkeley, writes in chapter 8 that higher education's soul may already have been sold: "What is new, and troubling, is the raw power that money exerts in higher education. . . . Nowhere in the university is this market mentality more on display than in the luring, caring, and feeding—and almost incidentally the educating—of undergraduates." He notes that more splendiferous residence halls, tennis courts, student unions, and athletic facilities add little value to serious learning.

In chapter 9, Murray Sperber, professor emeritus of English, Indiana University, traces the growth of research and other funding and its impact on the academy. The pursuit of research funding—whatever its source—has changed higher education for the worse. Today, he writes, "A non-aggression pact exists between many faculty members and students: Because the former believe that they must spend most of their time doing research, and the latter often prefer to pass their time having fun, a mutual nonaggression pact occurs with each side agreeing not to impinge on the other. The glue that keeps the pact intact is grade inflation: easy As for merely acceptable work and Bs for mediocre work."

We invited a number of writers, including Frank Deford, Arthur Levine, Roberto Suro, Richard Fry, and Heather Wathington, to address specific subjects, such as sports and race. In chapter 10, novelist and *Sports Illustrated* senior editor Frank Deford takes on athletics. "Big-Time Sports" and the myriad privileges that are afforded athletes corrupt the very purpose of higher education, he says. Deford argues that we have our priorities wrong. "How can anyone rationally argue that a baseball player should get a college scholarship, but a piano player should not? What does it say about a college's regard for art, literature, drama, and music if the finest young painters, writers, actors, and musicians are not eligible for the same rewards as are athletes?"

Coincidentally, in our research for this project, we spent many hours with Frank Newman, former president of the Education Commission of the States and author of the 1971 Newman Report on Higher Education, talking about such key issues as access, cost, and retention. Insightful, caustic, and yet always optimistic, Frank told us that big-time sports were, in effect, the canary in the mine for higher education. It is not only a story in itself, he said, but it is a warning to the rest of the system. Sports may have gone over the waterfall already, Newman believed, but the rest of the system does not have to follow. But in many ways, the system has begun to follow and become corrupted by more than sports.

From Arthur Levine's perspective, presented in chapter 11, students are higher education's customers, and he finds the academy paying scant attention to the notion that "the customer is always right." What the faculty wants is often at odds with what students want, and Levine, the president of Teachers College, New York, finds that at most institutions what faculty want comes first. The mismatch is profound: Students want to see their professors, who would rather do research. Students want courses taught by full professors but are likely to find a graduate student leading their class. Students, particularly part-time students, want courses in the evening, but that cuts into the professors' family time. Will the academy bend? It had better, Levine warns, because "*Tyrannosaurus rex* was once an outstanding brand name."

The issues of race and social class seem to matter more to three of our essayists than they apparently do for the academy. Roberto Suro and Richard Fry, director of and senior associate at the Pew Hispanic Center respectively, write persuasively in chapter 12 about Hispanic students, the fastest-growing college-going population in the United States. As they note, Latinos who finish high school pursue postsecondary studies at the same rate as whites, but in almost every other respect, the numbers are depressing: graduation, the kinds of institution attended, and academic attainment. In chapter 13, Heather Wathington, assistant professor of education at the University of Virginia, examines the gap between the rhetoric of most of higher education and the reality. Many pledge their commitment to diversity but, as Wathington notes, they fail to "walk the walk." Higher education's collective failures contribute to widening income and education gaps between Latinos and blacks and all other segments of the population.

Some problems are not higher education's fault. Julie Johnson Kidd suggests in chapter 14 that we have let students down long before they began filling out applications. We sell higher education as the only route to a "good job," we emphasize developing "networks for success" after college, and we talk about "the credential" and "the diploma," while rarely engaging in conversations about education or learning. Kidd, who has been providing foundation funds to colleges and universities for a quarter century at the Christian Johnson Endeavor Foundation, says we need leadership from the academy to help correct this problem but at the moment there is an ongoing "lack of vision, imagination, and boldness when we evaluate ways to improve our institutions of higher learning."

In chapter 15, Leon Botstein, president of Bard College, maintains that our colleges and universities have never succeeded in making the life of the mind and love of learning the centerpiece of campus culture. What dominates (and perhaps suffocates) intellectual life for students are the "extracurriculars" of campus life: sports and drinking are at the top of that list. He lays the blame for this disregard for the intellect at the doorsteps of faculty and administration. The faculty's primary loyalty is neither to students nor to their institutions, but instead to their disciplines. As for administrators, their quest for revenue and national attention leads Botstein to conclude that a "big business" mentality has overtaken higher education.

The decline in the quality of American undergraduate education has not yet become a major public issue. Americans may be cynical about their public institutions and public leaders, but their skepticism does not extend to the nature and content of a college education. Most students—and the public as a whole—assume without question that the subjects they choose to study in college do not really matter because they will learn what they need to know for today's competitive and complex environment. They accept, apparently unthinkingly, the existence of a one-to-one relationship between college and work, as if the entire purpose of going to college were to enable graduates to "get a good job." It is as if they somehow believe they will be working twenty-four hours a day.

The result of this mentality (we are resisting the temptation to label it "mental illness") is graduates who are narrowly educated—and often are "trained" for work in fields that will have changed before the ink on their diplomas is dry. These graduates have scant understanding of civic responsibilities or of the possibilities of life beyond work. Accumulating a sufficient number of courses and credit hours to earn a college degree is, in the public mind, synonymous with being educated. But having a diploma bears little resemblance to being educated. "Higher" education has been lowered.

This is not to say that all is wrong on American campuses. Indeed, much is right. Access to higher education (an essential part of the American Dream) has in fact advanced significantly in the past fifty years, but that success has only raised the bar, creating a new and higher standard for equitable access that is yet to be achieved. Concerned about the high number of students leaving college after only one year—it can reach 30 percent—many campuses are tackling the problem of retention, often with success. Campuses have created "learning communities" in which students take the same courses and live in the same dormitory, which provides them frequent opportunities to learn together and to "bond" with each other and their college.

Significant curricular change has taken place during the past quarter century, legitimately responding to advances in knowledge and to the demands of students. New disciplines and interdisciplinary programs abound. The new pedagogies of engagement—having students become actively engaged in their learning rather than being passive recipients of lectures—are beginning to take hold. Both civic engagement and community service have become well-established norms on most campuses. Advances in computer technology mean that not only the campus library but also the entire world of knowledge can be on every student's laptop.

We are writing this before completing the filming for our documentary, but in the more than three hundred hours of videotape we have profound examples of the power of higher education, at its best, to transform lives. We interviewed a woman in community college who, at age twenty-nine, now feels that she has "a free pass" to learn anything and everything; a mother at fourteen and a high school dropout, she now can see herself as a college graduate, a business owner, and a contributing member of society.

But ask fifty students in an upper-division university course in macroeconomics how many hours they study on a typical day, and you discover that more than half of them spend only an hour or less getting ready for all their classes! "We do what we have to do," one says. And these students say they have grade point averages well over 3.0.

In vivid contrast, a determined student at that same university holds down a full-time job, working the night shift at an automotive assembly plant, while also taking a full load of courses. She studies three hours a day and sleeps in snatches whenever she can.

Teaching runs the gamut as well: One professor gives all of his students "touch pads" so that he can quiz them during his lectures to find out whether he's getting through. If they are not getting it, he finds new ways to make his points clear.

But a colleague at that same university admits that she is teaching to only 25 of the 250 students in her class because the others do not do the reading, and another lecturer drones on, reading from old notes while many of his students sleep, exchange instant messages, and read newspapers.

The vacuum created by the sterile atmosphere inevitably will be filled, as any vacuum must be. Too often alcohol is the diversion of choice on campuses. This very night we are filming at a campus bar on the day of the week known on this campus as "Boozeday," which the rest of us know as Tuesday. It is not a pretty picture.

We have learned that the best in higher education, which we have seen on all our campuses and which has been affirmed by our essayists, occurs all too infrequently. What exists is, to be blunt, simply not adequate for twenty-first-century America. Too many—if not most—students are being poorly served. Undergraduate education is paradoxically both suffering from and simultaneously causing serious student *underachievement*. Students arrive at college less intellectually and emotionally well prepared than ever before, candidates for remediation. In response, higher education has lowered its expectations and changed its priorities. The academy seems to have constructed a new social contract with too many students: "If you don't bother us, we won't bother you." The end result, unfortunately, is that many students are leaving college with degrees declining in quality. American colleges and universities are essentially cheating their undergraduates, failing them educationally. This situation has clear implications for America's civic and economic future.

As critical as this conclusion may sound, it is meant to be a loving critique. Colleges and universities are crucial to both individual and societal development, but the *promise* of higher education needs to be more than an I.O.U.

The purpose of *Declining by Degrees*, both the PBS documentary and this volume, is to sound an alert and encourage a national conversation about higher education. No longer can our colleges and universities be allowed to drift in a sea of mediocrity. The stakes are high, but we know that many Americans want the crown jewel of our system restored to its former glory. This can be done. It *must* be done.

1

The Media: Degrees of Coverage

Gene I. Maeroff

Professors who study news coverage are fond of content analysis. One approach calls for measuring articles by column inches. Or, in the case of broadcast journalism, counting the number of minutes devoted to a particular topic. This is a crude form of analysis, but it bears some connection to the real world. A comparison of the coverage of higher education and K–12 education, for example, would almost certainly conclude that the space and time that the media devote to colleges and universities pales by comparison with that lavished on elementary and secondary schools. This is so for five reasons.

1. More Americans have an active link to K–12 schools than to higher education and, presumably, have more interest in K–12.
2. Taxpayers plow much more money into elementary and secondary schools, and have soaring property tax bills to show for it.
3. The news media perceive the issues in K–12 as more compelling—and therefore more worthy of coverage.
4. The media fail to see higher education as a landscape rich in story ideas and instead tend to focus on a few predictable subjects, giving far less attention to issues of teaching and learning.
5. This is the way it has always been, and the status quo counts for a great deal in journalism.

These truths add up to a situation in which higher education, surely among society's most valued public goods, escapes scrutiny by the media, one of the few forces with the authority to question the quality of a college or university education. Given higher education's social and economic importance to individuals and to the nation, one hopes that journalism will begin to take its responsibility as an agent for accountability more seriously. Yet the reasons why this has not happened are abundantly clear.

When it comes to the size of the enterprise, it is not surprising that journalists deem precollegiate education worthy of more coverage than higher education. After all, the number of students (53.8 million vs. 15.9 million), institutions (100,000 vs. 3,500), and teachers (3.5 million vs. 1.9 million) in elementary and secondary classrooms dwarfs colleges and universities. Such factors help determine news coverage—the size of the potential audience in terms of those affected and those interested in a subject. News organizations simply do not think that colleges and universities warrant the degree of coverage given to elementary and secondary schools.

As for expenditures, the best advice comes from the film character Jerry Maguire: Follow the dollars. If you ran along the money trail, you would see that precollegiate education is a monstrous $500 billion-a-year enterprise. That is the major part of state and local government expenditures. In most locales, the largest portion of property tax supports K–12 education.

How do schools spend this money? Do they adhere to high standards? What do the taxpayers get for their investment? The pursuit of answers to such questions drives the coverage of elementary and secondary education. Journalists quickly conjure up a plethora of possible articles fraught with the tension and conflict so attractive to the media: Why don't students score higher on tests? Why don't teachers do a better job? Why are members of school boards always squabbling? Why aren't reading, math, and almost every other subject taught better?

Journalists could ask similar questions about higher education, but they usually do not. They act as if it were an article of faith that America's higher education is the best in the world—almost beyond criticism—while considering precollegiate education seriously flawed and, therefore, ripe for scrutiny. The image of a supposedly high-quality system of higher education, operating with the precision of a fine engine, seems to awe journalists. Like most Americans, journalists do not see past the ivy.

Higher education's weaknesses and shortcomings remain largely out of sight to reporters, many of whom are quick to seize on almost any foible at the elementary and secondary level. In other words, higher education is Teflon-coated, remarkably immune to criticism.[1] It is easier to assume that when students do not succeed at colleges and universities, it is because high schools have not prepared them properly, not due to any deficiency on the part of institutions of higher education. Charles B. Reed of California State University and Edward B. Rust of the Business Higher Education Forum think that institutions of higher education can make themselves more accountable by defining their goals and providing evidence that they have met them.[2] Surely such steps would lead to more transparency in judging quality.

The implementation of the federal government's No Child Left Behind Act, however flawed it may be, forced journalists who cover elementary and secondary schools to delve into achievement as never before. Higher education has no analog to that law, though the renewal of the Higher Education Act could contain language that may compel colleges and universities to divulge a great deal more information than they do now about various performance indicators.

Journalists have shied away from using their power to examine how well institutions of higher education discharge the responsibility of educating their students, particularly undergraduates. Instead, similar stories, repeated over and over, dominate the coverage. Not counting college athletics, which is in a class by itself, the big two are tuition and admissions.

The news media convey the impression that nearly every college costs a potentate's fortune and that most institutions are so selective that only super-students need apply. "Reporters stalking and reporting on a handful of highly selective colleges have created serious anxiety that has incrementally escalated at the family dinner table and in high school corridors," according to two people who have served as admissions officers at elite colleges. They go on to say that students and parents "quite naturally (and mistakenly) infer that getting into any college, and paying for it, will be cause for frenzy."[3]

Coverage of this sort helps feed the public's misconceptions. In a 2003 poll by the U.S. Department of Education, 65 percent of students and 58 percent of their parents could not estimate yearly tuition costs or overestimated tuition by at least 25 percent. Those from the poorest families were least likely to know the cost of going to college.[4] The facts, according to College Board, are these: Average tuition and fees in the 2003–2004 academic year were $4,694 at four-year public institutions and $1,905 at community colleges. In the sector of the country with the lowest tuitions and fees, the West, the comparable figures were $3,737 at four-year institutions and $1,007 at two-year institutions.[5] These amounts are not the formidable obstacles that the media lead the public to believe. Of course, it costs a lot to go to Harvard, Stanford, Sarah Lawrence, and Duke. But these institutions are private and not typical.

Yet newspapers perpetuate distortions with such articles as the one distributed in August 2004 by Associated Press, which reported that colleagues of Tom Ridge expected him to resign after the November election.[6] His associates said he needed to find a higher-paying job so as to afford impending college tuitions for his two teenagers. Ridge's government salary as head of Homeland Security was $175,000. The article went on to deplore what it called the crisis in college costs.

As for admissions, a large number of postsecondary institutions admit virtually all applicants and exert no selectivity whatsoever. Only 8 percent of all four-year institutions accept fewer than 50 percent of their applicants. Half accept from 50 to 80 percent of their applicants, and the rest—fully 42 percent—accept at least four of every five applicants.[7] Community colleges, which 40 percent of first-year undergraduates attend, have open admissions. Yet daily newspapers act as if the nation's more than one thousand community colleges barely exist, seldom noting their open admissions and low tuition policies, and barely mentioning their academic programs. Journalists find Brown University eminently more fascinating than Northern Virginia Community College.

In an essay on the editorial page of the *New York Times* in June 2004, one of the newspaper's editorial writers reflected on his conversations with classmates at the fiftieth reunion of his graduating class from the elite Exeter Academy. He described how much easier it was to get into Exeter in the 1950s and how the school's graduates at the time could almost assume they would win entry to Harvard, Yale, and Princeton.[8] These thoughts led to the obligatory discussion of how difficult it has become to gain admission to Exeter and to highly selective colleges—yet the writer did not acknowledge that this kind of exclusivity does not figure in the experiences of the vast majority of Americans.

I mentioned sports coverage. The media are obsessed with sports and it is no wonder given that the American public—or at least the male portion—is consumed by sports. Editors think they give readers and viewers what they want with this gargantuan coverage, and perhaps they do. It would be grand, though, if only 10 percent of the space devoted to college and university athletics were converted to coverage of substantive academic issues at the institutions mentioned on the sports pages. Alas, this is not apt to happen.

It is hard to get newspapers to alter their ways. The industry is steeped in tradition. Of course, not everything has remained the same. Production methods for newspapers have changed vastly since the 1960s. Cold type has replaced hot type, banishing linotype machines to museums. Reporters use cell phones to communicate with the city desk from the field, and they write stories on laptops without returning to the office. Yet the news itself, or what constitutes news, has changed less than other parts of the business.

The issue therefore is how the media can foment a national discussion about quality in higher education, looking at more than whether colleges and universities adequately prepare legions of employees for business, industry, and the professions. How often do stories from the campuses overturn conventional wisdom to probe and challenge the very purposes of higher education?

Journalists—and, for reasons I will explain, basically I am talking about those who work for newspapers—need to focus more on questions of quality at colleges and universities, just as they are inclined to do in reporting on elementary and secondary schools. I submit that such a shift requires more sufficient coverage of higher education and better judgment by news organizations about which stories to cover.

How can we tell when and if higher education gets sufficient coverage? It's a tough call. Partisans in most fields do not feel that coverage is sufficient for the topic that they champion. Higher education is hardly sui generis in this respect. Consider issues in transportation, health, science, technology, labor, and the environment, to mention just a few subjects. Public discussion in all of these areas is woefully handicapped by the news media's scant coverage. It is a fact, for instance, that until 9/11, the news media had gradually reduced coverage of foreign affairs. Furthermore, news organizations assign far fewer reporters to cover the state government than in former years. Here are some questions, particular to higher education, that one might ask to determine if the public is sufficiently informed:

- Do people know enough to carry on cogent discussions of such topics as tenure, admissions standards, financial aid policies, affirmative action, academic pedagogy, and how students choose their majors?
- Can they evaluate the fiscal policies of their state legislatures in regard to allocations for higher education and the connection to quality of outcomes?
- How does the public make decisions about quality at colleges and universities?
- Can people pose solid questions about the worth and purpose of a college degree?

The other half of this equation involves the news judgment of reporters and editors and their ability to identify the most worthwhile story possibilities. Journalists on the beat ought to develop mental maps of the higher education terrain, recognizing where to situate their priorities. News people who parachute into a higher education story only occasionally are not apt to be able to make keen judgments about what to cover and how to cover it. Their coverage becomes largely reactive—dealing with ephemeral issues. Reporters and editors involved in higher education coverage should ensure that enough of the kinds of stories that the public needs to be sufficiently informed about issues of quality find their way into the paper or onto the tube. Supervising editors should be able to stand up and argue at the daily story conferences of their news organizations on behalf of such articles. Such a shift in approach would imply that those involved in higher education coverage have the confidence that comes from deep familiarity with a subject.

As I pointed out earlier, improved coverage of higher education, if it comes, will have to arise primarily from the print media. Commercial television, the source of news for most Americans, is addicted to the trivial and the inconsequential. Broadcasters dispense a surfeit of coverage about Scott Peterson, Michael Jackson (not to mention his sister Janet), Britney Spears, and other personalities posing for what Andy Warhol called their fifteen minutes of fame. Such stories, masquerading as news, consume space that news organizations might devote to matters of substance. Coverage of this sort insidiously undermines the ability of the public—especially younger viewers—to distinguish between real news and garbage.

Amusing viewers has grown more important than informing them. I like the way that David Shaw, the media critic of the *Los Angeles Times*, puts it when he casts his practiced eyes on this alarming phenomenon. He talks of the "four horsemen of the journalistic apocalypse: superficiality, sensationalism, preoccupation with celebrity, and obsession with the bottom line."[9] These four horsemen trample over intelligent, informed coverage of higher education and other topics of consequence.

Even coverage of politics, once regarded as a matter of gravitas, has been rendered the stuff of amusement. Look at Jay Leno, David Letterman, Dennis Miller, Jon Stewart, Al Franken, and Bill Maher—comedians all. And now they are America's experts when it comes to politics—commanding audiences far larger than those who provide serious punditry. Comedy shows were a prime source of information about politics for tens of millions of Americans during the election campaign of 2004. *Newsday*'s television critic observes that "CNN covers the news and Fox puts on entertainment shows in which news is a component."[10] Pity poor Jim Lehrer.

One must understand the inner workings of the news media and the pressures on reporters on the higher education beat to see how difficult it will be to get even the more serious print media to cover issues of quality in higher education. Consider the circumstances under which reporters, including those who cover colleges and universities, work. Many simply do not get enough time to produce articles. Moreover, some news organizations subject reporters to a quota system requiring them to turn in a specified number of stories a day, or a week. It is as if they are pressing pants at a dry cleaner's. How much time does such a journalist, however talented, have to explore questions of quality in higher education?

Think about the implications of these limitations: there isn't ample time to grasp the details of some of the more complicated stories. Journalists operating under such restrictions gravitate toward what they can comprehend and sum up easily and quickly. No wonder higher education coverage features articles about admissions and tuitions. These are relatively simple stories: Fill in the blanks, print the numbers, and shake up the reader.

One must also consider the turnover on the higher education beat, even at the leading news organizations, as a factor affecting coverage. The Hechinger Institute on Education and the Media offers an annual seminar for those who cover higher education. Let us look back to 1999 and some of the reporters who were on the beat and attended the seminar that Hechinger, based at Teachers College, Columbia University, sponsored at that time: Many of them are no longer reporting on higher education. And, remember, most dailies do not even maintain a higher education beat, instead leaving the episodic coverage to general assignment reporters, the Jacks and Jills of all trades.

Some of these journalists moved to different jobs at the same newspapers; some relocated to other papers; some left journalism altogether. An indication of the challenge of improving coverage is the fact that during one recent period of almost twelve months, the higher education post at the *Miami Herald* went unfilled. I am pleased to note, though, that a few of those who attended the 1999 seminar were still pursuing higher education coverage in 2004—Karen Arenson of the *New York Times*, Tanya Schevitz of the *San Francisco Chronicle*, and Kelly Heyboer of the *Star-Ledger* in Newark, for example.

Whether one's assignment is K–12 schools or higher education, it takes time to become a good beat reporter—to know the issues, the context, the history, and the contacts. Moving journalists, no matter how skilled they are, through this beat as if they were caught in a revolving door is not the way to do it. They simply cannot cover higher education the way it ought to be covered. Their lack of knowledge about the field undoubtedly makes some of those involved in covering colleges and universities reluctant to grapple with questions of quality.

Editors exacerbate the problem when they look at reporters as fungibles, no different from potatoes in a sack, one interchangeable with another. Everyone on the staff attended college, according to this kind of reasoning, so why would they not know all they need to know to cover higher education? Interestingly, editors don't regard all beats this way. Not just anyone is sent to the symphony to review a concert or assigned to write a complicated science story. Newspapers sometimes do recognize expertise. It would be good to get editors to appreciate the need for sustained specialization in the coverage of higher education, but the struggle will be a lengthy one. And forget about television; most news staffs are simply too small for specialization.

Moreover, as matters stand, journalists—including those who cover higher education—do not get all that much respect. The *Chronicle of Higher Education* ran the results of a survey by the Association of Governing Boards that asked the public how much confidence they had in society's various institutions. When it came to "a great deal of confidence," 65 percent had it in the military (which ranked first), 51 percent had that level of confidence in four-year private colleges and universities, 48 percent in the local police, 46 percent in four-year public colleges and universities, and 43 percent in community colleges. And so it went right down the list to 18 percent in local government, 17 percent in television news, 16 percent in newspapers, all the way down to 6 percent in large corporations.[11] And when one looks at the internal pecking order in the media, many beats command more respect than education. This fact may explain the inclination of many editors to treat education as a starting beat for younger, less seasoned reporters.

The public may be right about television news deserving scant respect, but it saddens me to think that people have so little confidence in newspapers. They ought to differentiate between the egregious failures of commercial broadcasting and the less offensive peccadilloes of newspapers. This lack of trust in newspapers is a serious threat to America's well-being. Most newspapers in this country can be a lot better, but still—even as they are—they form a bulwark of democracy. They comprise one of the few institutions that can help make other institutions, including the higher education establishment, more concerned about quality.

Meanwhile, daily newspapers, reluctant to delve more fully into issues of quality, have deferred to *U.S. News & World Report* and a host of guidebooks—many of questionable merit—that now line the shelves of Barnes & Noble and Borders. "Why is everyone paying so much attention to them?"[12] asked a scholar of higher education in a book chapter assessing the impact of guidebooks. *USA Today* seems to have a response on its editorial page when it says: "The popularity of the rankings tells us customers want more information about what they will be getting in return for the tens of thousands of dollars a college education costs."[13]

Perhaps the style of coverage has to change in the news media before quality becomes a topic of greater concern. The higher education beat needs more reporters who are comfortable taking an adversarial stance. Healthy skepticism is in order. The scandals in the Roman Catholic Church have demonstrated that no institution should be above scrutiny.

Journalists must not assume that quality always prevails at colleges and universities. They should not regard colleges and universities and those associated with them with reverence. They must remain neutral and impartial as they probe deeper in their coverage. In turn, news organizations ought to keep dedicated journalists on the higher education beat long enough for them to establish contacts and to know their way around the campuses they cover. Moreover, these reporters and their supervising editors should engage in professional development to deepen their knowledge of the issues.

Let us look at one example of how this would work. Administrators and faculty at publicly supported colleges and universities would like to see journalists do more to point out the inadequacies of legislative allocations for higher education. It seems to me, though, that a full discussion of this topic requires, for instance, attention to how faculty members spend their time and what students learn from them. Articles about allocations, in other words, should not be written in a vacuum.

Consider the articles that Patrick Healy wrote in 2001 in the *Boston Globe* about Harvard College's "dirty little secret," after he discovered that more than 90 percent of the school's graduates received honors, a portion almost twice that at Yale or Princeton. I do not imagine that the good folks around Cambridge welcomed this sort of coverage. Likewise, the *Pioneer-Press* in St. Paul embarrassed the University of Minnesota in 1999 with its reporting on varsity athletics. The *New York Times* did the same in 2003 to Ohio State with stories noting how academic rules were bent for athletes. Michelle Crouch raised questions in the *Charlotte*

Observer in 2001 about whether university research was becoming too commercial. And Daniel Golden of the *Wall Street Journal* took on admissions, winning the 2004 Pulitzer Prize along the way, for pieces that reshaped the affirmative action debate by pointing to the advantages enjoyed by legacy applicants. Coverage of this sort certainly does not originate in releases from public information offices.

Despite such examples of inspired reportage, Americans remain relatively uninformed about the state of quality in the academy. Accreditation, which could help lift the veil, has all the openness of the old Politburo. It is not as if these institutions were entitled to operate without accountability. Government funds, derived from tax revenues, benefit both public and private colleges and universities. Moreover, even the richest institutions receive tax-free status on the theory that they serve the public good. Students and, often, their parents are consumers, deserving the kind of information about quality that people crave whether the product is healthcare, sports utility vehicles, or houses.

The media have a special role to play in this regard. Journalists, when they rise to the occasion, can exert power in ways that serve the public interest beyond and above the capabilities of almost any other institution—except perhaps enlightened government. It is not a question of exposing scandal or wrongdoing so much as ensuring that people understand and are able to rely on something more than blind faith in determining where and how quality manifests itself in higher education, as well as where and how it does not.

Notes

1. John Immerwahr, "Doing Comparatively Well: Why the Public Loves Higher Education and Criticizes K–12," Public Agenda, April 26, 1999, p. 2.
2. Charles B. Reed and Edward B. Rust Jr., "A More Systematic Approach," *Chronicle of Higher Education* (September 3, 2004): B7–8.
3. Richard W. Moll and B. Ann Wright, "What College Selectivity Looks Like to the Public," in Gene I. Maeroff, ed., *Imaging Education: The Media and Schools in America* (New York: Teachers College Press, 1998), p. 149.
4. U. S. Department of Education, National Center for Education Statistics, "Families Overestimate College Costs, New Study Finds," October 1, 2003.
5. The College Board, "Trends in College Pricing 2003," October 21, 2003.
6. Associated Press, "Ridge's Big Fear: Tuition," August 10, 2004.
7. "Selectivity in Admissions," Table 2.5, undated research paper.

8. Philip M. Boffey, "The College Admissions Scramble: From Sure Thing to Anxious Ordeal," *New York Times*, June 6, 2004, editorial page.
9. David Shaw, "If You Were the Editor, What Would You Do?," *Los Angeles Times*, December 14, 2003.
10. Noel Holston, "The Two Flavors of Cable News," *Newsday*, September 1, 2004.
11. Jeffrey Selingo, "What Americans Think About Higher Education," *Chronicle of Higher Education* vol. 49, no. 3 (May 2, 2003): A10.
12. Don Hossler, "Everybody Wants to Be Number One: The Effects of the Media's College Rankings," in Gene I. Maeroff, ed., *Imaging Education*, p. 161.
13. "Rankings That Rankle," *USA Today*, August 27, 2004.

2

Ready or Not? Where the Public Stands on Higher Education Reform

Deborah Wadsworth

A growing host of critics, including legislators, business leaders, and many who believe deeply in the importance of an educated citizenry, have called on higher education to stop its obsessive competition for specious ratings and start looking seriously at its own assumptions. Does 120 credit hours really mean that an undergraduate student is educated? Does the structure of departments, increasingly professionalized and isolated from one another, really advance student learning? Is it really true that, as one professor interviewed for a Public Agenda study said, "teaching college is like playing a Mozart string quartet; 250 years later it still takes four people and can't be done any faster," or could technology revolutionize the delivery of higher education? Is there an alternative to the blame game, where K–12 blames higher education for poorly prepared teachers and colleges and universities blame K–12 for poorly prepared students? For that matter, what is the primary purpose of higher education? Is it to provide job skills for students and human resources and research for state economies, or is it to foster a spirit of inquiry and independence leading to the fullest possible realization of what it means to be human and a thinking, compassionate member of society?

Expert panels and commissions have waded into these matters and found higher education wanting in many respects. The late Frank Newman, director of Brown University's Futures Project, described institutions of higher education as having grown complacent and generally satisfied with the status quo. He criticized colleges for "focusing their energies on a form of competition based not on improving graduates' skills and knowledge but on institutional prestige and revenues."[1] One might raise two questions: Do the views of such experts truly resonate with those of "ordinary" Americans? And, because those responsible for higher education—administrators and faculty alike—are notoriously resistant to change and famously better at dishing out criticisms than receiving them, can reformers seeking allies look to the public as a source of support and pressure to pursue an agenda of reform?

In this essay I explore recent surveys of public opinion and what they can tell us about how Americans think about higher education, what value it holds for them, and whom people believe should be the recipients of a college or university education. I draw on a variety of surveys, many of which were developed in a ten-year collaboration between Public Agenda, a nonpartisan, nationally respected leader in understanding public thinking about complex issues, and the National Center for Public Policy and Higher Education. As president of Public Agenda over the decade in which these studies were conducted, I had the opportunity to follow this research closely. Recent surveys from other organizations also help round out the picture.

On the face of it, the public would seem to be a natural ally for reformers bent on change. Over the past twenty years, public opinion surveys have identified substantial majorities, across all demographics, as seriously critical of K–12 education and highly receptive to reforms that call for raising standards while insisting on the introduction of measures of accountability. Surprisingly, in contrast to the public's critical perception of K–12, higher education is remarkably immune to criticism. Not only is there no call for reform, but there appears to be widespread celebration of an institution people think of as a world-class act. Nevertheless, the research does indicate the start of a few ripples in this placid pond, which I will comment on a bit later.

Growing Importance

Research on the importance of higher education in the eyes of the public is unambiguous. Quite simply, among large random samples of the general public over the past ten years, it is clear that college education has replaced the high school degree as the ticket of admission to a good job and a middle-class lifestyle. Eighty-seven percent of 1,400 adults surveyed, and even higher percentages from random samples of African American, Hispanic, and white parents, support the statement that "a college education has become as important as a high school diploma used to be."[2] When Public Agenda started looking at attitudes toward higher education in 1993, respondents in focus groups often worried that the population was becoming overeducated. Too many college graduates were driving taxicabs, they would say, while good plumbers were nowhere to be found. Today that emphasis has shifted: more than three-quarters of the public (76 percent) says that the country can never have too many college graduates; now only 18 percent say it is possible to reach a point where too many people have a college degree.[3] People still complain about being unable to find a plumber; the difference is that now they think the plumber needs a college degree as well.

It stands to reason, then, that if a college degree has replaced the high school diploma, the public also might subject higher education to the same kind of scrutiny it so generously lavishes on K–12. The public, as we all know, has not been the least bit shy in calling for reform of public schooling. So, if higher education has replaced K–12 as the platform for achieving a productive life, why is the public not also putting post-secondary education under the microscope?

Important, But for Whom, and for What?

To answer that question, we need to examine two powerful and prevailing public mind-sets. Public Agenda focus groups and in-depth interviews conducted over the years suggest that, despite the typical media coverage of higher education that focuses on teenage high school graduates bound for competitive colleges, most people are aware that higher education is no longer restricted to "traditional" students between the ages of eighteen and twenty-four. Moreover, our respondents frequently described people of varying ages attending community colleges, four-year colleges and universities, predominantly local or state institutions, many with open enrollment policies.

Nonetheless, they also made clear that they believe that the most important function of higher education is what it can do for the youngster who is just graduating from high school. First and foremost, people say, higher education should provide these young people with the means to achieving a good job that will guarantee them entry into the American middle class. One hardly needs survey data to bear this out. Even the most casual conversations between many adults and college students devolve pretty quickly into a discussion of "What's your major?" "Where are you headed?" "I didn't know you could do prelaw at Wabash U," and "Why in the world are you wasting your time and money majoring in English?" Admissions literature and media marketing pieces often reiterate this mindset in describing available programs. The fragmentation and specialization of the disciplines of undergraduate education, compounded by the proliferation of certification programs of every kind, reinforce the tendency to view higher education as solely a province for career preparation.

A second mind-set, in some ways even more important for the public, has to do with a widespread belief that the college years should be a unique transitional time in early adulthood, a time to learn to be independent and responsible citizens. Therefore, people once more turn their focus to the stereotypical eighteen- to twenty-four-year-old. Focus group participants frequently speak with some emotion about the greater freedom (and greater distractions) that come with the college years, and they insist that the task for students is to learn how to manage their own time and to resist the many temptations created by higher levels of freedom.

Survey findings reflect this dual emphasis, preparing for careers on one hand and becoming independent on the other. Public Agenda asked people to rate a series of items, in terms of how important each was as a goal of higher education. At the top of the list is maturity and self-management, which is seen as important by an overwhelming 97 percent of those surveyed. Learning to get along with different kinds of people is almost as high, followed closely by career-related skills. Interestingly, gaining the responsibilities of citizenship or exposure to great writers and thinkers in literature and history are viewed as far less important outcomes of attending college. To put it more broadly, as shown in the chart that follows, the public expects higher education to help complete the transformation from childhood to adulthood and to lay the groundwork for a young person to become a self-supporting member of the middle class. Other goals are frills.

These are powerful and unambiguous mindsets, undisturbed by questions about quality or any interest in reform. Indeed, the public is basically satisfied with higher education pretty much the way it is. And in those rare instances where people begrudgingly acknowledge a potential problem, they exhibit a high degree of tolerance, basically giving the institution of higher education a pass and focusing the blame elsewhere. Unlike K–12, where every criticism seems to stick like Velcro, higher education, as one researcher put it, seems wrapped in Teflon.[4]

How important is each of the following in terms of what students should gain from attending college?

	Absolutely essential (%)	Important, but not essential (%)	Not too important (%)
A sense of maturity and how to manage on their own	71	26	2
An ability to get along with people different from themselves	68	29	2
An improved ability to solve problems and think analytically	63	34	1
Learning high-tech skills, such as using computers and the Internet	61	35	4
Specific expertise and knowledge in the careers they have chosen	60	35	4
Top-notch writing and speaking skills	57	38	4
The responsibilities of citizenship, such as voting and volunteering	44	47	9
Exposure to great writers and thinkers in subjects like literature and history	32	53	14

Source: John Immerwahr with Tony Foleno, "Great Expecations: How the Public and Parents—White, African American and Hispanic—View Higher Education," Public Agenda report for the National Center for Public Policy and Higher Education, Consortium for Policy Research in Education and National Center for Postsecondary Improvement, May 2000, p. 10.

Smooth Sailing for Higher Education . . . Here's Why

A High-Quality Product

In focus groups conducted across the country, we found that, despite the fact that people actually know little about what transpires in their local colleges, they believe higher education to be a quality product. While the critics of higher education may debate the quality of education, with many believing that what is being delivered is inadequate and getting worse, the public, for its part, does not seem to echo this concern. Respondents speak with great pride about their town's university and about the prestige of their local university medical center. People know that students come from all over the world to study at America's colleges and universities, and they interpret this as a message that American higher education is a world-class product.

Defects Are with the Consumer

As survey findings revealed respondents' beliefs that the main purpose of a college education is to inculcate a sense of maturity, it is not surprising that respondents also say that they do not expect colleges to make it easy for students; quite the contrary. Focus group respondents tell us that learning to negotiate obstacles in life is an important part of college education; indeed, it is probably even more important than the content of the education. Students must learn to cope with not always being able to have everything as they wish it to be. For example, the inability to enroll in a highly desired class or to study with preferred professors because of burgeoning enrollments or declining revenues are seen as problems for students, not failures of the institution. Indeed, an overwhelming 88 percent of respondents said that the benefit a student gets from attending college depends on how much of an effort he or she puts in, while only 11 percent thought that the benefit depends on the quality of the college.[5] College ought to be a test of motivation, according to the majority of respondents. As distinct from attitudes toward K–12 education, which Public Agenda has documented for over a decade and a half, in the case of higher education, the "consumer" should learn to adapt to the problems of the institution, not vice versa.

This is most apparent when we look at what people say about college "dropouts." Public Agenda asked survey respondents whom they think is responsible when students drop out of college. The results paint a vivid picture of the degree to which people are (or are not) ready to hold colleges responsible. The biggest group of respondents, 47 percent, placed the blame on students themselves as responsible for their inability to keep up with the work. Thirty-eight percent blamed the high schools for poor preparation. A minuscule 10 percent blamed the colleges for not doing more to help students.[6] Very interesting! Young adults come to college, in other words, precisely to grow up and learn to take responsibility. It is not the job of higher education to pick up the pieces.

In a series of focus groups in Philadelphia, we asked people to tell us how they felt about a student dropping out of high school, and most respondents equated such action with a virtual death sentence. Although the dropout might come back for a General Education Diploma (GED) at some point, respondents felt that it was unlikely that such a student would ever hold a really good job. In contrast, when we asked these groups how they felt about a college student who drops out, many said something like "Perhaps the youngster hasn't really found himself yet. He should go and work for a few years, and then come back to college when he is ready." Taking some time off is generally perceived as a good thing, a way for a student to gain additional maturity and motivation. Over and over again, it is striking to compare the degree to which survey respondents hold their local K–12 public schools responsible for failures, while giving higher education a free pass.

Glowing by Comparison

Over the past two decades, Public Agenda repeatedly has documented high levels of concern among large majorities of people across the range of socioeconomic, racial, and ethnic demographics about the failure of public schools, K–12, to deliver a basic education to all youngsters, to provide an environment conducive to learning, and to demand and enforce discipline and respect in the nation's classrooms. We heard nothing like this when we asked people to talk about higher education.

Indeed, so long as students appear to be making progress and getting decent jobs, people believe higher education is performing reasonably well. And although media today repeatedly report news of failing schools and failing students, people hear and read glowing stories of local colleges and universities, successful sports teams, and glorious and voluminous offerings of local continuing education programs. In a 2003 study for the Educational Testing Service, researchers Peter D. Hart and Robert M. Teeter confirmed this notion, finding that 56 percent of the public give colleges nationwide a grade of either A or B. By comparison, in survey after survey, year after year, no more than one in three give public high schools nationwide grades of A or B.[7] And even those who initially rate their local K–12 schools positively soon turn critical as they respond to questions about the nuts and bolts of public education.

Access and Affordability: The Achilles Heel?

Nonetheless, higher education is not entirely invulnerable in the public's mind. The problem that surfaces for most, however, is not the issue of the quality of the experience, but growing concern over *access* to higher education. Surveys show that the public regards the opportunity to go to college as a virtual right. Hart and Teeter found that an overwhelming 91 percent of the public think that "every high-school student who wants a four-year college education should have the opportunity to gain one."[8] Public Agenda documented an equally overwhelming 91 percent who strongly, or somewhat strongly agree, that we should not allow the price of a college education to keep students who are qualified and motivated to go to college from doing so.[9]

Public concern has clearly been heightened of late by reports in the media of escalating costs of a college education, and a 2003 Public Agenda survey (which I will discuss in just a moment) provides some very interesting findings on this subject. But despite growing concern about the affordability of higher education, I believe, nervousness about access has yet to translate into a call from the general public for reform of higher education.

In focus groups, respondents suggest why people—even parents—retain their optimism about higher education even in the face of growing concern about costs. They reason that there are many alternatives for students desirous of higher education, even if their preferred choice is not attainable. There is a small and consistent number, they say, who can opt for an elite private school with total costs of $40,000 per year, and various opportunities for financial aid. That same student, if need be, they reason, could live at home and attend a state school in the area, even, if necessary, on a part-time basis. It is also possible to begin at a reasonably priced two-year college and transfer later on. In each case, the student can end up with a degree, they say, and many cited success stories about people who "got what they needed over time."

In effect, respondents say that students and their families have the ability to insulate themselves from increases in tuition by "trading down." Public Agenda quoted one focus group respondent who explained it this way:

> It is like getting a new car. Almost everyone can get a new car, but now many people might only be able to afford a KIA. But suppose I want a Buick. That used to be a middle class car, but it isn't any more. So now people in the middle class can't afford to buy what used to be the middle class car, let alone something above like the Lexus. In the old days a middle class family could afford a better college, but now you are going to have to trade down. The same person who would have been going full-time before is now going part-time, or going to a community college for the first two years.[10]

It is far easier, they say, to "trade down" for education beyond high school than it is to do so for healthcare or housing, which may be another reason why people retain their optimism about access, even in the face of concerns about affordability. In effect, many people seem to feel that they can somehow work things out for their own children. In 2000 Public Agenda asked the parents of high school teens how likely it was that their oldest child would attend college. Three-quarters said that this was likely or very likely. When we asked about finances, the overwhelming majority of this group (93 percent) said, "Somehow we'll pay for it."[11]

Beware the Sleeping Giant

What all of these data suggest is that despite the experts' concerns about quality and some public nervousness about access and affordability, for now, at least, Americans are content to leave higher education on the back burner. Hart and Teeter put the question of reform squarely to the public and found little energy for change. Seventy-two percent of the public say that higher education works pretty well as it is or needs only minor reform. A fraction—19 percent—calls for major changes or a complete overhaul.[12] Nevertheless, as a result of a recent small-scale Public Agenda survey like Hart and Teeter's study, also conducted in 2003, just before the post-9/11 recession began to lift, I feel a slight stirring in the wind. Three small but interesting changes may presage a shift in attitudes on these matters.

Growing Concern about Access

In 2000 the public was evenly divided on the question of whether higher education is available to all qualified students. Although 45 percent said that the vast majority of qualified people did in fact have an opportunity for college, a comparable 47 percent said that many qualified people do not have that opportunity. By 2003, concern about access had increased to a healthy majority. Fifty-seven percent said that many qualified people do not really have the opportunity to go to college.[13]

Growing Emphasis on the Essentiality of Higher Education

As noted earlier, people have consistently stressed the *importance* of higher education. At the same time, they also tended to say that a college education was not the only path to success in America. Many people point to the success of individuals such as Bill Gates (a college dropout) to show that even though higher education is important, it is still possible to become the richest person in the world without a degree. The 2003 Public Agenda survey also found a change in this area. The study shows a small but significant growth in the number of people who believe that college is not only important but also essential, and a falling off (from 67 to 61 percent) in the percentage who think that it is still possible to make it without a higher education degree.[14] Although the perceived importance of a college education has been consistently high, we now see, in other words, a growth in the belief of the *necessity* of a higher education as well.

Taken together, the two items—the perceived decline of availability and concomitant greater necessity of a higher education—create a kind of "misery index"—borrowing the term coined in the 1970s to describe the convergence of inflation and unemployment. If college is increasingly viewed as absolutely essential *and* simultaneously less available, American society is approaching a much more unstable situation. Our society is predicated on an ideology of social mobility. At the heart of that tenet is the belief that hard work will pay off and that people can pull themselves up by their own bootstraps. It follows, then, that if higher education becomes the only path to success and, at the same time, less available to significant numbers of individuals, that sense of mobility will be threatened.

Lower Grades for Higher Education

Interestingly, these changes also were accompanied by a small but statistically significant drop-off in the favorable ratings for higher education. Or, to put it another way, an up-tick in the misery index occurred simultaneously with the decline in the public's approval rating for higher education. The percentage of people who say that higher education in their own state's colleges is doing an excellent or good job fell from 57 percent in 2000 to 53 percent in 2003.[15] We would need to test these results over time, of course, and to tease out the impact of temporary fluctuations in the economy from longer-term economic trends. Nonetheless, we can still speculate on the connection between the misery index and people's overall evaluation of how well colleges are doing and the impact of that on greater calls for reform.

Canaries in the Mine

The hypothesis that the increasing importance of higher education colliding with a decline in access will lead to less adulation and ultimately to growing criticism or calls for reform gains additional plausibility if we look at the views of several subgroups from Public Agenda's 2003 survey, especially those of blacks and the parents of high school students. These "canaries in the mine" are the groups that already appear to be sensitive to changes that eventually may affect large numbers of the general public. These are our findings.

Parents of High School Students

In 2000 high school parents were *more* likely to be optimistic about access than the general population, with 52 percent saying that the vast majority of people in their state have an opportunity to attend college. In other words, the group that was closest to the action was less worried than the population as a whole. Three years later this situation had reversed itself. By 2003 the parents were less likely to be optimistic than they had been and less likely than others to be optimistic. Only 34 percent now say that the vast majority has an opportunity for college.[16]

African Americans

African American views changed even more dramatically between 2000 and 2003. Blacks always have been more worried about college accessibility than the population as a whole, but the level of concern about access among blacks also jumped during this period from 60 to 76 percent.[17]

We also saw even greater increases in the percentage of blacks who feel that college is essential for success, with a jump of almost 20 percentage points (from 35 to 53 percent) in just three years. Hispanic attitudes also changed in the same direction, from 41 to 53 percent.[18]

From the perspective of African Americans, therefore, the situation is already grim. On one hand, they are convinced that college is absolutely essential for success. At the same time, concern about access is much more pervasive within the black community than in the public overall. My speculation about the connection between the increasing concern over access and positive evaluations of higher education is obvious here. In 2000, colleges and universities received high marks from blacks, with 64 percent saying that colleges in their state were doing an excellent or good job. Just three years later, as the misery index skyrocketed, positive evaluations dropped by almost 30 points, from 64 to 35 percent.[19] Indeed, this was the single most dramatic change noted by Public Agenda on any question over the three-year period. Although these findings cannot be considered definitive without further study, they do suggest one possible response to the question of what might evoke a call for reform of higher education from the general public.

A Troubling Analogy

The answer looks like this: For now, higher education is a public policy success story. From the public's perspective, it is doing what it is meant to do: providing access to decent jobs and therefore to the middle class for a significant number of young people. And, so long as there is a safety valve even for some of those who do not go to college, the public's priorities will focus elsewhere. But if higher education becomes simultaneously more essential *and* less available, the public's rose-colored glasses may begin to cloud over.

Healthcare provides a useful analogy. Long thought of as a service of the highest quality, healthcare was catapulted to the very top of the list of the public's concerns when the downturn in the economy caused many people to lose not only their jobs but also their health coverage. Today public concerns about cost and access to healthcare have replaced cancer and AIDS as the public's top health concerns.[20] The introduction of managed care has also created rising levels of frustration, leading many to believe that the quality of care for HMO patients is suffering as well.[21] Problems with cost and access triggered a change in public attitudes about satisfaction with the quality of health care. Higher education may suffer a similar plight.

The Perfect Storm

Some observers have predicted a future for higher education that might well evoke a public response similar to the one described above on healthcare. On one hand, colleges and universities are facing a deluge of new students, what Clark Kerr called a third tidal wave comparable to the earlier ones caused first by the GI Bill and later by the coming of age of the baby boomers. At the same time, many states are facing serious revenue shortfalls and an environment that is increasingly resistant to tax increases. In this "perfect storm" scenario, public higher education will face decreasing revenues and an onslaught of both greater numbers of students and more nontraditional students. Even private institutions, with the exception of those that are most heavily endowed, are likely to suffer from the impact of rising tuition costs on vast numbers of potential applicants.

As John Immerwahr, the author of many of Public Agenda's surveys on higher education, wrote recently, "Many Americans seem to fear that they will be caught in a 'squeeze play' . . . with college education becoming both more important and more expensive."[22] If access to decent jobs or entree to lucrative careers narrows, people who are now scrambling to address the cost of higher education may begin to feel that this ticket to a middle-class life is being priced out of their reach and respond with real hostility. I have few doubts that the emergence of such a scenario would lead to more public support for higher education reform. But critics should not presume that their agenda of reform will hold sway with the public.

Public Agenda research frequently captures striking disconnects between the views of experts and those of the general public. As noted, such a gap already exists on the subject of higher education; experts focus on the quality of education being delivered, and the public concentrates on the price tag associated with it. Indeed, our research in the late 1990s revealed an interesting difference between business executives and the public on the issue of the cost of higher education itself. While both groups were concerned, business executives in particular felt that higher education was much too bloated and inefficient. And, inasmuch as corporate America had undergone serious downsizing, they called for the institutions of higher education to do likewise. They did not, however, share the public's concern about the price of higher education. To the contrary, many believed that students and their parents should be paying more for higher education! The public felt that students and parents were already paying too much.[23] And these are but a harbinger of other gaps that are certain to reveal themselves should reform of higher education become a priority on the public's agenda.

Higher education, in all of its guises, has uniquely served the promise of social and economic mobility in America. No one today questions the ideal of mobility or the critical role of higher education in delivering on that promise for both the individual and society overall. Several candidates for election in 2004 spoke with passion about "being the first in the family to attend college," confident that people grasped the power of that story. Public satisfaction with higher education remains high. Those who are calling for reform would do well to recognize that, at present, only modest support for change exists.

Moreover, what support does exist is sure to dissipate if people begin to think that reformers have set out to fix what is not really broken. Problems with access and affordability are likely to be the galvanizing issues, and they could be especially divisive if they fall disproportionately on minority groups struggling to gain their chance to achieve the American dream. Such is the challenge for those who would attempt to lead the charge to reform higher education. To be successful, they must consider the public's concerns and priorities and find a way to address both the goals of increasing quality and ensuring access. Without this marriage, they have little chance of success.

Notes

I would like to acknowledge the significant contribution of John Immerwahr, senior research fellow with Public Agenda and associate vice president for academic affairs at Villanova University, and Patrick Callan, president, National Center for Public Policy and Higher Education, whose work has provided the inspiration and context for this essay.

1. Frank Newman, Lara Couturier, and Jamie Scurry, "Higher Education Isn't Meeting the Public's Needs," *Chronicle of Higher Education*, October 15, 2004.
2. The survey question was: "A college education has become as important as a high school education used to be. Do you agree or disagree? Is that strongly or somewhat?" According to the survey, 68 percent strongly agreed, 19 percent somewhat agreed, 8 percent somewhat disagreed, 4 percent strongly disagreed, and 2 percent didn't know. See John Immerwahr with Tony Foleno, "Great Expectations: How the Public and Parents—White, African American, and Hispanic—View Higher Education," Public Agenda report for the National Center for Public Policy and Higher Education, Consortium for Policy Research in Education and National Center for Postsecondary Improvement, May 2000, p. 38.
3. The survey question was: "In your view, is it possible for the U.S. to reach a point where too many people have a college degree, or is this one area where there can never be too much of a good thing?" Eighteen percent of those responding believed it is possible to reach a point, 76 percent believed there can never be too much, and 6 percent didn't know. See ibid., p. 7.
4. John Immerwahr. "Doing Comparatively Well: Why the Public Loves Higher Education and Criticizes K–12," Institute for Educational Leadership and The National Center for Public Policy and Higher Education, 1999, p. 1.
5. Immerwahr with Foleno, "Great Expectations," p. 16.
6. Ibid., p. 17. See also Peter D. Hart and Robert M. Teeter, "Quality, Affordability, and Access: Americans Speak on Higher Education," Educational Testing Service,

June 2003, p. 7, where only 35 percent say that high schools are doing well in pre-paring students to succeed in college. http://www.ets.org/aboutets/americaspeaks/2003find.html

7. Hart and Teeter, "Quality, Affordability & Access," p. 3.
8. Ibid., p. 5.
9. John Immerwahr, "Public Attitudes on Higher Education: A Trend Analysis 1993–2003," Public Agenda report for the National Center for Public Policy and Higher Education, February 2004, p. 5.
10. John Immerwahr, "The Affordability of Higher Education," Public Agenda report for the National Center for Public Policy and Higher Education, May 2002, p. 14.
11. Immerwahr, "Great Expectations," p. 23.
12. Hart and Teeter, "Quality, Affordability & Access," p. 3.
13. Immerwahr, "Public Attitudes on Higher Education," p. 4.
14. Ibid., pp. 9–10.
15. Ibid., p. 12.
16. Ibid., p. 4.
17. Ibid., p. 5.
18. Ibid., p. 10.
19. Ibid., p. 12.
20. Surveys conducted by The Gallup Organization, February 8–9, 1999, November 3–5, 2003.
21. An April 1999 study, Update on Americans' Views on Consumer Protections in Managed Care, by Princeton Research Associates for the Henry J. Kaiser Family Foundation and the Harvard School of Public Health found that 56 percent feel that HMOs have decreased the quality of health care for people who are sick, as compared to only 26 percent who say that HMOs have increased that care.
22. John Immerwahr, "Losing Ground: A National Status Report on the Affordability of American Higher Education," National Center For Public Policy and Higher Education, 2004, chapter 5, page 14.
23. John Immerwahr, "Taking Responsibility: Leaders' Expectations of Higher Education," report for the National Center for Public Policy and Higher Education, January 1999, p. 19.

3

College Admissions: A Substitute for Quality?

James Fallows

For the past several years the *Atlantic Monthly* has reported about the chaotic and stressful nature of college admissions in the United States. Apart from the challenge of paying for college and the uncertainty about what students learn (and do not) during the four or more years they devote to higher education, the process of matching student with institution is widely seen as a source of needless heartache and a distortion of both high school and college life.

The anxiety produced by college admissions is all the stranger, given several important realities of the process. One is that it affects only a relative handful of students and institutions. Of the nation's 3,000-plus colleges and other sources of post–high school education, only a few dozen are "selective" in the most basic sense, that of admitting fewer than half of all who apply. Of the almost 3 million American students who finish high school each year, at most 10 to 15 percent are involved in competition for these few selective schools. Most others do not go to college, enroll in community colleges, attend state junior colleges or four-year universities, or relatively easily find a place among the vast majority of private colleges that are open to most applicants. Even those who apply to the most selective schools benefit from admissions staffs that, with rare exceptions, are compassionate, amazingly hardworking, and sincerely committed to trying to find the right students for each college and vice versa. On the whole, the matchmaking process works very well. Most students end up satisfied with the institutions they attend; most colleges are satisfied with the balance and talents of the student body they attract. And in the long run, the stress about admissions is strange, since there is so little demonstrable connection between the selectivity of the school a student attends and that student's long-term success or satisfaction in life.

Fully explaining why some Americans should compete so hard for "positional goods" of such evanescent value is beyond the ambition of this chapter. Instead my purpose is to cover several of the trends that are shaping and misshaping college admissions and the bearing they might have on the process of undergraduate education.

The admissions system has become notably more "marketized," in the sense that all its elements increasingly think of themselves in business terms. A whole industry of "enrollment management" consultants has arisen to handle what is ordinarily known as "admissions" and was once quaintly called "crafting a class." For all but the richest ten or twenty universities, an important part of managing enrollment is simply being sure that enough paying customers will show up each fall—and that not too many students will take the school up on its offer to give financial aid to those who need it. (Most private colleges say they will provide need-based aid, but shrunken endowments mean that what they can cover is limited. In practice, this means that the colleges try to ensure that they do not enroll more needy students than they can handle.) Students are taught to think about the "package" of accomplishments they will present to admissions committees.

At the private schools and high-end public schools where admissions mania is most intense, counselors are expected to supply students and parents with a "product"—namely, admissions to prestigious schools. Many high school counselors can recount some variant on the following story. A student has just gotten into, say, Tufts or Pomona, both colleges that have become very selective. The counselor, hearing from the parents, starts to offer congratulations and is cut off by a bellow: "What happened with Yale?" A few counselors describe colleagues who were forced out, especially at private schools, because their record in college placements was not impressive enough.

As with other institutions that have become more marketized in the past decade—consider medicine, media, law—this change has brought some improvements. A more open market for college admissions, no matter how fevered, is still fairer than the old system, which petered out in the mid-1960s, whereby Exeter's headmaster could earmark a few dozen of each year's seniors for admission to Harvard. But as in these other increasingly market-minded fields, some of the changes undermine what had been fundamental ideals and values. Some aspects of this have been widely publicized—for instance, the rise of costly admissions counselors, especially in New York, who charge tens of thousands of dollars to advise students on where and how to apply. The most publicized of these is Katherine Cohen of IvyWise in Manhattan, who in 2001 was profiled at length in *New York* magazine. She offers a "platinum package" for students that lasts two years and at the time cost $32,995.[1] Colleges themselves have turned to enrollment-management firms for advice on how to attract the students they want. The best known of these is Noel-Levitz. As of early 2005, its Web site is almost beyond parody, with consultant-speak applied to the business of recruiting, admitting, and retaining students. For instance, the company's consultants can provide "Institutional Image and Competitive Positioning Analysis™"—a "complete enrollment research package [that] offers comprehensive decision data for image enhancement and strategic market positioning."

The marketization of the admissions process has intensified at both ends of the process. High school guidance counselors report that they are under ceaseless pressure to "produce" by getting students into exclusive colleges. This pressure is greatest at the most elite private schools, where parents feel they are paying extra for results. A sense that high school counselors are not doing enough has also led to booming business for private admissions consultants, most of them hired by relatively affluent families.

Meanwhile, nearly every college official the *Atlantic* has spoken with told us how some other college was playing the market, usually by aggressively prospecting for new applicants, many or most of whom it would ultimately reject. In addition to making a college statistically more "selective," attracting a larger pool may enable schools to find students with higher test scores and less financial need. A number of colleges were described as using this "attract-to-reject" strategy, but one was mentioned by numerous interviewees: Washington University in St. Louis, which has gotten itself into the top ten in the *U.S. News* rankings—ahead of Columbia, Berkeley, the University of Chicago, and Brown—largely by attracting more and more applicants. Nanette Tarbouni, the director of admissions at Washington University, denies any attempts to influence the ranking and says that the school's sky-rocketing applications are a result of good word of mouth from current students about the school's "exceptional experience."

DePaul University, the largest Catholic university in the country, has taken a very different approach: As the number of its applicants has risen, DePaul has grown. Its current freshman class of 2,350 is nearly two and a half times the size of the 1992 freshman class. Jon Boeckenstedt, DePaul's associate vice-president for enrollment management, points out that if DePaul had not changed its class size, it would be accepting only 28 percent of all applicants—a level of selectivity comparable to Johns Hopkins's—rather than the 68 percent it accepts now. Boeckenstedt says DePaul decided "to turn the extra demand into greater access, rather than greater selectivity," because part of its announced mission is to create opportunities for "first-generation" students—those whose parents did not go to college.

All this marketing is occurring at a time when the college-age population is increasing, meaning that applications are up, way up, at the minority of very selective colleges and universities. Last year Amherst College had about five thousand applicants with an average SAT score of 1,390, some of them, no doubt, attracted by Amherst's ranking and its marketing efforts. Amherst turned down all but a thousand of them. In an extended interview for the PBS program that is the companion to this book, Dean of Admission Tom Parker reflected on how rejected applicants react.

> Some of them . . . and this is the sad part of it . . . will think that they have failed, because they've never failed at anything. They have been terrific students, terrific athletes, terrific everything. And then for the first time they've run into a "No," and their first reaction is "I must not have done something, or I did something wrong. If only." When they write to find out why we rejected them, much of the counseling we do is to convince them that's not the way to look at this. I use the analogy of applying for a job. I say, "What you've done is applied for a job, and there were a lot of good applicants. And I'll bet you got another real good job, didn't you?"

Parker said he was concerned about the extent to which parents seem to measure their own worth by where their children are accepted. He said, "I don't understand why a father who went to college X and has prospered has suddenly decided that only Harvard will do for his son or daughter. I don't understand how we've found ourselves in this position in this time in our history. I just don't understand why this one part of education has exploded in importance and has so much anxiety attached to it."

The overemphasis on admission has two negatives, Parker said in his PBS interview. Those who were accepted may think they are set for life, while those who were rejected may feel they are failures. "Neither case is true," Parker said, "but if you [were] to listen to a lot of parents and students, you would suddenly believe that college admissions is the biggest thing in life—more important than marriage, more important than your job, more important than anything in life."

The solution—Parker called it "salvation"—is to expand the list of publicly recognized superb colleges and universities beyond the usual suspects.

> Our salvation is that kids who don't get into Stanford or Amherst do get admitted to another superb college that you might not necessarily equate with Stanford or Amherst or Harvard or Swarthmore, but that I know full well is an unbelievably good place, colleges like Grinnell, Carleton, and Macalester. And they go there, have an unbelievably good experience, as they always do, go home, and talk about, "Oh, I didn't get into Harvard or Princeton, but I got into College X and I love it." We have to expand our universe of superb places or we're all going to go nuts.

Parker's comments were no doubt sincere, as are those from most of his colleagues at very selective schools. But students and parents who know how sought-after Amherst and similar colleges have become, and how hard the schools work to enhance their standing relative to their competitors, may think that the process is more in the colleges' control than observations like Parker's might suggest. At the moment, most of them are doing so less by improving the day-by-day quality of the teaching and learning in their classrooms than by marketing efforts to enhance their prestige.

The presidents, provosts, and deans of these institutions would all say that they wish it could be otherwise. But this is where today's marketized pressures lead. Based on the reporting my magazine has done, I think the colleges have more leeway than they believe. To put it differently: Parents, students, high school counselors and teachers, employers, college alumni, and other members of the public at large should put pressure on our selective universities to change their emphasis. It is time to have a competition based on the actual process of education, rather than on prestige based on *Social Register*–style comparisons of how hard each school is to enter. Over time, the higher-education establishment would respond. People working in higher education generally are not in it for the money. They care about scholarship, they enjoy working with young people, and they believe that what they do matters. That may be why so many of the people we spoke with volunteered that the higher-education system was evolving into something less and less connected to any kind of public good. "Universities don't benefit society enough directly, on a day-to-day basis," consultant Steve Goodman says. "They're supposed to serve the public interest, but they've become no different from insurance companies."[2]

This line of reasoning has several strands. One involves a simple loss of ambition on the part of universities and their leaders. In 2003 Robert Zemsky, a professor of education at the University of Pennsylvania, wrote in the *Chronicle of Higher Education* that "colleges and universities are seen principally as providing tickets to financial security and economic status," rather than being involved in any larger public purpose. He noted that through the 1950s and 1960s, many university presidents were leading public intellectuals.[3] Agree with them or not, Clark Kerr, of Berkeley; Theodore Hesburgh, of Notre Dame; Kingman Brewster, of Yale; and others of their time played a larger role in public debates than almost any of their modern counterparts.

Many of the people we interviewed expressed concern that colleges are not fully serving their own students, who often take on considerable debt or draw heavily on their parents' savings in order to attend. "The amount of attention paid to undergraduates at the larger private and public research institutions is a national scandal," says admissions consultant Norman Puffett, who is also a dean at the College of Mount Saint Vincent, in Riverdale, New York, in a widely echoed sentiment.[4] Outside the academy, discussion of higher education usually involves what happens before students begin their undergraduate education (i.e., during the admissions process) and what happens after it is over (i.e., whether their degrees help them get appropriate jobs). What happens in between is largely a mystery.

Concern about these very expensive "lost years" has fueled the important "accountability" movement, which hopes to measure how well colleges actually perform when it comes to educating their students. The National Survey of Student Engagement (NSSE), has been a pioneer in this area, with studies that measure how often students at a given college do the things that have proved to be associated with real learning: writing papers, speaking in class, interacting with professors, and so on. Since 1999 NSSE has been used at more than 850 colleges and universities. Similarly, a group called the National Center for Public Policy and Higher Education, based in San Jose, has produced innovative "Report Cards" every two years since 2000, judging each state's public and private higher education on its affordability, the graduation rate of students, the contribution the graduates make to public life, and other factors. A still more recent effort, the Collegiate Learning Assessment, is measuring how well individual colleges teach their students to think and write.

In addition to the question of how well America's colleges and universities are serving their current students is the question of how well they will be able to serve those in the future. Many of our interviewees stressed a concern that few outside academia are aware of. It is that the next five or six years will see a big surge in demand for college enrollment, which will be as rapid and dramatic in some regions as the Baby Boom, and will be overwhelmingly Hispanic. The fastest growth in America's college-age population, in other words, will be in the group that has had the lowest college attendance rate. One in seven Hispanic Americans has a college degree, compared with one in two Asian Americans, one in three white Americans, and one in five black Americans. This "participation gap" will pose an enormous challenge for higher education in the near future. Moreover, higher education has been particularly unsuccessful with Hispanic American and black students. Retention rates for these students are far below those of white students. "The stakes for serving this new population are very high," says Peter Osgood, of Harvey Mudd. "If we invest in education as a society, we will produce a better, richer society, a better-educated electorate, and we may help lower costs for health care."[5] Or, if American colleges and universities cannot figure out how to serve this population, it may mean the reverse.

In sum, today's students are competing for places in a college system racked by debate about many of its basic values and practices—but more animated by questions of common good and public purpose than it has been in years. Sooner or later, educators and citizens must address the next question: how to do a better job of measuring real education quality, rather than using selectivity and prestige as crude, often destructive proxies.

Notes

1. Main profile of Katharine Cohen: *New York* magazine, April 1, 2001.
2. Interviews for James Fallows and V. V. Ganeshananthan, "The Big Picture," *Atlantic Monthly*, October 2004.
3. Robert Zemsky, "Have We Lost the 'Public' in Higher Education?" *Chronicle of Higher Education*, May 30, 2003.
4. Fallows and Ganeshananthan, "The Big Picture."
5. Ibid.

4

Caveat Lector: Unexamined Assumptions about Quality in Higher Education

Jay Mathews

> The University requirements for graduation transcend the boundaries of specialization and provide all students with a common language and common skills.

This is the opening sentence of Princeton University's statement of its general education requirements, the standard term for universities' efforts to give their students a rich dose of the major subjects of human inquiry. Clearly, the university is affirming its commitment to tradition.

Princeton's statement continues in the same vein: "It is as important for a student . . . to engage in disciplined reflection on human conduct, character, and ways of life or to develop critical skills through the study of the history, aesthetics, and theory of literature and the arts as it is for a student . . . to understand the rigors of quantitative reasoning and to develop a basic knowledge of the capabilities and limitations of scientific inquiry and technological development."[1]

It sounds good. An applicant skimming the Princeton course catalog would have gotten the impression that the university's undergraduate program was designed to give her the very best and broadest of courses. Who would doubt that the university that prepared novelist F. Scott Fitzgerald, Secretary of State George P. Schultz, and Senator Bill Bradley meant what it said?

Sadly, one would be wise to question Princeton—and probably every other institution of higher education—when it comes to statements about educational goals and outcomes. K–12 education is watched as carefully as a third grader crossing the street, but higher education's claims go largely unexamined. In most instances where independent assessments of college learning might serve the public, particularly when applicants are trying to find the right school, institutions of higher learning resist being measured by quantitative results. Until that changes, let the reader beware.

When Barry Latzer, senior consultant for the Washington-based American Council of Trustees and Alumni,[2] inspected the actual core requirements at Princeton, he discovered a gap between the words and the reality. The university did have composition and foreign language requirements that took those two subjects seriously, but when Latzer looked at other areas the university's own statement said were vital, such as literature, government and history, mathematics, sciences, and economics, he was disappointed.

Princeton had *no* required literature course that did not focus on exotica or just a single author. It did not require a comprehensive course in American history or government. It did not require a college-level math course. Nor did it require a course in sciences such as astronomy, biology, chemistry, geology, or physics. Economics? Forget about it.[3]

Princeton is not unique. A course called "Ghosts, Demons and Monsters" apparently satisfies Dartmouth's humanities requirements, while Duke students can meet that requirement by taking "Campus Culture and Drinking." Students who pass "Reasoning about Luck" meet Cornell's math requirement.

If an applicant was unwilling to slog through the fine print, she would think that Princeton undergraduates had to take a mathematics course under its Quantitative Reasoning requirement and a natural or physical science course under its Science and Technology requirement. But Latzer concluded that Princeton did not actually have a serious mathematics requirement because, he said, "The Quantitative Reasoning requirement may be satisfied by such courses as Math Alive (focuses on the mathematical concepts behind important modern applications, such as bar codes, CD-players, and population models); The Universe (astronomy for the non-science major; no prerequisites past high school algebra and geometry); and Computers and Computing (introduction to computers and computer science; emphasis is on understanding how computers really work)."

And as far as the science requirement went, he said, "The Science and Technology requirement may be satisfied by Freshman Seminars such as Sound, Music and Physics, or by courses in Anthropology or in the multidisciplinary program in Environmental Studies."[4]

In the white heat of competition for places in the freshman class at selective colleges and universities like Princeton, the nature and quality of the education being offered is often obscured. Few independent organizations attempt to look past the course catalog and website mission statements to see what is actually being taught. Those groups that do measure the weight of an undergraduate education do it quietly, and often decline to disclose their findings without the permission of the universities that would prefer to keep their failings to themselves.

Colleges often say they care about how much they are teaching students, but there is little evidence that they are as concerned about that as they say they are. A 1997 study by the National Center for Postsecondary Improvement at Stanford University found that few institutions of higher education linked what they knew about how much their students were learning to relevant data on what they were trying to teach and who was doing the teaching.[5] That same report by the center said assessment of student academic progress had "only a marginal influence" on college decision makers.[6] Perhaps the most damning fact is that there are so little data about student learning compiled at all by higher education. Pat Callan, President of the National Center for Public Policy and Higher Education, makes this point in summarizing MEASURING UP 2000, the Center's study of higher education quality in each of the fifty states: ". . . the national center could say next to nothing about the knowledge and skills of those who had completed at least some education beyond high school."[7]

Mark D. Soskin, associate professor of economics at the University of Central Florida, said, "It is convenient all around for students, faculty, taxpayers, legislators, alums, and donors to pretend that high quality and relevant learning is going on." He said

> Establishing standards or even publishing measured learning would reveal that the emperor, if not naked, has a much skimpier wardrobe than commonly

> presumed. Once such performance numbers are revealed, colleges would be faced with untenable choices such as the following: (1) either make colleges less sociable and fun or else be willing to flunk out many more and become less attractive to students interested in what a party school has to offer, or (2) force faculty to teach more classes (especially undergrads), not cancel as many classes or shuffle students off into teaching assistant discussion sections, hold more office hours and do more advising, spend more time learning to teach effectively (like developing lesson plans), cut back on status-based research in the non-sciences, channel resources into the classroom and instructional support, and change the incentives that over-reward non-educational activities.[8]

While researchers and policymakers produce mountains of data under the new federal No Child Left Behind Act showing where K–12 public schools are meeting and not meeting their teaching obligations, higher education is largely ignored. What investigations that are conducted are often written by university professors who, sincere or not, have a conflict of interest when writing about their own institutions. They tend to accept the general notion that universities are superior academic institutions because so many high school seniors want to enroll in them, whether they have data to confirm the quality of their work or not.

Quick to judge others, colleges are loath to question the value of their own efforts. A good example of self-regard involves Advanced Placement (AP) courses, through which high school students can earn college credit. Former college philosophy professor William Casement argues that AP courses are a poor substitute for the college introductory courses without questioning the quality of those undergraduate offerings.[9] Casement says many selective colleges have made it more difficult for students who took AP courses and tests in high school to gain college credit for their work. This trend has accelerated in college academic departments as the number of college freshmen who arrive annually with AP tests on their records has reached the one million mark and continues to climb.

"Selective colleges are increasingly wary of the program, and tightening further on the award of credit," Casement says. The AP exam is scored on a point system, 5 points being the equivalent of an A in a comparable college introductory course and a 3, the equivalent of a college C-plus, the lowest score that will earn college credit. One way colleges have tightened credit, Casement says,

> is to reject not only scores of 3 but also of 4, leaving only scores of 5 as credit worthy. In 2002, Harvard announced that a minimum score of 5 would be required for college credit for any of the AP exams. This move came after a study in two departments found that students who used AP credit to skip introductory courses fared significantly worse at the next level than students who took those courses. In 2003, the University of Pennsylvania also reached the level of accepting no score less than a 5 for credit. . . .
>
> Policies like these are not simple administrative fiats, but a collection of decisions by individual departments. The matter usually lies within departmental control, and at various other schools—William and Mary, Carnegie Mellon, Washington University (St. Louis), and Carleton, to name a few as examples—several departments now require a score of 5, although other departments do not.

Casement goes beyond the numbers on tightening credit to get at the attitudes fueling the change:

> AP is talked about in the meetings of the Ivy League deans, where the growth and quality of the program are a significant concern. One veteran of these meetings summarizes the group's misgivings: "I think that we are unanimous in wanting to see AP as a means of placing students in appropriate college courses but not as a substitute for the full experience of a residential college. . . . [E]ven when our faculty are willing to allow students with AP to place out of introductory courses, they rarely believe that the AP experience is equivalent to those courses."

Casement says that colleges have lost confidence in the ability of high school AP teachers to teach their subject matter as well as the instructors whose introductory courses the AP students want to skip. He says that because high school teachers do not have as many academic credentials as the college instructors, because high school AP students are often two or three years younger than college freshmen, and because average AP scores have not dropped as much as he would expect given the increase in the number of AP examinations, the AP program cannot be providing as demanding and useful an academic experience as introductory college courses. His conversations with college officials, such as the unnamed university veteran quoted above, lead him to conclude that these are the reasons that colleges are withholding or restricting credit.

And therein lies the curious double standard that college educators such as Casement accept when judging higher education. Like the Princeton statement about its core curriculum, the college view of AP is based on a wealth of information about Advanced Placement, willingly provided by the College Board, but almost no information about the college introductory courses to which the AP courses are being unfavorably compared.

Casement suggests that the College Board has not kept its AP exams at a college level. The College Board says it has, and offers as proof the fact that it gives AP tests to samples of college freshmen every five years or so and compares their introductory course grades to their AP scores. Casement complains that the five-year gaps are too large, since AP test taking is growing so fast, but he uses the College Board data anyway, without any apparent embarrassment, to buttress his points.

The questions that Casement does not consider are these: How many colleges give a nationally standardized exam to students who have completed their introductory courses to see how much they have learned compared to what they might have learned in an AP course? How can we be certain that the professors who organize those introductory courses and write the exams are not just teaching and assessing a few peculiar issues that interest them and ignoring the high-minded endorsements of a common body of knowledge found on the university website?

Casement told me he does not know of any colleges that give an AP-like test to confirm that their introductory courses are fulfilling their promises. I contacted ten colleges and universities around the country and could find no evidence of such an exam being given anywhere.

Officials at several of the colleges that are restricting credit for AP told me they have no research that would show if their introductory courses are better or worse than AP. Furthermore, few of them have any research that shows how well a student who *has* been given credit for AP does in the next level course, when compared to students who took the college's introductory course rather than skipping it with AP credit.

Casement cites one such unpublished study by two departments at Harvard that led the university to decide that only grades of 5 on AP tests could be used for credit in any department.[10] This was because students in three courses who got credit for scores of less than 5 did not do as well in follow-up courses as students who had taken the college's introductory courses.

That was one small study. Another selective college has done another small, unpublished study that reaches the opposite conclusion, at least for its courses.[11] At Claremont McKenna College in Claremont, California, students who skipped introductory calculus by getting a grade of 4 or 5 in AP calculus AB or BC had an average grade of 11 out of 12 points in its follow-up calculus course. This was better than the average grade of 9.51 for all students in that follow-up course. The same thing happened in Spanish. Students who skipped the equivalent course at Claremont McKenna by scoring 4 or 5 in AP Spanish had an average grade of 11.29 in the college's follow-up course, which was higher than the average grade of 10.68 for all students in that course.

Many colleges cloak the quality of their courses in respectful adjectives without much data to support their claims, and Casement provides cover for them by overlooking several possible explanations for their tightening of AP credit that have nothing to do with any decline in the quality of AP courses. College department heads, for instance, might be downplaying AP because they are unfamiliar with the AP program's strengths, since few of them have ever spent any time recently in an AP class. Or they might want to show themselves academically tougher than rival colleges also recruiting high-scoring freshmen. Or they might be concerned that too much AP credit would force them to cut back on their introductory courses, which provide jobs for their graduate students. There is not much research to back up these conclusions, but neither is there much to support Casement's argument about a decline in the quality of AP.

When challenged about the quality of teaching in colleges during an interview, Casement accepted their traditional position. They are respected institutions with long histories, college officials say, and that should be enough for everyone when compared to an organization like the College Board, which is trying to protect its franchise. Casement has been critical of colleges' overspecialization, but in this case he ignores colleges' own tendency to distort facts in their own marketing campaigns: "I would trust whatever assessments the colleges make, whether they have formal data or not, more than I would trust what the present College Board has to say about its data."[12]

The National Research Council, in a 2002 report, endorsed the same double standard.[13] The report, "Learning and Understanding," attacked the College Board for producing AP courses and tests that it said were too broad and shallow. But it overlooked the fact that the College Board was bringing to the high schools AP courses and tests that were virtually identical to the introductory college courses that the committee members, many of them college professors, chose not to criticize.

Similar assumptions about the quality of university core courses are exposed in the full American Council of Trustees and Alumni[2] report, "The Hollow Core: Failure of the General Education Curriculum."[14] It graded fifty colleges and universities on how many of the seven subjects the council considered essential to a liberal arts education—writing, literature, foreign language, U.S. government or history, math, natural or physical science, and economics—actually were required. Schools that had at least six of the seven subjects required got an A. Four or five out of seven earned a B, three a C, two a D, and one or none an F.

Twenty-four of the fifty institutions got Ds and Fs, and only one, Baylor, an A. Princeton received a D, but only two Ivy League colleges, Columbia and Dartmouth, did any better, scraping by with gentleman Cs. Two schools, Brown and Vassar, never even tried to have core courses—they say for very good reasons—and got zeroes. Ten schools also earned Fs by requiring only one out of seven subjects: the University of California—Berkeley, Colgate, Cornell, Iowa State—Ames, Mount Holyoke, Nebraska, Northwestern, Penn State, Smith, and Wisconsin—Madison.

Baylor earned its A with requirements for six of the seven subjects. Wallace Daniel, dean of its College of Arts and Sciences, said the school "is opposed to narrow specialization, to breaking the world into separate parts and viewing them as isolated."[15] Those specialized courses are what most university professors want to teach, which is one reason why so few colleges require many general courses. Baylor, however, promotes a retro image—no coed dorms, for instance—which may attract a student body more interested in the classic academic subjects.

The council's report describes some of the unusual courses that help obscure the weakness of the core requirements at many colleges. An undergraduate can meet the math requirement at the University of Illinois, for instance, with a course called "Principles and Techniques in Music Education," or the composition requirement at Nebraska with a course in "Instructional Television," or the math requirement at Cornell with the course "Reasoning about Luck," which "uses high school algebra." And the list of courses that meet humanities or social science requirements includes "History of Comic Book Art" (Indiana), "Love and Money" (Bryn Mawr), "Ghosts, Demons and Monsters" (Dartmouth), and "Campus Culture and Drinking" (Duke).

The report says a serious liberal arts education is necessary because graduates need analytical, writing, and quantitative skills to pursue their careers, even though 62 percent of the schools surveyed require no college math and 30 percent do not require a serious writing course. It says being an educated citizen requires a serious American history or government course, although only 14 percent of the sample require one. Having a rich life, Latzer said, requires an appreciation of great literature, but only 12 percent of the colleges studied "required a survey of significant works by numerous authors of acknowledged stature."

To be sure, many students arrive in college having taken AP or International Baccalaureate classes that would meet the council's requirements if they got good scores on the tests. But they often get no credit for them since these colleges, which often share Casement's distrust of AP courses, do not give AP credit for those courses or do not require them at all.

No one will be surprised to learn that many colleges reject the American Council's criteria. Meg Lauerman, spokeswoman for Nebraska, said she thought her school's entrance requirements ensured that students got much of what they needed in liberal arts in high school, including "a menu of courses which contribute to the concept of a liberal education."[16] Brown spokesman Mark Nickels said that his university's distaste for the whole notion of core courses helped make it very popular with very bright students. "By any reasonable measure, Brown's curriculum has been a brilliant success: alumni satisfaction, graduating seniors' admission to graduate and professional schools, student honors and achievements, consistent top-20 national placement in various independent quality ratings, size and quality of admission pools," he said.[17]

Most defenses of higher education use the same criteria—they have respected professors and brilliant students and do well in the rankings, even if there are not any systematic surveys of what they are actually teaching. Princeton alumnus Bradford R. Findell, who teaches mathematics at the University of Georgia, said the Princeton course "Math Alive" that Latzer demeaned ought to be accepted as worthy because it was designed by Ingrid Daubechies, a member of the National Academy of Sciences. And what matters in such a course, he said, is not the description in the catalog but "what happens inside the class, in the interactions among the teacher, the students, and the subject matter."[18]

College instructors often defend each other's courses. David McNeill, a lecturer in philosophy at the University of Essex, protested Latzer's characterization of the Cornell math course, "Reasoning about Luck," and made his case with a quote from Cornell chemist Benjamin Widom about the book of the same name, by Cornell mathematician Vinay Ambegaokar, on which the course is based: "'Reasoning about Luck'" is a beautifully written, highly original treatment of probability in the physical sciences—notable for its clarity, its wit, and its insights. It succeeds admirably in teaching the subject to any attentive reader, even one with no mathematics beyond high-school algebra, and yet can be read with pleasure and profit by professional physicists as well."[19]

McNeill is attempting to make a virtue out of the course being accessible to students who have no more preparation than high school algebra, even though such students would almost never be admitted to the Princeton freshman class. That indicates Latzer may be right in suggesting that "Reasoning about Luck" is a bit of academic fluff without a solid core.

There is one part of Latzer's critique that can be judged without a subjective argument over the character of a specific course. Latzer says that colleges should require economics because "it is hard to see how someone can compete successfully if he or she does not understand such fundamentals as the law of supply and demand or how the costs and benefits of diverse courses of action can be evaluated and compared. Whether one is introducing a product, creating a new business, or managing a national economy, understanding economics is no longer optional—it is essential." So he looked at the course lists of each of the fifty colleges to see how many required a general course in macro- or micro-economics, taught by faculty in the economics or business department. He did not find a single one.

There is some tentative movement toward measurement of what is taught in college courses. The National Survey of Student Engagement (NSSE, pronounced "nessie"), based at Indiana University, is used by more than 850 colleges and universities. It surveys undergraduates to determine the quality of their learning process. How many papers did they write? How often did they see a professor outside of class?

But most colleges participating in NSSE have refused to release the results of those surveys, preferring to use them for their internal decisions on which courses need to be improved or dropped. And even those colleges that have released their NSSE data have made it hard to locate the relevant numbers on their websites. In their current form, the NSSE surveys are not very useful in determining the worth of specific courses, since the questionnaires ask general questions rather than the differences between, for instance, the European history and Asian history courses.

An even newer attempt to assess college quality, the Collegiate Learning Assessment (CLA), is also focused on general skills, not specific courses.[20] The CLA researchers picked three dimensions of college learning—critical thinking, analytic reasoning, and written communication—to be assessed with an open-ended examination rather than a multiple choice test. From the Graduate Record Examination they borrowed a forty-five-minute essay in which test takers support or criticize a given position on an issue, and a thirty-minute essay critiquing someone else's argument. They adopted critical thinking tests developed in the 1980s by the state of New Jersey. And Stephen Klein, a senior researcher at the Rand Corporation in Santa Monica, California, created two ninety-minute performance task questions inspired by his work in the early 1980s enhancing the California Bar Examination.

For the initial trials, fourteen unidentified colleges of various sizes supplied 1,365 student test takers, lured with payments of $20 to $25 an hour to take the tests online. In a series of reports available on the Council for Aid to Education Web site, the CLA researchers say the tests worked. College seniors had significantly better CLA scores than freshmen with comparable SAT scores, suggesting that something that improved with college teaching had been measured. Some colleges with similar SAT averages had significantly different CLA averages, suggesting that the results had something to do with the nature of education at each school.

But it will be many years before these systems are developed to where they can measure the worth of specific courses, and even longer before the colleges involved are willing to let the results be made public. Until that time, colleges will continue to insist that what they do has to be good because their professors have fine reputations and their graduates go on to successful careers.

In many cases they will be telling the truth. But in some cases they will not, with no one but the undergraduates in the courses aware of what is wrong. And the applicant trying to discern the truth by reading a Princeton catalog will, as always, have no reliable way to determine if the rhetoric matches the results. Unfortunately, "Caveat Lector" is likely to remain good advice for years to come.

Notes

1. Quoted in Barry Latzer, "The Hollow Core: Failure of the General Education Curriculum," American Council of Trustees and Alumni, 2004, nd.
2. The American Council of Trustees and Alumni describes itself as a nonprofit educational organization "committed to academic freedom, excellence, and accountability on college and university campuses." Some college officials call it a conservative organization, and its national council includes people who would fit that definition—former U.S. Education secretary William J. Bennett, The Public Interest coeditor Irving Kristol, and U.S. Circuit Judge Laurence H. Silberman. But other council members would be considered left of center, such as two prominent Democrats, former Colorado Governor Richard D. Lamm and *The New Republic* editor-in-chief, Martin Peretz.
3. Latzer report.
4. Ibid.
5. Marvin W. Peterson and Marne K. Emerson, "Analytic Framework of Institutional Support for Student Assessment," National Center for Postsecondary Improvement, Stanford University, Stanford, California, 1997.
6. Ibid.
7. Patrick M. Calla and Joni E. Finney, "Assessing Educational Capital: An Imperative for Policy," *Change* (July/August 2002): p 27.
8. From a 2004 e-mail to the author.
9. William Casement, "Declining Credibility for the AP Program," *Academic Questions*, National Association of Scholars (Princeton, NJ: Fall 2003).
10. Casement, p. 15.

11. E-mail to the author, August 20, 2004, from Richard C. Vos, vice president and dean of admission and financial aid, Claremont McKenna College, richard.vos@claremontmckenna.edu.
12. Telephone interview with the author, August 2004.
13. National Research Council, "Learning and Understanding: Improving Advanced Study of Mathematics and Science in U.S. High Schools," 2002. Committee on Programs for Advanced Study of Mathematics and Science in American High Schools. Jerry P. Gollub, Meryl W. Bertenthal, Jay B. Labov, and Philip C. Curtis Jr., eds. Center for Education (Washington, DC: National Academy Press, nd).
14. Latzer.
15. Ibid.
16. Telephone interview with the author, May 2004.
17. E-mail to the author, May 2004.
18. E-mail to the author, May 2004.
19. E-mail to the author, May 2004.
20. The three-hour test, piloted at fourteen colleges and universities and about to be adopted by more than fifty others, was designed at the behest of former Trinity and Hobart and William Smith colleges president Richard Hersh and of Roger Benjamin, president of the Rand Corporation's Council for Aid to Education (CAE). Hersh is also coeditor of this volume.

5

Liberal Education: Slip-Sliding Away?

Carol G. Schneider

As the United States moves into the twenty-first century, a college diploma has become what a high school diploma became a hundred years ago—*the* widely sought and broadly expected passport to both economic mobility and contributing citizenship. Most of the new jobs being created in our society now look for a higher level of analytical and contextual thinking than was expected a generation ago. The knowledge economy places a premium on the ability to deal with complex questions, analyze new information, and advance workplace innovation. Employers further seek conversancy with diversity and with cross-cultural and global developments. Above all, they look for employees with the skills and dispositions that lay a strong foundation for lifelong learning.

Public life also requires richer knowledge and understanding than was the case a generation ago. Especially since September 2001, Americans have been catapulted into a powerful sense of engagement with peoples, places, histories, and worldviews that many previously knew only dimly. Our entire society is now caught up in quests for deepened understanding and in reexaminations of the most basic questions about international justice, world religions, cross-cultural encounters, and civil liberties.

Responding to these new realities, Americans are flocking to college. Across the nation, 75 percent of high school graduates already pursue some form of post-secondary education within two years of graduation.

Among today's high school students, fully 93 percent declare that they expect to seek higher education, with 73 percent of this group intending to pursue a bachelor's degree. Working adults also are going to college. Forty-three percent of all college students are age twenty-four or older, and these older students have become the new majority on many college campuses. Higher learning has ceased to be simply an elite or elective option. In the United States, as in some other industrialized countries, it is now becoming the baseline preparation for full participation in every sphere of life.

By any measure, this is a milestone development with potentially far-reaching consequences. The new importance of higher education creates an extraordinary opportunity for students—and, ultimately, for American society. As a nation, we are now poised to make an investment in intellectual, economic, and civic development that could be even more historic in its implications than was the GI Bill that sent World War II veterans to college. But how likely is it that we will fully harvest the possibilities of this milestone opportunity?

Facing Core Questions

Americans are increasingly cynical about their public institutions and public leaders. But their skepticism does not extend to the content of a college education. Most students—and the public as a whole—assume without question that whatever students choose to study in college, they will learn what they need to know for today's competitive and complex environment. But in practice, college figures in the public imagination as something of a magical mystery tour. It is important to be admitted; it is also important to graduate with a degree. But what one does in between, what students actually learn in college, is largely unknown and largely unchallenged.

The new importance of higher learning in our society ought to raise fundamental questions about what students—and society—should expect from a college education. What kinds of learning will serve graduates well over time? What kinds of learning do we need to continue to fuel a dynamic economy? If analytical skill, creativity, and problem solving are important to graduates' long-term opportunities, how are these capabilities best developed? What is the academy's role in preparing students both for democratic citizenship and for citizenship in a nation that now possesses unrivaled power all around the globe? And what about the most ancient rationale for a liberal arts education: the view that the unexamined life is not worth living?

These questions are fundamental, but there is no public debate about them. And in the prevailing silence, Americans should recognize the real and present danger that we may ultimately squander the opportunity now before us to provide this entire college-going generation with the full benefits of an empowering and horizon-expanding education. If this seems far-fetched, consider what happened when all eligible students began to enroll in high school nearly a century ago.

In the first decades of the twentieth century, as high school became expected for all, there was a decisive struggle over the high school curriculum. One group of educators thought that all high school students ought to take a strong academic foundation in history, literature, science, mathematics, and languages. But others—the progressives of their day!—thought the students who were not college bound would be better served by less academic forms of learning.

The proponents of a rigorous liberal education in the schools lost this battle. As a result, the public schools invented differential curriculum "tracks." There was an "academic" course of study in the liberal arts and sciences intended to prepare students for college; a vocational course of study designed to prepare students for employment in industry or trades; and a "general track" that fell somewhere in between. The dividing lines were, of course, economic, with the affluent moving in one direction and the poor, including people of color and first-generation families, moving in quite another.

The invidious consequences of these policy decisions against a strong liberal arts and sciences curriculum in the schools are with us even today. The contemporary dialogue around school reform might suggest that many public schools have simply fallen short of a once-expected academic standard. This is far from the case. The "standards-based" school reform movement now under way in every state is, in practice, a belated effort to dismantle the inequitable and discriminatory curricular pathways that were earlier established as a matter of policy. Citizens need only look at the reports from the National Assessment of Educational Progress (NAEP) to see how far we remain, even today, from eliminating an attainment gap that was once considered perfectly sensible educational practice.[1]

Which Road to the Future: Liberal or Illiberal Education?

Today, as higher education becomes the new norm, the core question confronting educators, policymakers and the public is whether to insist on an intellectually challenging and horizon-expanding liberal education for all college students. Or, following the pattern of the twentieth-century high school experiment, will we decide to offer "elite" education to some students while providing a *narrower* preparation—what policymakers now call "workforce development"—to others?

On the merits, the answer to this question might seem self-evident. Respected colleges and universities in the United States have always placed high value on what has traditionally been described as liberal or liberating education, that is, an education that helps students comprehend and negotiate their relationship to the wider world. While the practices that constitute liberal education have evolved over time, liberal education has been viewed since the founding of our republic as the nation's best investment in cultivating democratic freedoms and a sense of responsibility to ends beyond one's own advantage.

Benjamin Franklin railed against "liberall education" when he was a young man unable to enroll at Harvard College. But later, as one of democracy's founding fathers, he helped establish the University of Pennsylvania and proudly touted the connection between the liberal arts and the economic and civic needs of the young nation. College and university founders across the nation proceeded in much the same spirit. Liberal education became the premier tradition in American higher education. It has set the standard for educational excellence in the academy, and it is still what students expect to achieve when they enroll at the nation's most sought-after colleges and universities.

What is a liberal education? Characteristically, liberal education fosters the qualities of mind and heart that prepare graduates to live productive lives in a complex and changing world. There are many classic descriptions of liberal education, but collectively they all point to the importance of helping students develop:

- Analytical, communication, and integrative capacities;
- problem-solving, intercultural, and collaborative abilities;
- scientific, technological, and quantitative competence;
- cross-cultural, aesthetic, and historical knowledge;
- ethical and civic engagement and responsibility; and
- preparation for work in a dynamic and global economy.

Many of the capacities listed here also are the very qualities that employers now seek in the workforce, as one study after another makes clear. Employers, for example, recently have told engineering educators that it is not enough to prepare engineers who are well schooled in science, technology, and mathematics. To function effectively in the modern economy, the business community contends, engineering and technology employees also need strong communication and collaborative skills; knowledge of social, global, and diversity issues; ethical reasoning; and the ability to integrate these different kinds of knowledge with engineering solutions.

Leaders in other professions also are calling for graduates who are broadly prepared and who can contribute productively to the waves of innovation and change that are now the new reality for organizations and communities alike. From business, to health fields, to education, there is a new insistence that all professionals need the skills, knowledge, and responsibilities just listed to succeed in their chosen work.

In today's world, therefore, liberal education provides a strong foundation for professional opportunity while enhancing graduates' readiness to respond to the demands of a complex and changing environment. A good liberal education also gives students a strong grounding in the core concepts and methods of science, as well as an understanding of the pervasive role the sciences play in shaping contemporary society.

At the same time, liberal education enriches the life of the mind and prepares students for the responsibilities of citizenship, at home and abroad. It introduces students to the ideas and values that undergird democratic societies and increasingly, in the contemporary academy, engages students directly with searing societal challenges, from HIV/AIDS to global hunger. As the University of Chicago's Martha Nussbaum has said, liberal education cultivates a "narrative imagination," the ability to enter into worldviews and experiences other than one's own.[2]

A liberal education further includes advanced study in one or more fields, studies that prepare students to grapple with the new and unscripted problems they can expect to find in every sphere of life. And finally, a liberal education helps students develop the ability to connect different parts of their learning: from different disciplines and courses, between academic and community-based learning, and between the different spheres of their own lives. Indeed, historian William Cronon has argued that if he had to pick just a single phrase to capture the essence of a liberal education, it would be E. M. Forster's famous injunction: "Only connect."[3]

This is the knowledge and these are the competencies that prepare one to prosper in our society. As the better part of a generation now heads to college, however, there are no guarantees that all of today's students will achieve this kind of education.

The public, vaguely and with few details about the particulars of educational excellence, still may assume that the commitment to provide this kind of life-enhancing education to all students remains intact. But, in fact, numerous trends in postsecondary education are moving in a very different direction. Not that there has been a policy debate about denying liberal education to some fraction of the college population. Far from it. Rather, there has been an insidious acceleration of countervailing developments that, collectively, have had the effect of marginalizing liberal education, moving it off the policy and public radar screen altogether.

Market Challenges

One of the most important countervailing trends has been investor interest in higher education as a form of "big business." With for-profits jumping into the competition for students, there are now some two thousand so-called career colleges that are not accredited in the traditional way, through peer review by colleagues from long-established regional accrediting associations. Instead, the career colleges have set up their own "national" accrediting organizations. They also have invested unprecedented sums in political lobbying activity. Virtually none of these institutions purports to provide a liberal education, nor do any employ many faculty with a strong foundation in the liberal arts and sciences. Instead, these career colleges offer professional programs only: business, accounting, finance, technology, and the like. Some of the career colleges assume that students will have taken a general education foundation in arts and sciences courses at another institution; others dispense with any arts and sciences expectations altogether.

Each of these career colleges promises students a degree. But the meaning of these degrees is very different from what students would experience at universities that value their commitment to liberal education.

Not surprisingly, there is widespread skepticism within the academy about the value of these alternative degree programs. But the academy has been silenced because business leaders and political figures love these career college programs. Their overhead is low, since they make no pretense at advancing scholarship or even of sustaining a full-time faculty. Their business plans are reassuring since they offer only high-profit majors, while more costly fields, such as the sciences and the humanities, are left to mainstream institutions. The for-profit schools even have pioneered in new assessment and accountability strategies that business leaders also find reassuring. The traditional academy knows perfectly well that career college assessments do not address liberal education outcomes. But because the traditional academy is itself weak on assessing the quality of liberal education outcomes, it has been ill-positioned to raise this very basic objection.

Self-Inflicted Wounds

The threats to liberal education do not come only from for-profit competitors. The erosion of liberal education also is proceeding apace within the established academy, despite the best efforts of many well-intended faculty members and academic leaders who continue to believe that liberal education is the defining difference between excellence and mediocrity.

The root of the problem is a curriculum model that was originally intended as a design for liberal education but that, over time, has evolved in ways that frequently make it an impediment to the very goals it was initially created to achieve. Put in place throughout the academy nearly one hundred years ago, this prevailing curriculum model is familiar to most college-educated people as an educational plan for "Breadth" and "Depth," with "Breadth" to be attained through a series of introductory or "general education" courses in arts and sciences fields, and "Depth" achieved through completion of a major or concentration in one of these disciplines.

When first invented, the Breadth/Depth plan took it as axiomatic that students would select one of the arts and sciences disciplines as a major and that "Study-in-Depth" in a disciplinary major would by definition both define and foster liberal education. This view was so widely held that, for many years, institutions were classified—as liberal arts or not—by the percentage of their undergraduates who chose arts and sciences majors.

Classification systems notwithstanding, however, the fact is that "Depth" and the disciplines soon took off on a trajectory of their own. As the twentieth century progressed, the arts and sciences disciplines became absorbed in their own scholarly questions and drew back from overt concern with the broader aims of liberal education such as civic engagement, ethical reasoning, or integrative learning. Faculty members in the arts and sciences disciplines certainly value these capacities and generally believe that college should develop them. But they do not see it as their own primary responsibility or a role for their departmental curricula.

Over time, moreover, the curricular dominance of the arts and sciences disciplines has waned. Today's students are notably pragmatic about college, and close to two-thirds of all graduating college students choose preprofessional fields rather than the arts and sciences as their primary focus of study. There is no inherent reason, of course, why business, engineering, health, or education cannot be taught in ways that advance the broad aims of liberal education. But like the arts and sciences departments before them, the professional fields also have other priorities. They too believe that liberal education outcomes may well be important, but are not their particular responsibility.

If disciplines and departments are not considered responsible for the broad outcomes of a liberal education, who is? The answer to that question is the same on virtually every college and university campus.

From the Ivy League to the nation's growing system of two-year colleges, the academy has lowered its sights for liberal education from the entire college curriculum to that small fraction of the undergraduate experience known as general education. The aims of liberal education and the goals of the "Breadth" courses in general education are now one and the same. General education requirements vary from one-quarter to one-third of the undergraduate curriculum but on the great majority of college campuses, this small set of courses is the only part of the curriculum held collectively responsible for liberal education outcomes.

Liberal education, in sum, has been downsized. Where once a liberal education encompassed the entire college curriculum, now the conventional design for liberal education—that is, general education—calls for students to take a "distribution" of courses in the humanities and arts, the social sciences, and the sciences, with additional requirements in mathematics and English composition. Indeed, this basic framework has been locked in by legislative or regulatory fiat within public higher education in the majority of the fifty states.

The systemic quality problems with this downsized design for liberal education are pervasive and spreading. There are, to be sure, some wonderful models for general education: rigorous programs with high standards, strong organizing principles, and an ethos of shared intellectual inquiry and community. But these are the exceptions that prove the rule.

On the whole, faculty know that the academy rewards academic scholarship, not educational leadership, and that their contributions to the quality of general education are simply a form of pro bono enterprise. Faculty priorities follow the academic reward system. Faculty do spend time on the quality of their own individual courses. But on most campuses, they are neither expected to spend time on the quality of the collective general education curriculum nor rewarded for doing so.

As a result—at both selective and unselective colleges and universities alike—general education is an orphan curriculum, fragmented and incoherent. Frequently, required courses are taught by adjunct faculty or graduate assistants rather than full-time senior faculty. Sensing the lack of strong intellectual purpose in their general studies, many students have come to view general education as an obstacle to surmount rather than a resource for their own lives.

Campus slang tells the true story about the unraveling of this twentieth-century design for liberal education. Rather than valuing this "liberal education core," both students and faculty routinely speak of getting general education requirements "out of the way" as soon as possible.

For many years some well-intentioned faculty have fought to bring educational focus and coherence to the general education curricula, despite the absence of campus rewards for their efforts. But today general education is facing an additional set of problems that are only accelerating the tendencies toward curricular fragmentation and incoherence.

The new reality on campus is that 60 percent of all students who earn a four-year degree transfer courses from one college or university to another, sometimes attending three, four, or even more institutions on their way to a diploma. With student transfers skyrocketing, many campuses find that their graduates have taken their introductory general education courses somewhere else, while the students who actually completed their general education program have since departed for other colleges or universities.

In addition, the new popularity of advanced placement and other accelerated high school courses means that many students are satisfying their general education distribution requirements with courses they took in high school. In Fall 2004, some state governors announced their interest in shaving a semester off the traditional four years of college by encouraging students to take at least a semester's worth of college courses while in high school. Although the governors do not say so, the course reductions will almost surely count against general education requirements rather than departmental majors.

In other words, even when a campus manages—against all odds—to design a coherent general education program, that program may serve only a small fraction of the institution's students. A growing majority of students are cobbling together their general education courses from multiple institutions, including high school.

And yet, as we have seen, the prevailing commitment to Breadth/Depth means that general education is the typical college or university's only shared program for liberal education. More by default than design, liberal education is eroding.

Hidden Differences

Although these above problems affect virtually every college and university, some additional obstacles to liberal education are particular to community colleges. As half the nation's college students first enroll in community colleges, these additional problems are significant, especially for first-generation students and students from underserved communities who often know the least about what to expect from a college education.

Community colleges certainly offer a general education curriculum in arts and sciences courses to students who want to transfer to a four-year institution; in this sense, they share in the now-standard "Breadth" approach to liberal education. But many community colleges also make a basic distinction between their associate degree programs, which were designed to support transfer, and their "applied" or "technical" degree programs, which were not. These applied programs range from office administration, to tourism, to real estate; they convey a degree, but their intent is to prepare students directly for job placement rather than for further academic work. At best, such programs may include a few general education courses, but they were never designed to meet the existing standards for "Breadth," much less to meet the ambitious goals for liberal learning that both the academy and employers endorse today.

When college students enroll in these applied programs, they are pursuing a degree—an applied degree—but not a liberal education. The public does not understand this distinction; students may miss it as well.

Many community college students, of course, start in applied programs and then discover that they want to transfer to a baccalaureate degree program. Frequently, however, these students encounter difficulties transferring their courses for the applied degree toward a four-year degree. Sometimes the four-year colleges' objections are warranted; sometimes they are not. But the discovery of these barriers has not led policymakers to ask whether all college students are being fully prepared for a complex and changing world. Rather, discovering that community college students have "wasted" their credit dollars, legislators are rushing to the rescue with an outraged insistence that colleges should recognize one another's credits, a principle they also apply to courses that students may want to transfer from one or more of the career colleges.

The result is that public colleges and universities are under considerable pressure to homogenize their academic standards and to recognize courses as essentially equivalent, whether they actually are, or not. In this new environment of student swirl, what is needed is a fresh effort to rethink the work of the first two years of college in relation to goals for liberal education. But this is not what is happening. Rather, the policy inclination is to insist that the academy treat college courses as if they are Lego pieces, one interchangeable with another.

Far from focusing on the quality of the general education program, regulators are focusing instead on students' credit accumulation. Students, policymakers contend, should be able to collect their diplomas when they have the right number of course credits collected in their shopping carts. Do the accumulated course credits signify that students have achieved the outcomes of a rigorous and challenging liberal education? This is not a question that policy leaders and legislators are asking. Instead, some national leaders are even considering the desirability of a national "credit registry" so that students' courses will be permanently on record and seamlessly transferable from one campus to another.

Such a credit registry would certainly be a consumer service. But is education the same as any other consumer product? Or is this much the same mindset that, in an earlier period, made all high school diplomas superficially equivalent, even when they represent dramatically different levels of challenge and accomplishment?

What is missing, in the new environment of student and credit transfer, is any set of organizing principles for ensuring equivalency either for liberal education as a whole or for the individual courses that should contribute to liberal education. Many states have ensured that courses with the right titles—English 101, Biology 202—will transfer readily from one institution to another. But very few states have asked faculty to establish what students are supposed to know and be able to do after completing Biology 202. So long as the course is "approved," and the student passed, state expectations are met.

Off the Radar Screen

In the current policy and political environment, where the degree is all important, but no one wants to look too closely at what level of learning it represents, the very concept of a strong liberal education is slipping off the nation's radar screen. The organization I head, the Association of

American Colleges and Universities (AAC&U), commissioned a series of focus groups with college-bound high school seniors across the country to find out what they thought about liberal education. Every one of these students hoped to enroll in one of the nation's traditionally accredited four-year institutions. But scarcely one of these students had even heard the term "liberal education." Those who thought they knew something about it assumed that liberal or liberal arts education was some special species of education found mainly at small residential colleges—the so-called liberal arts colleges—which today educate fewer than 5 percent of all college students.

The college-bound students who took part in these discussions were not opposed to the broad aims of a liberal or liberal arts education, once these aims were explained. Indeed, they found them attractive. But it was clear that most had never taken part in a discussion of the larger goals of a college education before. No one had told them that the broad aims of a liberal education are the same educational outcomes that future employers routinely endorse, in survey after survey. Like everyone else, the students in these groups were focused on getting into college and getting out. As one said candidly, "I think that college is expecting you to not know what's going on. . . . But I'm not really concerned. . . . Everyone is going to be in the same situation." In other words, we are all going to college. None of us knows what we will actually do there. But that is how things are.

Any college admissions office would be able to explain these students' mystification about liberal or liberal arts education. "Liberal" is a problematic term in today's political environment, and, as a consequence, many admissions officers have quietly retired the term—even for their general education curricula—unfazed by the thought that liberal education is the nation's premier educational tradition and philosophy. Moreover, current wisdom in college marketing assumes that the best way to attract applicants is through a strong focus on career preparation, reinforced by an appealing array of amenities and services and a nearly unlimited choice of curricular and life options. No one wants to "market" the news that college is, at its best, a process of challenging intellectual and personal formation. The aims of liberal education are demanding as well as life and career-enhancing. But "demanding" is not a concept that admissions offices have learned how to sell.

Many analysts and policy leaders are very comfortable with the marginalization of liberal education. They declare without apology that markets are keyed to short-term outcomes and have no patience for forms of learning that pay off over a lifetime. Practical studies that prepare students for specific jobs will sell; the rest will just wither away at all but a small set of "elite" institutions. First-generation, low-income, and adult learners in particular, such observers contend, need job training rather than intellectual development. Like their predecessors in the schools debate, these higher education realists are content to provide "elite" education to elites and vocational skills to everyone else. And, in virtually every state, it is these realists who sit at the table with governors, legislators, and university trustees.

Reclaiming the Commitment to Liberal Education

It is in our national interest to reclaim our commitment to the aims of liberal education—for all college students, not just a fortunate minority. We live in a world of change in virtually every sphere of life; all citizens need and deserve the intellectual skills and the foundational knowledge that can help them successfully ride the waves of change—at work, in civil society, and in their personal lives.

Yet, as we have seen, many of the trends in higher education are moving in just the opposite direction. What then is to be done?

The answer, I believe, is the creation of a new partnership between the academy and leaders in the business and civic communities. That partnership needs to focus once again on the broad aims of a good education and to provide vocal leadership for the importance of these aims in every sphere of life: the workplace, the public square, the global community, the home. We need a new alliance for liberal education, an alliance that works simultaneously to prepare graduates for the challenges of the workplace, of citizenship, and of fulfilling personal lives.

But it will not be enough simply to argue for the importance of an empowering and horizon-expanding college education. As I have suggested, we also must recognize that the twentieth-century design for liberal education—that long-sanctified combination of Breadth and Depth—no longer works. The goals for liberal education are ambitious and expanding, as our society becomes more global and technologically savvy. But the terrain of general education has been limited by design. Moreover, general education is now buffeted by too many centrifugal forces—the tendency toward early college courses in high school; the new student patterns of multiple institutional enrollments; the lack of powerful intellectual leadership—to provide for itself a coherent and empowering liberal education. The twentieth-century design for undergraduate education is simply too frail a vessel for the challenge of liberal education.

What would a new national alliance for liberal education actually do? Recently the AAC&U has been asking just this question, in candid and probing exchanges with academic, business, and civic leaders from across the country. Eight key proposals have emerged from these dialogues:

1. Promote a new understanding that the traditional distinctions between the liberal arts and preprofessional studies no longer hold. The professions require people who have mastered the liberal arts, while the liberal arts and sciences gain new value when they make a difference in the world. Liberal education—redefined to include practical learning—is needed in every sphere of life.
2. Build public and academic support for the broad aims of a twenty-first-century liberal education—intellectual, social, practical, civic, and ethical—and insist that these aims be addressed across the entire educational experience, beginning in school and culminating with the final year of college.
3. Create new partnerships between schools and the academy so that school reform and higher education reform focus together on helping students prepare for the multiple challenges of a complex and changing world.
4. Hold every college and university responsible for focusing the entire educational program—students, faculty, and staff alike—on the important aims of liberal education and for achieving these aims in the contexts of students' most advanced studies—that is, their chosen fields or majors.
5. Reframe students' majors so that each provides focus, context, and integration, the enabling conditions for liberal education.
6. Institute milestone and capstone requirements and assessments—opportunities for students to demonstrate their progress in achieving the

larger aims of education, and for institutions to make transparent the quality of work they expect as evidence for a liberal education degree.

7. Create and sustain a broad public dialogue about the purposes of education. Challenge and change the mind-set that views higher learning as an accumulation of courses, credit hours, and grades. Seek and value tangible evidence of liberal education in practice—raising questions, solving problems, making a difference.
8. Seek out and make visible the campuses, programs, and practices that already help students achieve the aims of liberal education at a high level of quality. Liberal education is under siege, but it is not totally vanquished. There are many campuses where it is already being reinvigorated through innovative new curricula and teaching practices. Most of these promising innovations are unknown to the public. They deserve new visibility and new support, because they point the way toward a new design for the undergraduate experience, a design that breaks free of the traditional silos and the traditional problems with the Breadth design for liberal or general education.

American higher education stands at a fundamental crossroads. A new generation is heading to college. But to ensure both access and excellence, we will need a new generation of leadership and public support to overcome the significant barriers that impede students' access to educational excellence.

Campuses will have to make far-reaching and even dramatic changes to their established practices to ensure that all students graduate well prepared for an era characterized by greater expectations in every sphere of life. They can and will make these changes when the public learns to insist that liberal education is the best and most practical preparation for every American.

Notes

1. National Center for Education Statistics, "The Nation's Report Card," http://nces.ed.gov/nationsreportcard/naepdata/.
2. Martha C. Nussbaum, *Cultivating Humanity: A Classical Defense of Reform in Liberal Education* (Cambridge, MA: Harvard University Press, 1997), p. 85ff.
3. William Cronon, " 'Only Connect': The Goals of a Liberal Education," *Liberal Education* vol. 85, no. 1 (1999): 6–13. Article adapted and reprinted from *The American Scholar* vol. 67, no. 4 (1998).

6

Six Challenges to the American University

Vartan Gregorian

When I was at Brown University, I welcomed each new class of students by citing Richard Sheridan, whose late-eighteenth-century play, *The Critic*, has one of my favorite lines about the paucity of independent thinkers. He wrote, "The number of those who go through the fatigue of judging for themselves is very small indeed!" I urged students to undergo this necessary fatigue and to resist pressures to conform from teachers, peers or those with simplistic political or religious catechisms promising to provide instant solutions to complex problems. I told them that their own thoughts, convictions, beliefs, ideas, and principles—their identities and their characters—are their most precious possessions. Change them if you must, I said, but do not abdicate your intellectual prerogatives, your independent thought, and free will. And please, please, be neither victims of cynicism and nihilism nor passive adherents of so-called political correctness. That trivializes, marginalizes, and ignores our society's real issues and challenges, including poverty, racism, sexism, discrimination, and injustice.

The university has long provided a place to undergo the "necessary fatigue of independent thought." Thomas Jefferson saw universities as sanctuaries of ideas, where, he said, "We are not afraid to follow truth wherever it may lead, nor to tolerate any error so long as reason is left free to combat it." Today our colleges and universities, these vital "sanctuaries of ideas," face at least six major challenges:

1. The information-glut (hereafter referred to as "info-glut") and the fragmentation of knowledge;

2. the curriculum crisis, including the liberal arts;
3. the commercialization of research;
4. the evolution of a two-tier system of faculty, with full-time and part time members;
5. concerns about quality, especially in schools of education; and
6. the changes that distance learning and e-learning may bring.

Failure to answer these challenges will transform our society and threaten our democratic republic.

The Information Challenge

The first of these challenges, impacting all others, is that our world is overwhelmed with information and "underwhelmed" with knowledge. This is an old problem, grown worse, as Neil Postman reminds us in his "Informing Ourselves to Death." He maintains that the Information Age really began "in the late 15th century when a goldsmith named Gutenberg, from Mainz, converted an old wine press into a printing machine, and in so doing, created what we now call an information explosion. Forty years after the invention of the press, there were printing machines in 110 cities in six different countries; 50 years after, more than eight million books had been printed, almost all of them filled with information that had previously not been available to the average person."[1]

The Information Age, now the Information Revolution, parallels the Industrial Revolution in its impact and far-reaching consequences. It is extending our brains and imaginations into the deep unknown with computers and the World Wide Web. Information of all varieties is speeding toward us from all directions. We are bombarded by fragments of information without much context. T. S. Eliot could have been describing aspects of the twenty-first century when he wrote to the effect that hell is a place where nothing connects with nothing. Elsewhere, he also asked two important questions: "Where is the wisdom we have lost in knowledge? Where is the knowledge we have lost in information?"

The glut is very real. More information has been created in the last thirty years than in the previous five thousand. Given this amount of information, English astronomer Sir Martin Rees says, "It's embarrassing that 90 percent of the universe is unaccounted for."[2] According to a 1984 estimate, at least a thousand books are published internationally every day, 365,000 a year. We are told that the total amount of collected information doubles every five years, yet some investigators believe that we are unable to use 90 to 95 percent of the information that is currently available. For example, Internet search engines can give you hyperlinks to well over 20,000,000 web sites pertinent to the term "Information Age."

In his book *Information Anxiety*, Richard Saul Wurman notes that all this information is tantalizing, but very frustrating. He writes: "We are like a thirsty person who has been condemned to use a thimble to drink from a fire hydrant."[3]

The Information Revolution puts a great burden on the educational establishment to provide some kind of intellectual coherence, connections with our past, our present, and our future. Today, however, our universities are themselves prodigious information machines and, unavoidably, contributors to the info-glut. Two overlapping trends worsen this problem: First, there is, by necessity, an increasing importance of the specialist, and this specialization is accelerating the fragmentation of knowledge in all academic and professional fields; and second, there is decreasing respect for the generalist and, I believe, a consequent decline in our society's ability to provide coherence and synthesis. Universities face a major challenge in refining their philosophies of education and the structure of their curriculum.

Clearly, in an age of extraordinary specialization and fragmentation of knowledge, we cannot abandon specializations or subspecializations or even sub-subspecializations. After all, the division of labor has greatly advanced the cause of civilization. Specialization is an instrument of progress. Complexity, by necessity, requires specialization.

So we need specialists. But for greater understanding, we also need generalists trained in the humanities, sciences, and social sciences. The challenge is to provide synthesis. We need to create a common discourse, a common vocabulary among the various disciplines. We need to rethink the way we pursue knowledge and education, and this means we need to reorganize the content of the curriculum to give coherence to our specialized and fragmented base of knowledge. More than ever, then, liberal arts is necessary as one of the remaining tools of general education, interdisciplinary education, and multidisciplinary education that bring science, the humanities, social sciences, and arts together.

The Technical and Preprofessional Challenge: The Curriculum Crisis

A second, related challenge arises from the growth of technical and preprofessional education. To survive and prosper in an Information Age, we must try to balance technical studies with general and liberal education. When Oliver Wendell Holmes was a professor at Harvard in 1872, he commented on this need for balance, saying "Science is a first-rate piece of furniture for a man's upper chamber, if he has common sense on the ground floor."

In this balancing endeavor, I believe that institutions of higher education are losing ground. We witness the extraordinary growth of technical and preprofessional studies at the expense of the sciences, humanities, and social sciences—in short, true liberal arts. In 1970, 50 percent of the baccalaureate degrees awarded were in a liberal arts discipline, including the sciences. By 1995, that percentage had shrunk to about 40 percent, and about 60 percent of the degrees were in preprofessional or technical fields. The largest number of bachelor of arts degrees granted in the 1990s were in business. For the most part, people in the technical and preprofessional schools and those in the liberal arts schools exist in separate worlds on campus, in complete intellectual isolation.[4]

We must remind ourselves that the value of a liberal arts education and education in general is to enhance people's powers of rational analysis, intellectual precision, independent judgment, and mental adaptability. After all, a proper and balanced education is neither a passive act nor an end in itself. It is important not only to be able to engage in new ideas, but also to be willing to make public declarations of one's convictions and one's commitments—and then to be able to translate them into written words and action. Education must make us more than well-ordered puppets in the passing show, making gestures with no sense of the significance of the human drama, moved only by the strings that tie us to material things.

The experience of attending the university—and here I mean the broad sweep of the enterprise, from a large research institution to the community college—must make students familiar with the best our culture has taught, said, and done—as well as the dead ends and aberration—that clutter our history. Education must help us understand the sweep of our culture, the achievements, the problems, the solutions, and the failures that mark our history. This kind of knowledge is critical to our understanding of who and what we are. A proper education must serve as a tool of enlightenment. It can be an instrument for enhancing individual as well as collective self-determination. It can provide liberation from political, economic, and social ills. It can help us understand the American polity—which is no small task in our pluralistic and multicultural society that allows the unique to participate in the universal without dissolving in it. Finally, this kind of education serves as the vehicle of American democracy as well as its engine, providing a powerful way to tackle our country's unfinished agenda. After all, education promises every sort of advancement to those who, on the basis of their sex or race or age or disability, have not been able to partake in the benefits of our society.

A liberal education is needed to integrate learning and provide balance; otherwise students will graduate into a world in which dependence on experts of every kind will be even more common than it is today. With that trend comes an even greater temptation to abdicate judgment in favor of expert opinion. Unless we help our students acquire an identity, they will end up not just dependent on experts but at their mercy—or at the mercy of charlatans posing as experts. If students' knowledge is limited to their subspecialized area, they are vulnerable in most aspects of existence. It is the equivalent of dressing a child in the warmest hat possible—but no other clothing—and sending him out into a snowstorm.

As a people, we need to understand where we were, where we are, and where we are going. Without liberal arts to provide a context for technical training, young people cannot be expected to understand the general nature and structure of our society, the role of the university, the necessity of academic freedom, or the importance of values—all their education will have no ethical, moral, or societal context. There will be confusion. On campus, for example, freedom will be confused with license, and tenure will be confused with job security.

The Commercialization of Research

I fear the University's unbridled search for financial stability and new revenues is at the heart of the challenge. Just as students are drawn to fields that seem to promise lucrative jobs, much of higher education pursues grants and contracts wherever they may be. Just as the university is bending its educational mission to meet the demands of specialization and the job market, so too is the university's research being pulled out of its orbit of free inquiry by research contracts from industry and business.

Universities find themselves competing for business investment as federal and state support for research shrinks. The loss of public support prompted Mark Yudof, president of the University of Minnesota, to wonder—in print: "Is the Public Research University in America Dead?" Between 1986 and 1996, he noted, state spending on higher education fell 14 percent, with universities losing budget share to other priorities, including prisons and healthcare. Similarly, federal spending on university research declined for more than a decade, even as the cost of research has risen rapidly. But in the last two decades, industry-funded university research grew an average of about 8 percent a year, reaching $1.9 billion in 1997. By comparison, federal support for university research was softening, falling to $14.3 billion by 1997.[5]

As the nation's pioneer in basic research, the university faces a difficult challenge. How can it maintain leadership in pure research if distracted by research for the marketplace? In the past, the university's challenge was maintaining independence from federal regulators; the current challenge to academic freedom in research is to keep some degree of independence from industry and business. As James Bryant Conant, one of Harvard's illustrious presidents, once wrote, "There is only one proved method of assisting the advancement of pure science—that of picking men of genius, backing them heavily and leaving them to direct themselves."

Clearly, the increasing commercialization of university research has the potential to be a corrupting influence whenever economic necessities force faculty to surrender prerogatives. Industry sponsorship of university research, after all, can affect the faculty's research agenda in ways that directly and indirectly discourage pure research in favor of research with commercial applications. The challenge for the university is to balance theoretical and practical research—and to protect the individual rights of the faculty, the collective rights of the university, and the integrity of research.

This, again, is a question of balance, because university research always has mixed the theoretical with the practical. As Yudof reminds us, university research brought us the sound motion picture, artificial joints, the pacemaker, Teflon, earthquake-resistant buildings and countless other practical inventions.

The challenge is for universities to maintain their integrity, even as the lines between industry and university research are blurring. A controversial example of this is the alliance created between Novartis, the life-sciences company based in Switzerland, and the Department of Plant and Microbial Biology at the University of California at Berkeley. Since 1999 the company has been paying the department $5 million a year for the right to license a portion of what the researchers discover. Some say this funding will strengthen the department; others worry that research with less commercial potential will inevitably be phased out. No matter what does or does not happen under the glare of publicity at Berkeley, the contract may set a bad precedent. As Clark Kerr, the former president of the University of California system, once commented, "At a place like Berkeley, the situation is much more likely to go well than it would at lesser places, where faculty aren't as sure of themselves. I'm much more concerned about Novartis 2 and Novartis 3."[6]

The Part-Time Faculty Challenge

If the faculty is the core of the university, as I firmly believe it is, then it follows that the university is only as strong, or as weak, as its faculty. Anything that fragments or diminishes the faculty also fragments and diminishes the university. Hence the widespread trend toward part-time faculty threatens to undermine the strength of the university.

Today at most institutions of higher education, most newly hired teachers are either part-timers, adjuncts, or graduate students. Administrators rely on these part-timers to reduce class sizes and to teach more subjects at more times, including nights and weekends.

The growth of part-time faculty nationwide has been phenomenal, nearly doubling between 1970 and 1995, from 22 percent of the faculty to 41 percent. What this figure suggests is that in many institutions, the majority of faculty members are part-timers. The percentage of part-timers also has continued to edge up, and part-time faculty teach about one-quarter of all college courses. Although an estimated 85 percent of part-timers are not eligible for tenure, they are not temporary workers. Part-timers work for the same institution for an average of 5.4 years and teach an average of almost two classes in each enrollment period.[7] This reliance on part-time faculty reduces university costs—a major goal—because part-timers, adjuncts, and graduate students are paid a small fraction of what tenured faculty earn for a similar amount of work. As the PBS documentary that is this book's companion notes, most freshman English classes at the University of Arizona are taught by graduate students. That practice is, unfortunately, becoming the rule, not the exception.

Unfortunately, the university's shortsighted gains may cause long-term losses. Universities cannot afford to have a growing underclass of part-timers in the ranks of the faculty. The plight of part-timers is all too well documented, but Bryan Konefsky helps personify the trend. He teaches five classes in film and video at the University of New Mexico. He has worked at the university since 1996, but his rank is adjunct and he earns less than half of what his tenure-track peers earn. "In many ways it's a class system, and we're the untouchables," he says. He makes ends meet by doing freelance work and relying on his wife's health insurance.[8]

Let's be frank: Part-timers are piece workers, often paid just a few thousand dollars per course. Few are paid for any academic research they conduct. When a class is canceled for lack of enrollment, which can occur a few weeks into the semester, adjunct instructors may not be paid. They typically receive no benefits, do not have the use of a computer or office, and, in some places, are not even allowed to buy an on-campus parking permit or have their names listed in the campus phone directory. This is the employment market into which universities are sending their newly minted PhDs.

If this is how the nation's universities treat their recent graduates, how long will it be before graduate school enrollments wither away?

The lack of opportunity for tenure-track positions is already maiming the liberal arts. Consider one indication of this problem: Between 1990 and 1995, 55 percent of the 7,598 PhDs who graduated in English and foreign-language programs could not obtain full-time, tenure-track positions during the year they received their degrees, according to the Modern Language Association of America.[9]

In her review of research on higher education faculty, Adrianna Kezar reports, "Perhaps no other trend was more evident in the literature than the condition of and growth of part-time faculty . . . Part-time faculty has roughly doubled over the last 20 years, with temporary faculty especially prevalent in English, History, Modern Language and Mathematics." Is education becoming a business, ruled by the law of supply and demand? Kezar suggests it is, saying: "With most of the observable trends in higher education moving in the direction of responding to the demands of business, new technology, distance education and building partnerships with nonacademic communities, the humanities and the centrality of classroom teaching are being side-stepped."[10]

The increasing shift to a part-time faculty also poses a major threat to academic freedom. The *Chronicle of Higher Education* noted the growing threat: "Here's a news flash for people who care about academic freedom: Half the professoriate does not have it. Adjuncts are getting dumped for things tenure-track scholars do with impunity—teaching controversial material, fighting grade changes, organizing unions. One part-timer was dropped after trying to talk about pornography in an ethics class. Another was ditched after racist words came up in a communications course. Then there was the professor who got fired for harassment after he mentioned tampons and anal sex in a pathology class."[11]

In this type of situation, of course, the controversial statement or research project is not mentioned in the letter of dismissal. The offending part-time instructor is simply told that his or her contract is not being renewed because of declining enrollment, a scheduling conflict, or some other administrative excuse. We all know tenure is not a perfect system. Many things are wrong with it, but on the whole it has protected academic freedom. I am less concerned with the problems of tenure than with the problems of inadequate job security and related issues about income and professional advancement. These concerns can nurture the worst kind of censorship—self-censorship. And I believe that self-imposed censorship is a significant reason why we hear so little from faculty members about national issues confronting the United States. I have sometimes thought that faculties, not young adults, should be known as Generation X.

The lack of job security and of academic freedom inevitably take their toll on the quality of teaching by part-timers. P. D. Lesko, the head of the National Adjunct Faculty Guild, has said that "part-timers are terrified of being rigorous graders, terrified to deal with complaints about the course materials, terrified to deal with plagiarists. A lot of them are working as robots. They go in, they teach, they leave. No muss, no fuss." But Lesko adds: "If you're afraid to give an honest grade or an honest opinion, you're not teaching."[12]

Professional organizations also are limited in their ability to protect the academic freedom of so many part-time teachers. While serving as the general secretary of the American Association of University Professors' academic-freedom committee, Jordan Kurland said that part-timers with concerns about academic freedom are "entitled to a hearing, but we don't insist on the same full procedures that a faculty member with more equity in the place has."[13]

Essentially, the challenge posed by the trend of part-time faculty is the erosion of quality in institutions of higher education. Academic freedom cannot thrive in a setting where half the faculty members do not have secure jobs. Universities cannot easily separate economic security from academic freedom and autonomy.

The Challenge of Mediocrity

Higher education simply cannot afford to dedicate the first two years of college to remedial studies. But, make no mistake about it, remediation is a growth industry on most campuses. Higher education must contribute to strengthening K–12 schooling, which it can do by raising admission standards and requirements. But it must also get its own house in order, and here reform begins in schools of education.

Weak schools of education are contributors to the weakening of the university. It has long been the fashion to criticize teachers while ignoring their training, but the fact is, the quality of their preparation has a direct bearing on how well they teach. And if they teach poorly, their students tend to arrive at universities ill-prepared for higher-level courses.

Although universities should not institutionalize mediocrity and tolerate substandard schools of education, many allow their (perhaps unaccredited) schools of education to recruit education majors knowing very well that the schools cannot meet students' needs and career goals. The universities know their education schools cannot provide students with the knowledge, skills, and competency they need to fulfill their professional obligations or society's aspirations for them.

Schools of education have no excuse for offering substandard courses and programs. In one dismal indication of the problem a recent study estimated that of every 600 students who enter a four-year teaching program, only 180 complete it, only 72 become teachers, and only about 40 are still in the classroom several years later.[14]

Perhaps most shocking of all is that even inside many schools of education, the training of classroom teachers is routinely considered low-prestige, entry-level work—a responsibility given to the most junior faculty members, part-time professors, and teaching assistants. Reflecting this bias, a 1997 study found that nearly two out of three education professors acknowledge that their programs "often fail to prepare teachers for the challenges of teaching in the real world."[15] In many schools of education, prospective teachers never even have a chance to practice-teach in a K–12 classroom.[16]

Too often, the shortsighted management practice requiring every school to be financially self-sufficient exacerbates the problem. In these circumstances, schools of education, which often have no endowment, find it expedient to increase enrollments, which may require lowering standards for admission and graduation. They have created a self-contained curriculum and have increased course requirements in education as a way to avoid losing tuition revenue to other schools on campus. As part of the effort to discourage students from taking courses with the arts and sciences faculty, schools of education have hired their own professors of psychology, philosophy, or history. Thus, financial incentives often sustain the schools' intellectual isolation. No wonder that these trends have produced some poor results.

The poor preparation many teachers receive in schools of education is reflected in our K–12 schools. There we see horrifying statistics, ranging from low scores on student achievement tests to high levels of turnover among schoolteachers.

Another result is that higher education is forced to meet the remedial educational needs of its incoming students. We are told that one in three college students had taken a remedial reading course and that many of these remedial readers had taken three or more other remedial courses, including mathematics. For those who attended two-year colleges, the situation is worse: 63 percent of the students took at least one remedial course.[17] Not surprisingly, students needing remedial work are less likely to earn a degree. This is a disgrace. American higher education cannot afford to be in the remedial education business.

Technology's Challenge

Technology presents another major challenge to the university. Can technology strengthen the university and its faculty, or will it undermine the enterprise? Around us, an electronic university is emerging, one that promises to enrich teaching and make education more affordable and accessible around the world. But in our love affair with technology and in our culture's rush to say "Out with the old, in with the new," we must not blindly ignore the flaws in our gadgets or thoughtlessly spurn principles, practices, and values developed over the past eight centuries.

Today, advances in educational technology can transcend the limits of space and time so that students may study anything, anytime, anywhere. Electronic courseware, as it is called, can be accessed on campus, across the globe, or, in due time, on the moon. Will these advances in communications do away with the need for residential universities? What will be the role of the faculty in the cyberage?

Peter Drucker, the management guru, gives the traditional university only thirty years. Frank H. T. Rhodes, president emeritus of Cornell, is also among those who seriously question whether the residential university will survive. Writing about it, he said, "I wonder at times if we are not like the dinosaurs, looking up at the sky at the approaching asteroid and wondering whether it has an implication for our future."[18] Predictions and prophecies aside, the challenges posed by electronic learning are both real and major. Some interesting trends have brought us to this place.

Higher education is increasingly dominated by older students. These older students (by some estimates already a majority) typically are employed and taking courses at night and on weekends. They want their education to be convenient and inexpensive. At the same time, the rising generation of students who have used computers and the Internet since preschool expect electronic learning in one form or another. For them, having access to the world's store of knowledge is a given, not a marvelous miracle.

One scholar who has pondered the university's future is James Duderstadt, professor of science and engineering and director of the Millennium Project, the University of Michigan's research center concerned with the future of higher education. It was Duderstadt who sought to open our minds to the unimaginable by reminding us that the rapid advances in science almost seem to be keeping pace with science fiction. In one essay he writes: "A communications technology that increases in power a hundredfold decade after decade will soon allow human interaction with essentially any degree of fidelity we wish—3-D, multimedia, telepresence, perhaps even directly linking our neural networks into cyberspace, ala *Neuromancer*, a merging of carbon and silicon."[19]

In an essay entitled "Can Colleges and Universities Survive in the Information Age?" Duderstadt predicts that higher education is due for a fundamental restructuring, similar in its breathtaking scope to the restructuring that American industries underwent in the last two decades as they responded to deregulation and global competition. After the dust of restructuring settles, he believes that many institutions of higher education will have closed or merged with others and many universities will be operating exclusively in cyberspace.

To add some details to this futuristic picture, Duderstadt gives us a glimpse of what a leading information services company sees in its crystal ball. He writes:

> Their operational model of the brave new world of market-driven higher education suggests that this emerging domestic market for educational services

> could be served by a radically restructured enterprise consisting of 50,000 faculty "content providers," 200,000 faculty "learning facilitators," and 1,000 faculty, celebrities who would be the stars of commodity learning-ware products. The learner would be linked to these faculty resources by an array of for-profit service companies handling the production and packaging of learning-ware, the distribution and delivery of these services to learners and the assessment and certification of learning outcomes. Quite a contrast with the current enterprise![20]

Without endorsing this particular model, he argues that the university is still living in the preindustrial age and that its "hand-crafted" courses and teaching practices do not meet contemporary needs. He writes: "As distributed virtual environments become more common, there may come a time when the classroom experience itself becomes a true commodity product, provided to anyone, anywhere, anytime—for a price."

Duderstadt is right to warn us that this "brave new world" may well bring some harmful trade-offs in higher education. If universities evolve from faculty-centered organizations to market-driven enterprises, "we could well find ourselves facing a world in which some of the most important values and traditions of the university have fallen by the wayside." Later in the essay, Duderstadt notes that higher education "may be driven down roads that could lead to an erosion of quality." As an example of what could happen, he cites the consolidation of the broadcasting and publishing industries and notes "commercial concerns can lead to mediocrity, an intellectual wasteland in which the least common denominator of quality dominates."

His warning should be taken seriously, but I do not share his pessimism. After all, distance education is just a medium in need of content. As long as the faculty stands for excellence and controls the content of their intellectual property in teaching and research, they will not become guest workers, so to speak, hanging around the neighborhood waiting for companies to hire them to teach specific courses at specific times and places.

At the same time, the university clearly has its work cut out for itself: to reinvent itself in the cyberage. Already we are deluged with puzzling questions. Are faculty members to be reduced to the role of "facilitators" and "content providers"? For that matter, who would determine a course's content? What happens, for example, if people in

China or France object to some part of a world history course that an American university distributes over the Internet? Does the history professor or the sponsoring university modify the course to make it more marketable? Who holds the copyright on the content?

Will faculty members teach at multiple universities? If so, to whom will they be accountable? This issue came up in 2000 when Harvard Law professor Arthur Miller agreed to teach an online course for Concord Law. Harvard objected, and subsequently issued guidelines saying that faculty should not be "deflected from their primary commitment to educate Harvard students by assuming competing obligations to teach for other institutions." But in this electronic age, Miller maintains that videotapes of his lectures, which he already sells, should also be his to sell to Concord as a lecture course.[21]

Never before have so many fundamental questions been raised about the role of the faculty or the university itself. These very exciting and difficult times produce an impatience for simple answers. But, as H. L. Mencken once cautioned, "There is an easy solution to every human problem—neat, plausible, and wrong."

There is a common thread in these challenges: The info-glut cries out for the university's help with synthesis, and rebuilding the liberal arts will improve synthesis. Similarly, strengthening the entire faculty means strengthening every aspect of the university—from the quality of teaching and research to academic freedom. Strengthening the faculty will also, I believe, help the residential university continue to make its essential contribution to the nation in this cyberage.

Our first big challenge is how to transform undigested data and information into structured, integrated knowledge and make that knowledge widely available. As daunting as these challenges are, technology itself is reason for optimism. For one thing, the new technologies, a primary cause of the info-glut, also offer promising opportunities to create, integrate, and disseminate knowledge. Information scientists are making greater uses of artificial intelligence to automate information management tasks, including data mining, the practice of having a computer continuously monitor, filter, and collect information according to set parameters. The new technologies stand to deliver unheard-of benefits to seekers of information, instruction, knowledge, and community. But it will take time to integrate these tools into the historical identity of the university and, conversely, to accommodate the university's traditional organizational and social structures to these media.

University faculty also must recognize that the info-glut and the fragmentation of knowledge call for reorganizing the curriculum to create more coherence and more strength in the liberal arts, especially by renewing the centrality and interaction of sciences, humanities, social studies, and arts. After all, just because technical and expert knowledge are in high demand now, we should not lose sight of the important role that the liberal arts play in our society. Higher education, of course, is not just "hire" education, as in job training. One of the great advantages of a liberal arts education is that it teaches us to think and to learn. Today more than ever, we are confronting ethical challenges in technology and science: Human cloning, stem cell research, and other difficult issues require informed deliberation and action in public policy.

The faculty has been the heart and soul, the bone marrow and blood, of the university for centuries. We cannot undermine the quality of the faculty without undermining the quality of the university. Therefore, faculties and universities have to courageously face the issue of part-time teachers. We cannot have a two-tiered system, especially one so unequal, without promoting the idea that the whole faculty could be part time. This two-tiered system has a demoralizing effect on our own graduate students, who see, on one level, a completely insecure future as an adjunct and, on another level, an overly secure future, with no mandatory retirement age, for the full-time tenured faculty. We could speculate that this system helps explain why—until recently—so many of our nation's graduate students were from abroad.

The faculty and the university administrations must reassess the whole issue of tenure and part-time appointments. There are many ideas. In 1999 the American Association of State Colleges and Universities issued a report saying that the large number of part-timers was inevitable—and, because of that, universities should train them, evaluate them, and pay them more like full-time professors.[22] I believe the report should be given serious consideration.

I also believe that faculty members, including part-timers, must have some sort of job security for academic freedom to flourish. Tenure is not the only answer, and may not even be the best answer either. I often wonder whether it is reasonable to assume that twenty-first-century universities will remain accepting of the idea that an individual appointed in his or her thirties or forties should enjoy life tenure, defined literally as guaranteed employment until the age when senility sets in. Perhaps it would be better to guarantee term appointments of five, ten, fifteen, or twenty years. These appointments could be renewable if a peer review finds that the individual's teaching and scholarly work warranted it.

It seems, unfortunately, that many faculties in our universities are not engaged with these challenges to their profession. In her review of research on faculty issues, Kezar concluded, "The literature in this group is quite rich and many important new models and ideas are being developed related to faculty roles and lives. Unfortunately," she adds, "these discussions are for the most part happening outside of the faculty, among legislatures, college presidents and administrators."[23]

The faculty has three options: take a leadership role; abdicate responsibility; or go it alone and let outside factors and forces dictate the future structure of the university. My preference must be obvious.

In a similar vein, the faculty also must take the leadership role in monitoring and addressing the increasing corporate presence on campus. This change in tradition needs careful attention, but as yet does not seem out of control. According to the National Science Foundation, the amount of basic research conducted in universities has remained fairly stable since 1980, the very same period of increasing corporate investment in the university.[24]

The oldest challenge, which the university has swept under the carpet for decades, can no longer be ignored. Whether by design or by benign neglect, universities have created a culture of mediocrity, particularly in schools of education. What is true in nature is true on campus: One weak link weakens the whole chain. In the twenty-first century it is also crucial that universities recruit high-achieving graduate students, nurture this talent, teach them well, and be on the cutting edge of science, technology, and scholarship in the humanities and social sciences. We must remember that the entire university faculty—every member of every school—is part of the university. The schools should not be treating each other as isolated silos, because the strength of the university is in its totality.

Distance learning and electronic learning offer major benefits, ranging from expanding access to education to making educational materials more suitable for individual needs. But swept up in this electronic wave is the false notion that an education can merely be a bunch of courses when, in fact, an education requires following a well-constructed curriculum of study.

For now, and I believe forever, technology will supplement education, but never replace the need for the residential university, especially for students coming from high school. A university education, after all, represents a universe of activity, a four-year process of learning—with the faculty and curriculum at the center. It is about living with your peers; learning from them; participating in classrooms, athletic fields, and laboratories; questioning guest lecturers as well as attending political rallies, poetry readings, and exhibitions. Students are exposed to the diversity of races and religions and opinions; indeed, the whole world comes together at the university. The university also serves as a social melting pot, as the nation's campuses, in the absence of a military draft, are the only places left in America where different ethnic groups, races, and economic classes of people mingle. The university is also about developing networks and making lifelong friends. Universities and colleges are not way stations but are a part of our communities and as such are central to our economy, tradition, and culture.

However, I fear that half-baked responses to marketplace pressures and to the other challenges may warp the university beyond recognition. The university has not come eight centuries to evolve, almost overnight, into a Home Depot of courseware where there is no differentiation between consumption and digestion or between information and learning. The nation cannot afford to turn the university into an academic superstore, a collection of courses marketed much like sinks and lumber.

Throughout our history, the university has risen to challenges, whether it was the democratization of knowledge, the Depression, Sputnik, or affirmative action. No challenge has been too daunting, and I believe the challenges I have described here can be met imaginatively—so long as we hold constant to our commitments to academic freedom and the centrality of the faculty. Institutions with excellent, high-quality faculty will survive and thrive. Those with a mediocre faculty will not likely survive the competition. During times of revolution, the strong prevail. The weak coalesce, merge, or disappear.

Will faculties and universities respond to the challenges or retreat from them? Universities—which invented the computer, the Internet, and distance learning—are not derivatives, in stock market lingo; they are a primary source of knowledge, inspiration, and invention. Universities will survive provided they do not undermine themselves; I believe that they are not so much at risk from external threats as they are from internal ones of our own making. As Walt Kelly's comic-strip character Pogo observed, "We have met the enemy, and he is us."

As we face higher education's challenges, we must remember that the university in the West is the result of some eight centuries of struggle, oppression, perseverance, and endless refinement. The university is a living institution, and change it must. But as we make changes, we must be careful not to inadvertently undermine its foundations, muddle its architecture, or reduce its priceless value to society.

Notes

1. Neil Postman, "Informing Ourselves to Death," speech given at a meeting of the German Informatics Society, Stuttgart, October 11, 1990, p. 5.
2. Martin Rees, Second Hitchcock Lecture, delivered at the University of California at Berkeley, February 28, 1995, and cited in Timothy Ferris, *The Whole Shebang: A State-of-the-Universe(s) Report* (New York: Simon & Schuster, 1997), p. 14.
3. Richard Saul Wurman, *Information Anxiety* (New York: Doubleday, 1989).
4. Carol M. Barker, "Liberal Arts Education for a Global Society," 2000 Carnegie Challenge Paper, Carnegie Corporation of New York, p. 4.
5. Mark G. Yudof, "Is the Public Research University in America Dead?," unpublished article, July 2001.
6. The University of California at Berkeley, College of Natural Resources, Web site: www.cnr.berkeley.edu/srr/Alliance/concerns/htm/; see also http://plantbio.berkeley.edu/PMB-TMRI/Background.html/; see also Goldie Blumenstyk, "A Vilified Corporate Partner Produces Little Change (Except Better Facilities)," *Chronicle of Higher Education* (June 22, 2001): 24.
7. A. Berger et al., "Institutional Policies and Practices: Findings from the 1999 National Study of Postsecondary Faculty," report for the U.S. Department of Education, National Center for Education Statistics (NCES 2001-201), Washington, D.C., 2001, pp. iii and v.

8. Pamela Balch, "Part-Time Faculty Are Here to Stay," *Planning for Higher Education, Society for College and University Planning* vol. 27, no. 3 (Spring 1999), pp. 32–40.
9. Ethan Bronner, "Study of Public Universities Advises Changing Faculty of the Future," *The New York Times,* January 13, 1999, p. B9.
10. Adrianna J. Kezar, "Faculty: ERIC Trends 1999–2000," ERIC Clearinghouse on Higher Education, U.S. Department of Education, Institute for Education Policy Studies, ERIC #ED-446652, 2000.
11. Alison Schneider, "To Many Adjunct Professors, Academic Freedom is a Myth," *Chronicle of Higher Education* (December 10, 1999): A18.
12. Ibid.
13. Ibid.
14. Richard W. Richburg et al., "How Much Does it Cost to Train World-Class Teachers?," *International Journal of Innovative Higher Education,* n.d., as cited in a Report of the National Commission on Teaching & America's Future, "What Matters Most: Teaching for America's Future," Teachers College, Columbia University, September 1996.
15. Steve Farkas et al., *Different Drummers: How Teachers of Teachers View Public Education* (New York: Public Agenda, 1997).
16. Ibid.
17. *The Condition of Education 2001,* "Postsecondary Persistence and Progress," National Center for Education Statistics, U.S. Department of Education, p. 49. (A summary of the High School and Beyond Longitudinal Study of 1980 Sophomores, "Postsecondary Education Transcript Study," NCES, U.S. Department of Education.).
18. Postman, "Informing Ourselves to Death," p. 2.
19. James J. Duderstadt, "The Future of the University in the Digital Age," *Proceedings of the American Philosophical Society* vol. 145, no. 1 (March 2001): 56. Duderstadt's reference is to the so-called cyberpunk book by William Gibson.
20. Duderstadt's revised essay is in *Dancing with the Devil: Information Technology and New Competition in Higher Education,* a publication of EDUCAUSE, Richard N. Katz and Associates (Washington, D.C.: Jossey Bass, 1998), p. 20.
21. Harvard University, Office of the Provost website, "Statement on Outside Activities of Holders of Academic Appointments (effective July 2000)."
22. Bronner, op.cit.; see also, Denise K. Magner, "Report Urges Post-Tenure Reviews for Professors and More Pay for Part-Timers," *The Chronicle of Higher Education,* January 22, 1999, p. A10.
23. Kezar, "Faculty," p. 7.
24. Business-Higher Education Forum, a partnership of the American Council on Education and the National Alliance of Business, *Working Together, Creating Knowledge: The University-Industry Research Collaboration Initiative* (Washington, D.C.: American Council on Education, 2001), pp. 23, 27.

7

Beyond Markets and Individuals: A Focus on Educational Goals

Howard Gardner

> When an institution determines to do something in order to get money, it must lose its soul.
>
> —Robert Maynard Hutchins

Cross-Eyed Colleges

If a person familiar with the college scene in the 1950s were to alight on a campus in 2005, much would seem familiar. To be sure, structures scattered around the periphery might seem overly modern; but the red-brick buildings near the center, the grassy campus, and the athletic fields would look unchanged. Peering into the classroom, he would see a great deal of lecturing, punctuated by occasional seminars. Nor would the calendar, the catalog, the departmental organization shock the visitor. He might be told that the conservative pace of change is a virtue. After all, colleges and universities (hereafter, colleges) have lasted for many hundreds of years, far longer than entities (such as totalitarian regimes) that might have predicted their disappearance.

Beneath the surface, however, higher education has changed dramatically in two ways. First of all, colleges (like most of the rest of the society) have been influenced by the model of the market and now think of themselves primarily in terms of competition, supply and demand, profitability, and other features of classical economics. Second, the needs, interests, and "person" of the students have come to dominate the thinking of those responsible for the college—the senior management, admissions officers, development officers, and much of the faculty. Unfortunately, the twin foci are in many ways incompatible.

I see the vast majority of American colleges as cross-eyed creatures. One eye is focused on the financial status of the college, the other on the desires of the student. This dual focus has caused harm and requires a correction in course. To the extent that colleges become indistinguishable from other commercial entities, they lose their reason for existence. When Harvard.edu morphs into Harvard.com, it should lose its tax-free status and be classified with Disney and Wal-Mart, rather than with the Sorbonne in Paris or Xinhua in Beijing.

Every profession must confirm the reason for its origin and the rationale for its continued existence (or its eventual demise). In terms of my metaphor, colleges need to focus with both eyes on their principal educational mission. Stripped to its essentials, postsecondary education—and, specifically, the traditional form of education termed liberal arts—exists to convey to students the most important intellectual knowledge and skills that have been developed to the present moment; to develop in students deep disciplinary knowledge in at least one area; to foster critical thinking, analysis, and expression across a range of topics; to contemplate the relation between accumulated knowledge and skills, on one hand, and the issues facing contemporary society, on the other; to prepare students—in a broad rather than narrow sense—for civic life and productive work. A tall order! Over the years other religious, civic, personal, and societal goals have been pursued but I consider these optional rather than required considerations in a focused academy of the twenty-first century.

Evidently, the two features that dominate conceptions of college today and that threaten to overwhelm its educational mission are not wholly independent. When one thinks of an institution in market terms, one naturally thinks in terms of one's customers—in this case, students and their paying parents. Similarly, the more that one knows the needs and desires of the students, the more one can fashion an institution that directly addresses these demands. Yet, on analytic grounds, these are separable factors. One could know a great deal about students without making that knowledge the basis of market thinking.

For example, one could try to meet students' needs even when it was not economically feasible to do so. By the same token, one could market an institution on grounds that do not take undue consideration of one particular client. Military academies could stress the importance of defending the nation; technology schools could emphasize the infrastructural needs of the society.

In what follows, I consider factors that gave rise to the current cross-eyed foci on markets and individual students. I then note two vital considerations that have diminished over the years: (1) a set of alternative models of how societies can work, and (2) a sense of confidence about what colleges have to offer, arrived at independently of market or student considerations. I outline what colleges should properly do, if they felt relieved of pressures of the market and ignorant of the "demands" of students. Using data obtained from an ongoing research project, I suggest some ways in which it might be possible to highlight the supply side of the market equation, thereby confirming the fundamental importance of higher education viewed in its own terms.

The Triumph of the Market and the Individual, American Style

Markets have always been with us, of course. Except in the most totalitarian environments, institutions vie for support, customers, longevity—and, at least in a loose Darwinian sense, the fittest survive. In the late nineteenth century, for example, hundreds of institutions purported to train physicians. In the wake of the epochal Flexner Report on Medical Education, issued in 1910, the number of degree-granting medical schools was radically reduced.

Over the last fifty years, market considerations have become the dominant consideration in nearly every sphere of American life. The model of the corporation—with its hierarchical and centralized organizational structure, profit-and-loss ledgers, venture capital, dividends to shareholders, and the like—has influenced professions ranging from law and medicine to education and the arts.

Perhaps even more dramatically, the ways in which Americans evaluate individuals whom they know from a distance and even those whom they know personally occur increasingly in market terms.

The salary an individual makes, her disposable income, her potential for moving up in an organization loom ever larger in how such a person is judged. Just think of how we monitor the salaries of movie stars, CEOs, athletes, and, yes, even college presidents and faculty. My own observations suggest that many, if not most, younger Americans are unable to think of the occupational realm *except* in market terms. It is as if the market model has become the triumphant meme, the dominant metaphor, of our time.

In comparison to most other societies—and particularly ones in East Asia—America has always had a focus on the individual—his background, his strengths, his desires. It took nerve to leave the homeland voluntarily; it took courage to explore unknown territories; accordingly, the "lone cowboy," the "frontier wife," and the "pioneer family" deserved any rewards that they accumulated. In the last fifty years, this focus has been exacerbated by two factors. On one hand, the majority of Americans have seen a steady improvement in their standard of living, and this economic jag has allowed them greater choice about where to live, whom to live with, what to purchase or exchange. On the other hand, factors that counter an individual focus—communal, family, and religious ties—have been on the wane. In the phrase of political scientist Robert Putnam, more of us are "bowling alone." To be sure, a great many Americans describe themselves as religious and exhibit the proper accouterments of piety. Yet this religious description in no way detracts from a focus on the individual: Indeed, residents of the so-called red states put equal emphasis on both—even as individuals who are less overtly religious (in the United States as well as Scandinavia) often prove more sympathetic to communitarian or socialistic forms.

To be sure, these foci have yielded some positive dividends. Colleges should compete not merely on reputation or prestige but also on the "good" and the "goods" that they actually can demonstrate. By the same token, the "person" of each student is important. Indeed, as architect of the idea of "multiple intelligences," I sympathize with the notion that students think and learn differently from one another; they are best served when these differences are taken into account in curriculum, instruction, and assessment. But I am concerned that the two foci have become so dominant that distinctly educational goals often are marginalized.

The Importance of Countermessages

In my view collegiate educators—whether permanent or transient faculty—should be deeply knowledgeable about their subject matter and continue to bone up as needed; know how to teach their subject to novices and journeymen; relate that subject to issues of the time; be mindful of the postcollege trajectories of their students; and value the generic features of a liberal arts education (as sketched above). Teaching art or engineering in a college becomes a different matter from teaching art in an arts academy or engineering at a polytech. Both administrators and trustees ought to have as a primary goal the creation and maintenance of an institution that facilitates the achievement of these educational goals.

Why foreground these educational goals? Three reasons stand out. First of all, human knowledge is among our most precious possessions; we owe it to our predecessors and successors to privilege this human creation. Second, education is the sphere designated by society as the guardian, transmitter, and accumulator of that knowledge; if colleges do not carry out this mission, no other body can step into the breach. Third and often forgotten, the greatest gifts that we can provide to our students are the appreciation of such knowledge, the capacity to think with and about it, and the potential to add to that knowledge in whichever sphere they eventually enter. All the rest is incidental.

The central dilemma facing "cross-eyed" educators rises sharply with respect to teaching of classical Greek or Sanskrit. The utility of these subjects in the contemporary world or in postcollege education is limited, and few students arrive on the scene with a burning desire to pursue either. From a strictly market perspective, both should be dropped immediately. From an individual-centered perspective, these courses should be maintained only if, for some idealistic or eccentric reason, a significant number of students have a desire to pursue them. The major justifications for offering these subjects (and for hiring specialists in them), then, have to do with the values of educators and their conception of what it means to be an educated person. Citing the three reasons just introduced, I could mount arguments here, with the case for classical Greek being different from, but not in any absolute sense stronger than, the case for Sanskrit. But it is the principle that is important—we should not decide on course offerings simply on the basis of their cash value. After all, we are dealing here with bodies of knowledge and not with species competing for survival on a tiny landmass.

Here is where countermessages or alternative conceptions are urgently needed. It is possible—and desirable—to think of colleges in ways far different from the market model, with its emphasis on profit and its reflexive assumption that "more is better." One can think of them, for example, in terms of places that preserve and extend that knowledge which has made the most difference in human history, either for the better or the worse. Or as sites that develop individuals who will challenge the orthodoxy. Or as institutions that adopt a monastic rather than a market orientation. By the same token, it is possible to direct the lenses in directions quite different from that of student wants and needs. For example, one can ask what the chief needs of the society are today and how can they be met; or the chief needs of society in the future; or the populations that most need to be served; or the skills that students should acquire so that they can bring about a better world, without reference to the campuswear of the month.

Note that these nonmarket foci might well end up having market appeal. For example, some students might be attracted to a school like St. John's, which emphasizes the great written works of the past. Other students might be attracted to a place that shuns creature comforts in favor of transmitting knowledge and skills to those in poverty. But these would be by-products—externalities, in the terms of economists. Colleges would make these decisions on the basis of principles and not in a Machiavellian or Rube Goldbergian effort to increase market share. And to the extent that market thinking intruded, it would be limited to the need for *survival* and not for accumulating the biggest possible endowment or paying the highest possible salaries to faculty, staff, or managers of the investment portfolio.

The Current Scene: A Need for "Good Work"

Evidence for the increasing marketization of the college scene is ubiquitous and indisputable. Responding to the ever-rising costs of an education and the never-ending desire for expansion, the development offices of both private and public colleges have increased dramatically in size and budget. Mirroring this growth, far greater efforts are expended in attracting prospective students to learn more about the school, recruiting them to apply, furnish pleasurable visits to the college before and after admission, providing ample rewards for those—athletes, artists, academic stars—whose attendance promises to reflect glory on the institution. Colleges devote vast efforts to conforming to the requirements for a high ranking in the annual *U.S. News & World Report* sweepstakes and other tabulations, and more than a few are thought to massage their statistics in ways that add to their lure. Marketing surveys are ubiquitous and unchallenged. Colleges seek to build up those departments and attract those faculty that are newsworthy; they are proud to see news coverage of their successes, even as these same successes sometimes can prove embarrassing for departments or faculty that are not so garlanded. Finally, there are the most obvious signs of marketing: dorms, eating rooms, computers, iPods, and campus stores that promise a pleasurable, resortlike existence at the school, along with the predictable sweatshirts, caps, banners, and decals.

While I have been deeply involved with college and university life for over four decades, my own familiarity with the current scene has been enhanced by my involvement with the GoodWork Project.[1] This ambitious research project, carried out in conjunction with psychologists Mihaly Csikszentmihalyi and William Damon, and our research colleagues at four institutions, is an empirical examination of professional life in America today. We define "good work" as work that is excellent in quality and ethically responsible—work that any society should desire and honor across the professional landscape.

The question undergirding our research program can be crisply stated: How do individuals and institutions that seek to carry out good work succeed or fail at a time when conditions are changing very rapidly, market forces are extraordinarily powerful, and few if any forces can compete with these market pressures? We carry out extensive, in-depth interviews with leaders of various professions; these interviews are then subjected to careful qualitative and, when appropriate, quantitative analyses. So far we have interviewed over a thousand individuals; our findings are reported in several books and many articles, described at goodworkproject.org. In the last few years, we have been studying "Good Work in Higher Education."[2] In what follows, I draw on the testimony of the approximately one hundred individuals whose protocols have been analyzed so far.

What most surprised me, as it would have surprised the mythical campus visitor introduced earlier, is the extent to which the most admired individuals in contemporary colleges focus on the needs of students. Across a wide variety of undergraduate institutions, these informants stressed how important it was to know their students well. At least four-fifths of those interviewed explicitly described the need to know the backgrounds, limitations, and aspirations of their students. Equally, they emphasized the importance of students knowing themselves—their own strengths, needs, goals. Indeed, among the ten institutions, it was only at the University of Phoenix—an unusual noncampus institution that admits only those students who are age twenty-three and older—that the focus on knowing the students was absent.

An analogous portrait emerges when one examines the missions of the schools. Of course, missions vary across and even within schools. But across these exemplary campuses one repeatedly encounters the theme of interpersonal and intra-personal growth. Informants speak about the importance of satisfying the needs of each individual and of students' learning how to interact with others, engage in dialogue, and develop a more open mind, particularly with reference to those of a different background. Indeed, our analysis confirms that the goal of learning to interact with others is as important as the development of knowledge and skills; and the majority of nominated good workers saw their own personal mission as oriented more toward the development of the human being than the transmission of any kind of canon or, indeed, anticanon. Although this trend was discernible across campuses, it was especially pronounced at the less academically oriented institutions.

Let me underscore that I do not object to a deeper understanding of students, nor to missions that include personal growth. I consider it a positive development that educators are incorporating the human dimension into their thinking and articulating their aspirations for themselves and their students. Moreover, I understand why such a focus is appropriate, at a time when the student body is growing ever more diverse, and many students arrive at school with personal or academic challenges. Nor do I believe that the focus on students necessarily represents pandering, or marketing—though I do not exclude those factors. Indeed, with reference to my own four children, an interest in each student has represented a plus in the selection of a college for matriculation.

But note the dramatic shift in the prevailing "mental model." One hundred years ago, attendance at college was restricted to a tiny elite. Schools saw themselves as institutions with a religious mission and a limited canon of offerings. The intimacy of the school was exemplified by a practice where the president of the college taught a culminating course for seniors. Students with means had a good time, but it was up to them to determine how they spent their hours and their money. Fifty years ago, in the wake of the GI Bill, colleges expanded dramatically in their size, the wealth of their offerings, the diversity of their student bodies—particularly in terms of age and geographical dispersion. Electives had become more common. It was assumed that students attended college for a range of purposes. But student affairs and activity offices were small, where they existed at all; selection of college was largely by convenience and reputation rather than by market competition; and at least some consensus obtained on what subjects should be taught and how they should be taught.

Today most colleges have given up a religious orientation as well as any notion of a rigorous core. To be sure, few colleges have gone so far as Brown University or Wesleyan University in the 1970s, where students could create a curriculum virtually from scratch; but equally few have dared to specify the courses to be taken, in what order, and with what specified curriculum and mandated form of assessment. Rather, even as students confront a large number of choices in the school dining halls, so, too, can they put together an intellectual meal that is personally satisfying, with little need to attend to disciplinary restrictions or priorities in their intellectual diet.

We are left with a disquieting situation. The looming image of the market pervades the thinking of the architects of higher education today, even as it may well represent the only model of society known to students. Those most respected within the university place overwhelming importance on knowing their students well and on seeking to anticipate their expressed and inferred needs. This emphasis on personal knowledge is well motivated and provides a needed counterbalance in institutions that were once rather cocky and authoritarian; but less happily, this emphasis is not balanced by an equivalent preoccupation with the kind of education that students need today (and tomorrow) and the kind of society that educators hope will emerge tomorrow (if not today). Countermessages are absent, or at least muted.

Lessons from the GoodWork Project

Good work—work that is both excellent in quality and ethically meritorious—is never easy to carry out; it proves especially challenging in times like these, when conditions are rapidly changing and market forces are powerful and largely unchecked. Higher education finds itself in just such a situation today. Across the various professions that we have examined, we have identified several conditions that encourage good work—and these lessons can inform those entrusted with the governance of our colleges.

Good work is most readily carried out when all of the interest groups connected to a profession want the same thing from that profession. We observed this condition of *alignment* in genetics at the end of the twentieth century. Scientists, the bodies that supported their research, and the general public all wanted the same thing from these researchers: findings that lead to better health and a longer life. In contrast, journalism emerged as a profession that was very poorly aligned. Journalists wanted to research important stories in depth and present them fairly; but they felt pressured, on one hand, by readers and viewers who want their news quickly and sensationally; and, on the other, by publishers and shareholders who sought ever greater profits from this once-quiet corner of the business world. Under such conditions it is difficult to carry out good work; risks abound for compromised work—as documented in recent scandals at the *New York Times*, *USA Today*, and other news outlets.

A second factor affecting good work concerns the duties and responsibilities of the individual worker. To use a convenient metaphor, it is easier to carry out good work if you only have to wear one professional hat. The doctor who tends to his patient's needs, the lawyer who seeks to serve his client well, the scientist who observes the canons of research scrupulously—all these workers have their proper marching orders. But nowadays, only the extremely fortunate professional experiences no pressure to don multiple hats. Most physicians belong to large health maintenance organizations that impose limits on the type of patient interaction and permissible prescriptions; most lawyers are part of huge firms or multinational corporations with multiple missions, including relentless bottom-line pressures; scientists enjoy somewhat more flexibility, but particularly in the biological sciences, many succumb to the lure of major positions in profitable biotech companies. They find themselves in the odd position of wearing the hat of an National Institute of Health–supported scientist in the morning and the hat of a venture capital–supported executive or adviser in the afternoon. All too often, compromised work results when professionals are uncertain about which hat they are wearing at what time.

At a more microscopic level, we have identified three factors that increase the likelihood of excellent and ethical work on the part of the individual worker. *Vertical support* features examples and guidance from older, more knowledgeable individuals: initially one's parents and teachers, later one's first supervisors, ultimately, the wise "trustees" of a profession. *Horizontal support* comes from one's peers at work or in the wider profession. *Periodic inoculations and booster shots* come from experiences that either confirm the value of good work or document the risks of compromised or frankly bad work. To some extent, these are factors that one cannot control; one cannot choose one's parents, and one has limited choice in terms of supervisors and peers. Still, it is misleading to think that one's associates and experiences are totally a matter of chance. Mentors and mentees are both involved in a selection process; and employees have the option of confronting objectionable peers or supervisors and, in the ultimate case, leaving a flawed institution.

Now consider the complexity of achieving good work in higher education. On alignment: Those who want to study or teach classical languages clash with those whose eyes fix on the enrollment in such classes. And on "hats": It is difficult to focus on the preservation and refinement of knowledge while at the same time catering to students' desires for comfort and fun. Various kinds of support are desirable but cannot be assumed; many educators have had little exposure to exemplars of "good work," and the many individuals who want to achieve good work cannot assume that their peers, or their institution as a whole, are similarly disposed. And even when all of these enabling conditions are present, the issue of what constitutes good work can itself be contentious.

Toward Better Work in Higher Education

A thought experiment: Let us say one were planning a college from scratch, with unlimited endowment, no knowledge of student desires, but a commitment to good work; how might one proceed?

To begin with, an educational institution must be concerned first and foremost with what it means to be an educated person at the present time. The institution should be explicit about this central mission, and those who represent the institution on a regular basis must be in sympathy with it—just as a physician must honor the Hippocratic Oath and a journalist must embrace his or her organization's code of ethics. The institution should also be specific about its educational goals. For a liberal arts college, those should include the capacity to appreciate and to engage the major disciplinary ways of thinking—scientific, mathematical, historical, humanistic, and artistic. The content by which these ways of thinking is conveyed can reflect choice; but the contents should always be determined by considerations of quality, and not by expedience, conveniences, or political correctness. Interdisciplinary courses and majors should be reserved for those who have demonstrated disciplinary mastery, before or during college. Postcollege work life and preprofessional training must never be allowed to dominate. Other benefits of college—civic engagement, self-knowledge, familiarity with other cultures, ability to get along with others—should be acknowledged but considered externalities or benefits secondary to the scholarly goals. That is because, unlike the scholarly goals, each could be achieved without attendance at college.

Such a focus will necessarily foreground ways of conceiving the world that extend beyond a market view. The pursuit of knowledge for its own sake, for the sake of curiosity, or for broadening one's own perspective is different from the pursuit of knowledge for primarily pragmatic or instrumental ends. Moreover and crucially, as one assumes a humanistic, artistic, or historical perspective across time and space, one comes to appreciate that markets are but one way of construing experience. Societies have existed, and have thrived, when the principal considerations have been religious, spiritual, ideological, communal, pacific, egalitarian—as well as considerations that are less benign, such as thought control, militarism, or imperialism. Individuals have been judged in terms of their morality, their trustworthiness, their humility, their generosity, their spirituality, their beauty, and not simply in terms of their salary or exchange value. And institutions have endured on the basis of charity or communal support or sheer faith even when they have failed the most obvious dictates of the bottom line. Awareness of these alternatives should encourage debate: not that market models are necessarily worse than others, but rather that there are "competing" models, each with its own assets and liabilities. And faculty should be prepared to articulate these alternative visions, and especially so when students seem never to have considered life under any other model than that of the United States of America, circa 2005.

So far my focus may seem to fall on the excellent aspect of good work. However, there are clear ethical implications in this formulation. First of all, to the extent that educators take seriously their mission, they are realizing that sense of calling that constitutes the ethical core of any profession. Second, in being excellent teachers and advisors, educators should model care both for the curricular materials with which they are working and for the students whom they are seeking to educate. Finally, by exposing students to various ways of thinking, and to bodies of thought that embody diverse historical and cultural traditions, educators are conveying the most important lesson of all: One cannot be an incisive thinker unless one has grappled with various perspectives, appreciated their strengths and weaknesses, and reached one's own tentative conclusions about which formulations make the most sense—at least for now. Indeed, in today's atmosphere, I would consider an education a success if it helped students to question both the hegemony of market thinking and the assumption that colleges exist to serve the students' own (perhaps unreflected-upon) desires.

A focus on educational ends need not overwhelm a consideration of the backgrounds, needs, and desires of students. But the proper assumption—which should be made explicit—is that *the educational ends must come first.* They are what distinguish college from other institutions. Interest in the students does not arise in a vacuum: rather, it is germane because—indeed *just because*—such knowledge can help the institution to achieve its educational goals. In other words, we need to know students' needs and backgrounds primarily so that we can more effectively educate them in our lights, not because we want to sculpt an education to serve their aspirations, legitimate or not. Study after study documents that more students are studying business and other applied fields, while fewer enroll in core disciplinary tracks; indeed fewer than 10 percent of high school students and their families express any desire to study the humanities. A market- or student-oriented model would suggest that humanistic study be eliminated or severely curtailed. Such a decision would undercut the essence of higher education. We need to understand the resistances and hesitations of students and families so that we can better help them appreciate *why* humanistic studies are more important than ever—that, indeed, students will become neither good workers nor good citizens unless they can bring to bear in thoughtful ways the value considerations that suffuse the humanities.

Although I cannot detail a program that will enable colleges to correct course, a promising starting point emerges from our GoodWork Project. Individuals and institutions should ponder four considerations—all (as it happens) beginning with the letter "m":

1. *Mission.* It is essential to define, and periodically to revisit, the core notions of what it means to be an institution of higher education and a college educator. Such a consideration must go well beyond the by-now mandated formulation of a mission statement. It must feature a perennial grappling with what is most important to this particular calling and why.
2. *Model.* It is most helpful to bear in mind positive models, ones that come closest to what one hopes to achieve. In education, these models may come from the past—Plato's fabled Academy, Mark Hopkins on one end of the log and the student on the other—or from institutions (like the ones that we have studied, or others, such as Alverno College in Milwaukee or Berea College in Kentucky) that merit our respect today. By the same token, individual educators should strive to identify teachers

and mentors who epitomize the beliefs and actions that they most admire. It is sometimes salutary to bear in mind "anti-mentors" or "tor-mentors"—the educational equivalents of Enron or the Internet gossip sheet, the Drudge Report—institutions or individuals that undercut the core identity of a profession. When few positive models come to mind, this situation should serve as a wake-up call.

3. *Mirror Test, Personal Version.* With regularity, all of us, as individuals and as members of institutions should pose the following questions: If we look at ourselves clearly and transparently, are we doing the best job that we can? If our efforts were fully described on the first page of the *New York Times*, would we be touched with pride or wracked with regret? And if we are not satisfied with the current portrait, what can we do to improve it and how can we judge whether we have succeeded?

4. *Mirror Test, Profession-wide.* When you begin professional work, it is hard enough to satisfy your own standards. As you gain in expertise and maturity, however, it is appropriate to consider what is happening in your profession. Even if you are personally meeting the standards of an excellent and ethical higher education, what are the implications if other institutions are falling short? Do you have a wider responsibility? Following the French playwright Jean-Baptiste Molière, you should heed the aphorism "You are responsible not only for what you do but for what you fail to do."

Higher education remains one of the most respected institutions in our society, and not without reason. One consideration is that in the past strong leaders have been willing to invoke the considerations just described and, when necessary, to correct course. They may not have been oblivious to market considerations or to the interests of their student-clients, but they did not allow these factors to overwhelm their own individual and collective aspirations. University of Chicago president Robert Maynard Hutchins and publisher John Dewey may have differed deeply on their vision of the educated person in the first half of the twentieth century; but neither would have looked to the college's ledgers when articulating their respective positions. Given the strength of current market forces, it is more important than ever that the counterforces be recognized and, as appropriate, activated. The survival of a civil society depends on a pursuit of work that is both excellent in quality and ethical in its orientation. Because of its location at the juncture of youth and work, higher education should recognize its pivotal role in determining whether graduates are proceeding along the path toward good work.

Notes

For comments on earlier versions of this draft, I thank James Freedman, Richard Hersh, John Merrow, Jeanne Nakamura, Henry Rubin, and Ellen Winner. The GoodWork Project study of Higher Education has been generously supported by the Hewlett Foundation, the Atlantic Philanthropies, The Ford Foundation, and Carnegie Corporation of New York.

1. At the start, we conducted an extensive nomination procedure that identified ten institutions that are widely and justifiably admired for their excellence: Carleton College (MN), DeAnza Community College (CA), Indiana University, LaGuardia Community College (NY), Morehouse College (GA), Mount Saint Mary's (CA), the University of Phoenix (various locations), Princeton University (NJ), Swarthmore University (PA), and Xavier University (OH). Then, within each nominated institution, we carried out an additional nominating procedure designed to identify individuals who best exemplified the excellence of the institution.
2. For information on the GoodWork Project, see H. Gardner, M. Csikszentmihalyi, and W. Damon, *Good Work: When Excellence and Ethics Meet* (New York: Basic Books, 2001). See also goodworkproject.org.

8

This Little Student Went to Market*

David L. Kirp

"No matter what it is called, who does it, or where in the institution it is being done, universities are engaged in marketing." When this claim was first made in 1972, in an article that ran in the prestigious *Journal of Higher Education*,[1] most academics dismissed it as heresy. Those who ran and taught in universities saw themselves as members of a community of scholars committed to the generation and transmission of free thought, not as pitchmen.

That Mr. Chips's view of college life gave reality a romantic gloss. Dollars have always greased the wheels of higher education; were it otherwise, the term "legacy" would not have a meaning specific to universities. And the then-new "multiversity"—what University of California president Clark Kerr described as an academic city, not a village—was designed to be in sync with the needs of the market. Nonetheless, the romantics had it basically right. Three decades ago, the business side of running a university was viewed as a necessary evil, properly consigned to the institutional periphery, while at the heart of the institution the professoriate reigned supreme. To these sovereigns, the concept of marketing—more generally, the notion that higher education bowed to the marketplace—was foreign. It was also antithetical to the bedrock principles of higher education.

What is new, and troubling, is the raw power that money exerts in higher education. Even as public attention has been riveted on matters of principle like affirmative action and diversions like the theater-of-the-absurd canon wars, many American colleges and universities have been busily reinventing themselves as a reaction to intensified market forces. The pursuit of money, formerly a necessity, has become a virtue. "The business of the University of California," its ex-president proclaimed, "is business."[2]

These days priorities are determined less by academic leaders than by multiple "constituencies" and managerial mandarins. The new vocabulary of customers and stakeholders, niche marketing and branding, and winner-take-all embodies this sea change in the higher education "industry." In this brave new world each academic unit is a "revenue center," each party a "stakeholder," each student a customer, each professor an entrepreneur, and each institution a seeker after profit, whether in money capital or intellectual capital.

Nowhere in the university is this market mentality more on display than in the luring, caring, and feeding—and almost incidentally the educating—of undergraduates. The 1972 *Journal of Higher Education* article insisted that what colleges called recruiting was really a euphemism for advertising, financial aid was pricing, and the bloodletting ritual of revamping the curriculum was nothing more than product development. This was shock treatment, rhetoric meant to attract attention, but nowadays the emphasis on marketing to recruit top students is unapologetic. Universities on the make hire consulting firms to give themselves an academic face-lift, what the trade calls a new "brand." Schools at the top of the ladder battle, sometimes unscrupulously, to maintain their elite position. As reported widely in the media in the spring of 2002, staff members at Princeton's admissions office went so far as to hack into Yale's admissions website.

"The objective of the enrollment process," says William Elliott, Carnegie Mellon's vice president for enrollment management (good-bye admissions director, hello corporate-speak), "is to improve your market position." And as Alvin Sanoff, who used to edit *U.S. News & World Report*'s annual college guide, points out, "The pressures on admissions folks and on schools to get the best candidates is enormous."[3]

Sanoff should know, since the statistically dubious *U.S. News* ranking system, launched in the mid-1980s, has become the bible in higher education. Although there had been college guides before, now—crucially—there was a definite pecking order. To those who devised the rankings, prestige was essentially equated with selectivity: What percent of applicants does a college reject? What percent of those that it admits choose to attend? There are, of course, much better measures of the *quality* of a college education: What do students learn? Do they acquire the intellectual skills of analytical reasoning and critical thinking? What is the "value-added" of the education a college delivers? But only a few schools, among them Reed College in Oregon and Alma College in Michigan, contended that they, rather than an otherwise little-read newsmagazine, should determine their priorities. Those schools refused to supply *U.S. News* with the data the magazine demanded, but their principled stand proved costly, as they found themselves crucified in the rankings.

Almost every institution in the land embraced the *U.S. News* criteria as its own. The competition for students turned into a donnybrook as universities rushed to claw their way up the ladder. To attract students with the best academic credentials, colleges increasingly award scholarships on the basis of test scores rather than need. Financial aid offers are deployed strategically, to lure more desirable (or reluctant) applicants, rather than to help talented students from poor families attend college. There is greater reliance on admitting students through early decision, not because this makes sense in educational terms but because applicants who are accepted early usually enroll—this makes the college appear more selective, and hence more prestigious.

Historian Roger Geiger has calculated which schools have been the big winners in the star student sweepstakes. Colleges that recorded the largest percentage increases between 1995 and 2000 in enrolling students with 700-plus SAT scores— among them Pennsylvania, Duke, New York University, Boston University, University of Southern California, Washington University (St. Louis), Rochester— excel at what economists (and college presidents) Michael McPherson and Morton Schapiro call the "student aid game." Some universities have ventured into the realm of the unethical, manipulating the system by inflating students' SAT scores and the proportion of alumni donors (a factor in the rankings)—even stooping so low as to recruit applicants who have no chance of being admitted, just to make the school look more selective.[4]

Today, sought-after applicants are treated like pampered consumers whose preferences must be *satisfied*, not as acolytes whose preferences are being *formed* in the process of being educated. In this rivalry, much more is at stake than bragging rights for trustees and alumni. Prestige brings tangible benefits, and in this winner-take-all world small differences in reputation have large consequences. Although slippage in the rankings has an immediate impact on the following year's class, the more highly regarded the institution, the more top students and prized professors it attracts and the more readily it can secure the biggest gifts. (It is a truism among fundraisers that money follows money, not need.) Such successes reinforce a school's place in the hierarchy. "To those who have," as the Book of Matthew intones, "more shall be given"—in other words, "the more, the more."

College applicants have responded with alacrity to these signals of status, treating the *U.S. News* rankings as gospel. What matters most in picking a college, a survey of students at elite schools finds, is not the caliber of the education it delivers but rather its prestige.

Sixties-style idealism has long since given way to pragmatism. These aspi-rants regard an elite pedigree as their ticket to the new aristocracy. During the past thirty years, the percentage of freshmen that expect their college years will bring them better jobs has quadrupled, from 20 to 80 percent. Meanwhile, those who anticipate that college will help them develop a philosophy of living plummeted by precisely the same extent—from 80 to 20 percent. In 2002 the objective most often identified by male freshmen was "being *very* well-off financially." These Jay Gatsbys in training do whatever they can—and their families spend whatever it takes—to distinguish themselves from the crowd. They see it as a blue-chip investment.[5]

This frenzied activity is entirely consistent with what the model of rational economic behavior predicts. More information is becoming available in the form of rankings; colleges and applicants, the buyers and sellers, are doing the best job they can to promote themselves; and money talks. But neither the colleges nor the students have much incentive to emphasize the life of the mind.

Consider the plight of Beaver College in the late 1990s. Beaver had historically been a women's liberal arts college a cut below the elite "girls' schools" known as the Seven Sisters, but as that niche vanished in the 1970s, it suffered what one longtime faculty member describes as an "ongoing identity crisis." With enrollment dropping and an endowment of just $400,000, it was obliged to use deposits sent in by the following year's incoming class to pay off its creditors.

Beaver College did exactly what many schools do these days: It turned for rescue to a consulting firm. Embracing the consultants' recommendations, the college revamped the administrative structure; recruited a vice president for enrollment management; started awarding scholarships on academic merit, rather than need, to tempt applicants with better SATs; and adopted "total quality management," an idea lifted from the management textbooks. (This means, among other things, making the campus visit a more "memorably pleasant" experience.)

Still, there remained the ticklish problem of the school's name. Pop culture had long since turned an innocent animal into a double entendre, and the vice president for enrollment management argued that the name scared off prospective applicants. Back came the consultants to help the school find a new name—one that, as Beaver president Bette Landman said, would "reflect the brand." This meant something short and punchy, its first letter coming at the beginning of the alphabet to ensure early mention in college guidebooks; something pleasing sounding, easy to say and read—something, as Landman put it, that could "become a strong trademark."[6]

Arcadia University was the preferred choice in the focus groups on which the school relied for inspiration. It evoked pastoral images—"artistic, in a pretty setting," a focus group participant said—and "sounds like a fun place to be." Similarly, the college morphed into a university because the focus groups believed "university" sounded more serious.

Companies give themselves new names all the time, so why not a college? Yet whatever the institution's name, what should matter is the substance behind the symbol. However, instead of seeing the occasion of a name change as an opportunity to rethink the academic mission, Arcadia opted to distinguish itself by promoting a heavily subsidized spring break trip to London for its freshmen. This "London Preview" is just the sort of gimmick that a consultant would concoct: "Arcadia = Fun."

The name change and niche marketing have worked: The number of applicants has grown substantially, and in the fall of 2002, Arcadia enrolled the biggest freshman class in its history. Whether they are receiving a better education, though, is anyone's guess.

Once tuition revenues started flowing in, Arcadia's first priority was to build a new campus center. In this the school is hardly unique—it is hard to find a university that is not investing heavily to spruce itself up. "It's not a hardship to go to college," says Kevin Kruger at the National Association of Student Personnel Administrators.[7] That's a considerable understatement.

At Michigan State, lucky students can watch big-screen TV while lounging in the therapeutic bubble jets in their dorm rooms. "There's a putting green and batting cages at the new indoor tennis and track center at DePauw University," Mary Leonard writes in a front-page *Boston Globe* article surveying the playing field.

> At Saint Xavier University in Chicago, students can work out with a personal trainer in the fitness center and then pick up a Krispy Kreme doughnut and a Starbucks double latte, all under one roof. . . . The first college ESPN Zone at the Rochester Institute of Technology [offers] sports on plasma televisions and a broadcast desk to let students practice doing play-by-play on camera. . . . The feeding of this flock has become big business. The University of Cincinnati has hired a master chef to create gourmet menus. . . . Georgia Tech in Atlanta has a greengrocer in a residence hall. . . . The campus center at Babson College has vegan and sushi stations and a full-time person preparing specialty coffees.[8]

As Kevin Kruger acknowledges, "This is definitely driven by a competitive marketplace."[9] Amid the 2003 recession, Moody's, the bond-rating service, noted that universities floated $13 billion in bonds, betting their fiscal futures on frills.

This spending spree responds to demands being made by the current generation of undergraduates. These students, who were born in the mid-1980s, were brought up (at least until 9/11) in an era of unparalleled peace and prosperity. What undergraduates from an earlier era would regard as pampering, these adolescents take for granted. They see themselves as savvy consumers, and in picking a college they are looking for the sybaritic pleasures of gated-community suburbia. For them, monasticism is out and hedonism is in.

What students and their parents *do not* pay much attention to is especially telling. Applicants fixated on prestige and seeking to be cosseted are unlikely to ask about the number of books and journals in the campus library. (Who needs books, many of them believe, when everything's on the Internet?) Nor do they inquire about how many of their teachers are actually full-time members of the community rather than adjunct instructors, the so-called freeway flyers and subway strap-holders who do not have secure jobs from one year to the next.

This generation also has a clear—if in many instances wrong-headed—idea about academic life, and most universities have acceded to the students' wishes. Undergraduates regard good grades as a birthright. Grade inflation is the result: at elite institutions, the "gentleman's C" has morphed into a B. As consumers, students typically want a Chinese menu of courses from which to choose. In the past quarter-century, there has been a mass migration away from the traditional academic core and toward what is seen as useful; the biggest enrollment increases are recorded in such fields as business administration, recreation management, and public safety. Liberal arts professors, much like Swiss watchmakers, offer something that is widely regarded as a luxury item to a shrinking clientele. In order to best the competition, even the most prestigious universities have been attentive to these demands for the practical: During the 1990s, when Harvard began losing top applicants to Stanford because of its Silicon Valley connections, it devised its own high-tech program and allowed entrepreneurial undergraduates to operate businesses out of their dorm rooms.

To be sure, competition has motivated some schools to do a better job in the classroom. A handful of universities, including Syracuse and Arizona, recast themselves as "student-centered research universities." Princeton increased the size of its undergraduate enrollment and eliminated all loan requirements in its financial aid package. Those changes, which sent tremors through the Ivy League, have meant that more students, and more applicants from needy families, can enroll there. Across the land, many universities have added freshman seminars to the curricular bill of fare, and almost every school has gone about reviewing its general education requirements. Although there are exceptions, these ventures are mostly marketing devices designed to make a college look good. The professor sitting under a tree, surrounded by a gaggle of adoring students, is more a viewbook staple than the sign of genuine educational reform.

Academic consumerism is not just an accommodation to students' desires—it has been elevated to the status of an educational philosophy. In this Brown University led the way. Until the 1970s Brown had suffered through a long, inglorious history as the doormat of the Ivy League. Situated in the crime-ridden backwater of Providence, Rhode Island, it was the safety school for students rejected by Yale or Princeton, an unhappy place because it was the third or fourth choice for most of its students.

This situation turned around completely in the span of a decade. From being the least selective of the Ivies, Brown became one of the most picky. "Harvard University," a T-shirt reads. "Didn't get into Brown."

The main reason is the introduction and smart marketing of something called the New Curriculum. It is more accurately described as the No Curriculum, and reads like an undergraduate's wish list. All distribution requirements are abolished, the number of courses needed to graduate is cut, majors are eschewed in favor of individually tailored concentrations, and students can opt to take all their courses on a pass-fail basis. "Brown's curriculum is structured in such a way," the college viewbook declares, "as to teach students the lessons of *choice* and *responsibility*." One could also say that the Brown curriculum puts the inmates in charge of the asylum.

This "choice and responsibility" model has been widely emulated. Brown's experience showed that laissez-faire appealed to many students: If it works in Providence, the thinking ran, it can work at our school as well. The idea of "choice and responsibility" also appealed to many professors, especially in the humanities and qualitative social sciences. The No Curriculum is ideologically compatible with these faculty members' rejection of the Enlightenment, or modernist, commitment to the search for truth through the exposure of error, in favor of the relativism of postmodernity. The new guard trashed the fundamental belief that their calling was to transmit knowledge to the next generation. On the contrary, they insisted, all knowledge was relative and no approach to the universe of wisdom was better than any other; for that reason, requiring students to learn any given body of knowledge was arbitrary. More pointedly, it reflected the imposition of Dead White Male orthodoxy, or embodied neocolonialism, or enshrined heterosexism, or racism, or . . . —the litany of postmodern pejoratives is seemingly endless. Since no one could say with confidence what the young needed to know, these professors argued, why not turn the keys of the asylum over to adolescents?

The free-form curriculum is defended on pedagogical grounds, as accommodating students' desires to dive straight into what most interests them. Conveniently, it also frees professors to concentrate on what most interests *them*, rather than obliging the faculty to teach students how to think critically for themselves. In this respect, it represents a response to another market force—the insistence by the most-sought-after professors that their teaching focus on their specialized research interests, rather than on encouraging critical thinking among the young.

This is a relatively new development. Until World War II, the academy was a parochial world, one where professors fastened their loyalties to their institutions. But during the postwar era, in what has been labeled an "academic revolution," these loyalties began to shift, away from the campus and to the discipline. Mr. Chips became a vanishing breed, as esteem among one's fellow biologists or economists grew to matter more than esteem at Siwash U.

Now there are signs of another seismic shift in loyalty among the academic elite—toward the individuals themselves. Mirroring the aspirations of their own on-the-make institutions, these superstars see themselves as academic entrepreneurs. Although no one outside the world of higher education used to notice professorial changes, star faculty members have turned into media darlings whose comings and goings are sometimes front-page news. When a university lands one of these public intellectuals or a professor who is widely esteemed by fellow scholars or someone who attracts large research grants, the result is buzz and prestige—valuable intellectual capital for the institution. In this era of free-agent professors (some of whom retain agents to represent them in their negotiations with the university), faculty mobility in the senior ranks is greater, and salary differentials between the most hotly pursued professors and everyone else are larger than ever before.

When it comes to what and how much they teach, these professors typically get what they want. Although superb teaching can bring popularity on the campus, no one becomes a superstar because of classroom prowess; no one makes a reputation, either in a discipline or as a media sage, by introducing twenty-year-olds to Wittgenstein or Einstein. It is not surprising, then, that many luminaries are not interested in offering introductory courses. If they are willing to teach undergraduates—and some are not—it is usually in their narrowly circumscribed area of expertise.

The recent history of New York University's philosophy department illustrates this tension between star faculty members' interests and the quality of undergraduates' education. Since the mid-1990s, the department's reputation has risen with a speed unprecedented in the annals of higher education: A department without an accredited PhD program in 1995 was ranked number one in the world just five years later. This transformation has not come about because NYU's professors are teaching Descartes and Kant with renewed vigor. Quite the opposite: Such "history" courses are regarded as outside the "science" of philosophy, the province of graduate students and adjunct instructors rather than the "real" academics. One old-line philosophy professor with a reputation as a superb teacher was hounded out of the department. "He's certainly very popular and charismatic," an ex-colleague says damningly, but what he teaches "doesn't seem like philosophy to me."[10]

The cadre of internationally known scholars who migrated to NYU perceives its responsibility as carrying forward a tradition of analytic philosophy—currently the most prestigious area of philosophical endeavor—whose style deters all but the most persistent of outsiders. The newcomers' teaching loads are light, consisting mainly of specialized seminars for advanced undergraduates and PhD students. Undergraduates are likely to take most of their philosophy courses from part-time instructors.

It may be true that adjuncts and graduate students make the best teachers. These part-timers must see teaching as their calling, since otherwise they would not put up with the terrible working conditions and measly salaries. But it is surely true that, because of the circumstances under which they labor, these instructors cannot provide the students with the intellectual continuity that is essential to a first-rate education.

Because they have no job security, they are constantly on the lookout for their next classroom gig. There is no reason to expect those who are not on the path leading to tenure to be loyal members of an academic community that shows no loyalty to them.

These are wretched circumstances under which to mount an undergraduate education of quality. A well-crafted curriculum demands a major commitment of time and energy. Courses must be designed with painstaking care, and course sequences that trace a coherent pathway of knowledge must be set. The expectation that students do a great deal of reading, writing, and experimenting—work that is crucial to their intellectual development—demands a comparable investment by the faculty. For entirely different reasons, neither the academic entrepreneurs nor the strap-hanger adjuncts make the necessary investment.

There are, of course, some schools where teaching still matters. Professors at liberal arts colleges, even elite colleges like Swarthmore and Amherst, are expected to take their classroom obligations seriously. But the liberal arts colleges are swimming against the market tides. Every year the number of these schools shrinks, as does their enrollment. They have had a hard time competing with state universities that, aided by state subsidies, have created "honors colleges." Striving regional universities like the University of Richmond, which used to emphasize the quality of teaching, are now fixated on the quantity of their faculty members' publications. Emulating the prestigious universities whose ranks Richmond would like to join, the university has cut faculty members' teaching loads, while expecting them to have written two books before coming up for tenure. (One can only pity the trees pulped for these epistles.) Meanwhile professors in the leading graduate programs are actively propagating themselves. They discourage their best students from considering careers in liberal arts colleges, instead preparing them for positions in research universities—that, after all, is where academic reputations are made.

A few leading universities, most famously Columbia and the University of Chicago, are also known for their dedication to undergraduates. (Not coincidentally, these were the only two schools, among the top twenty nationally ranked universities, where students did not specify that prestige was the main reason for enrolling.) Sadly, those reputations are largely smoke and mirrors.

Columbia has long contended that its liberal arts college is the jewel in the university's crown. Resisting the conventional wisdom, it maintains its widely admired required core curriculum. Yet when graduate students and part-time faculty went on strike in a dispute over wages in the spring of 2004, the college was forced to shut down. The university's dedication to undergraduate education was exposed as a sham: Just as at many leading universities, many of Columbia College's core classes are taught by graduate students and adjunct faculty, not full-time professors. In educating undergraduates, Columbia turns out to be little different from NYU; the main difference is Columbia's pretension to be something special.

Like Columbia, the University of Chicago fetishizes the education of its undergraduates. Chicago is more self-absorbed—more precisely, self-obsessed—than any other institution of higher learning in America. A passing remark made long ago by the philosopher Alfred North Whitehead is still widely recited: "I think the one place where I have been that is most like ancient Athens is the University of Chicago," and the university claims as its own any Nobel Prize winner who has ever taught there.

Curricular reforms are blood wars in Hyde Park. In 1998, when the university's administration proposed cutting back the required core curriculum, opposition was vociferous and venomous. Seventy-four senior professors sent an open letter to the trustees, warning darkly that "the intellectual tradition and academic organization of our university are being put at risk by its present leadership." Ten academic ancients—icons such as Saul Bellow, David Riesman, and Mortimer Adler, the intellectual midwife to the core curriculum sixty years earlier—weighed in against this "dangerous" venture. "Making academic decisions on the basis of marketing," they intoned, "is itself a crime against the mind."[11]

"The administration did not understand that if they cut the core curriculum, the natives would get restless," anthropologist Marshall Sahlins thundered in a widely circulated broadside. For faculty, students, and alumni alike, "the University itself, as mediated by their own identity with it, has been put at stake."[12]

The rigors of the college experience are indeed pivotal to Chicago's identity. The quarter system is designed to cram a semester's worth of work into ten weeks. Most courses in the humanities and social sciences are conducted as discussions, with no more than thirty students in a class. In this spartan academic environment, where pallor is beautiful and reading Nietzsche at three in the morning is a badge of honor, it is not easy for a lazy student to hide. This is the school where, as students say, "fun comes to die."

The centerpiece of the undergraduate education is the common core curriculum. Its premise is the exact opposite of Brown's "freedom and responsibility" approach. At Chicago all students are supposed to master certain habits of mind, so that they can become independent critics of each of the major intellectual domains. This approach, argues Chicago sociologist Andrew Abbott, "forces"—forces!—"students to achieve a breadth of knowledge and experience they would not necessarily elect for themselves."[13]

On the surface, the drama that played out in Hyde Park, and on the front page of the *New York Times* as well, appears to emblemize the struggle between the values of the marketplace and those of the academy. In fact, the situation is far more complicated.

Chicago's traditionalists assumed that more was better. Yet what was being taught in those courses, and by whom, received no public attention, even though there was widespread faculty unhappiness with their content. Moreover, the biggest threat to the common core did not come from the administration—its proposal entailed sensible pruning, not decimation—but from the faculty, whose members had largely given up on the project.

Only senior professors should teach the core courses, Andrew Abbott argued, because only a widely published academic can stand as a "central authority figure who can model for students the discipline of rethinking ideas."[14] What a marvelous notion—Kant and Mill interpreted by Mortimer Adler or Allan Bloom—but you would have to go elsewhere to find it. At Chicago, the ideal of a college where intellectually obsessive undergraduates are instructed in small classes collides with a shabbier reality. Science courses are delivered lecture style, and few sections are led by faculty members. Even in the humanities and social sciences, nearly two-thirds of classes are taught by graduate students and adjunct instructors. Marshall Sahlins's enthusiasm for a substantial diet of required courses was rooted in his fear that if undergraduates had more opportunities to take electives, people like him—a self-described member of the *graduate* department of anthropology—would have to teach them.

"What we are doing has intellectual integrity!" was the rallying cry of the traditionalists. "But you can only go so far," observes one professor, "before you have to point at the faculty and ask, 'Why aren't you teaching?' " For all its rhetorical pretensions, the University of Chicago turns out not to be very different from NYU.

For parents, politicians, and the public, the mounting cost of a college education is the major higher education topic these days. That is entirely understandable. Tuition hikes of 10 percent and more each year are a big reason why many prospective candidates from middle as well as working class families cannot afford college. Smart poor kids, as one knowledgeable insider summarizes the data, are no more likely to get a college education than dumb rich kids.

Yet too little attention is being paid to another critical issue: How are undergraduates actually being educated? What are they learning in college? The answers are beginning to emerge through careful studies of the "value-added" of a college experience, and those answers are dispiriting. The batch-processing universities, the big state schools that enroll four out of five undergraduates, are generally failing in their teaching obligations. The elite schools seem to do a better job of certifying top students than educating them.

This situation ought to provoke public outrage, but it does not. Instead the public, which when polled gives higher education top marks, accepts the soothing assurance that American universities are the best in the world. Nor is there widespread discontent among undergraduates; overwhelmingly, they praise the college that they attend. That should not be a surprise. Market-driven colleges are going out of their way to assure that students have a good time. Undergraduates can take any course that catches their fancy, whatever its academic worth; moreover, they have no benchmark against which to assess their experience. Surveys of college professors—at least those who are lucky enough to have found a place on the academic career ladder, rather than having to eke out a living as guest workers—show that they too are generally happy with their lot.

In short, the higher education market seems to work for most of the participants. But that market has unhappy consequences—what economists call "negative externalities"—for the nation. Because of the generally shabby quality of undergraduate education, the United States is not getting the educated citizenry that is required if the country is going to stay competitive in the international competition for talented knowledge workers. Those who inveigh against the outsourcing of high-tech jobs should take a closer look at the skills possessed by the current crop of college graduates.

This is how the world seems naturally to work when, as now, the zeitgeist is the market. If healthcare, museums, even churches have been reshaped by intense competitive pressures, why should higher education be any different? In all those instances, the best answer is the same. Even as higher education was awakening to the reality that it engaged in marketing, economist Arthur Okun was pointing out the importance of balancing the values of the market against the values of the commons. "There is a place for the market," Okun wrote, "but the market must be kept in its place."[15]

In years past, academic statesmen such as Clark Kerr at Berkeley, Derek Bok at Harvard, and Theodore Hesburgh at Notre Dame could influence public opinion. Yale president Kingman Brewster was such an eloquent critic of the Vietnam War that *New York Times* columnist James Reston urged the Democratic Party to draft him as their 1968 presidential candidate. That is unimaginable now—because university presidents are constantly seeking money from power, they can hardly speak truth to power.

The critical question is this: Is there anyone with sufficient stature to persuade the public that, at their best, institutions of higher learning offer something of such great value that the enterprise is worth subsidizing, even in the face of market pressures? Is there anyone who can convincingly make the case that, as NYU president John Sexton (who is working hard to reinvigorate the academic commons at his own university) has said, there need to be spheres where "money is not the coin of the realm"?

Lacking such a principled defense of nonmarket values, higher education may degenerate into something far less palatable than a house of learning that—as a prophetic report on undergraduate education put it nearly two centuries ago—is "attuned to the business character of the nation."[16] It may degenerate into just another business, the metaphor of the higher education "industry" brought fully to life. Should that scenario come to pass, America's undergraduates will be among the biggest losers. But if there is to be a less dystopian future, one that revives the soul of this old institution, who is to advance it—and if not now, then when?

Notes

* David L. Kirp is Professor of Public Policy at the University of California at Berkeley and the author of *Shakespeare, Einstein, and the Bottom Line: The Marketing of Higher Education* (Harvard University Press, 2003), from which this chapter is adapted. The chapter draws on the superb contributions of Jeffrey Holman, PhD candidate in the Economics Department at Berkeley, and Jonathan Van Antwerpen, PhD candidate in Berkeley's Sociology Department.

1. A. R. Krachenberg, "Bringing the Concept of Marketing to Higher Education," *Journal of Higher Education* 43 (May 1972): 370.
2. Richard Atkinson, "It Takes Cash to Keep Ideas Flowing," September 1998, http://uc-industry.berkeley.edu/news/president/ittakes.htm.
3. Steve Jecklow, "Colleges Manipulate Financial Aid Offers, Shortchanging Many," *Wall Street Journal*, April 1, 1996, p. A1.
4. Roger Geiger, *Knowledge and Money: Research Universities and the Paradox of the Marketplace* (Palo Alto, CA: Stanford University Press, 2004).
5. Michael McPherson and Morton Shapiro, *The Student Aid Game* (Princeton, NJ: Princeton University Press, 1998).
6. *The American Freshman,* the annual report by the Cooperative Institutional Research Program at UCLA's Higher Education Research Institute (HERI), 2003.
7. Interviews conducted at Arcadia University. See David L. Kirp, *Shakespeare, Einstein and the Bottom Line: The Marketing of Higher Education* (Harvard University Press, 2003), pp. 12–14.
8. Mary Leonard, "On Campus, Comforts Are Major Colleges' Hope Perks Can Boost Enrollment," *Boston Globe*, September 3, 2002, p. A1.
9. Ibid.
10. Interview with Professor Peter Unger, conducted at NYU. See Kirp, *Shakespeare*, p. 74.
11. Letter from the Faculty to the Trustees of the University of Chicago, March 21, 1999. See Kirp, *Shakespeare*, p. 36.
12. Scholars for the University of Chicago, April 14, 1999. See Kirp, *Shakespeare*, p. 36.

13. Marshall Sahlins, "The Life of the Mind and the Love of the Body; Or, the New 'Chicago Plan,' Now With Added Balance," March 1999. See Kirp, *Shakespeare*, p. 37.
14. Andrew Abbott, "Futures of the University," Forum: Newsletter of the Faculty Committee for a Time of Reflection, October 1996. See Kirp, *Shakespeare*, p. 37.
15. Arthur Okun, *Equality and Efficiency: The Big Tradeoff* (Washington, D.C.: Brookings Institution Press, 1975), p. 19.
16. *Reports on the Course of Instruction in Yale College,* 1828. http://www.higher-ed.org/resources/Yale/1828_curriculum.pdf.

9

How Undergraduate Education Became College Lite—and a Personal Apology

Murray Sperber

The love of money may or may not be the root of all evil. However, I can say that it played a major role in the decline of American higher education. This I know to be true, because not only was I there, I also contributed.

How did American undergraduate education, particularly its state university version, go from its halcyon past—higher standards and low tuition—to its present predicament—highly questionable quality at an unquestionably high price? One answer can be found in my own experiences: Purdue in the late 1950s, graduate training at University of California, Berkeley, in the 1960s, and my teaching career at Indiana University from 1971 to 2004. In tracking my academic career, I am struck how it represents many faculty lives, particularly those of my generation.

The Research Imperative

The year 1957 was a crucial one in the history of higher education in the United States. When the Soviets put Sputnik in orbit, it forced Americans to acknowledge the high level of Soviet science. I arrived on the Purdue campus in the fall of 1957, pre-Sputnik and preexpansion. Sputnik prompted demands for more and better science, which the Eisenhower administration and the Congress translated into money for higher education. Money meant expansion. When I started at Purdue, the school did not grant a B.A. degree in English. Ten years later it was possible to earn a B.A., an M.A. and a PhD in that subject—and many others. Like many universities, Purdue fell in love with research and felt impelled to grant advanced degrees in almost all areas, not just fields where it traditionally specialized. Purdue's motto was "Science, Technology, and Agriculture," and, as a land-grant institution, its faculty had done pioneer research work in the areas of its motto. (Some of the first astronauts graduated from its aeronautical engineering program.) But why did Purdue decide to award advance degrees in English and other humanities areas? Didn't Indiana University, down the road in Bloomington, have long established and prominent graduate programs in English and other humanities fields? Indeed it did, but Purdue believed that to succeed as a university, it had to possess graduate programs in almost every area, not just its traditional specialties. Wasn't that the way the greatest public university of the period, the University of California at Berkeley, did it? Clark Kerr, the UC president at the time, called Berkeley the "multiversity" and boasted about its strength in all academic fields at every level. If it was good enough for Cal, it was good enough for Purdue and every other wannabe institution. Besides, the money was there.

Like Purdue in this period, Indiana University started or expanded various programs in some areas of Purdue's strengths and also enlarged its traditional graduate programs to stay ahead of its competitors. Similarly, Michigan State University, a land-grant school like Purdue, began or enlarged graduate programs in areas where the University of Michigan had a national reputation. In response, Michigan expanded to keep its lead over MSU and to reach Cal's level. Smaller colleges with a mandate to teach undergraduates followed suit and aimed for university status so that they could have research programs and grant graduate degrees. The "Academic Arms Race" was on—and it continues to this day.

Expansion created unprecedented employment opportunities. New or enlarged PhD programs like Purdue's and Indiana's needed faculty, particularly for research. For example, Indiana's English department ended the 1963–1964 academic year with sixty-three faculty members. It added ten the next year, nine the following year, and eight more the year after that. Other universities (and other departments at IU) were also expanding by 10 to 15 percent every year. This was the *only* time during centuries of American higher education when there were more jobs than candidates. However, to this day, some members of this extra cohort of faculty do not realize or acknowledge the historical anomaly of their professional histories. Indeed, they possess a sense of "research entitlement" and see higher education through their research bias. Because of their numbers and prominence, their research imperative has had a disproportionate influence on universities, and it has been central to the decline of undergraduate education.

(Incidentally, I am not convinced that this explosion of graduate education has produced significant benefits in the form of substantial research. As I read history, most of the quality work has continued to come from long established—that is, pre-Sputnik—research programs. The new empires turned out to be mainly Potemkin villages. What a sham and a shame!)

In the 1960s, a funny thing happened on the way to research paradise: The Civil Rights movement and the Vietnam War divided the country, often with student rebels on one side and enraged taxpayers on the other. Various politicians articulated the fears and hopes of the protestors and the taxpayers; Ronald Reagan became governor of California by promising to punish the student rebels at Berkeley and to gain control of the university. Reagan succeeded and part of his control was to cut funding to the university. Thanks to him, a University of California education was no longer free, and, by the time he left office, it had started to become expensive. A majority of the public approved his moves, and other politicians in other states imitated him. The era of cascading taxpayer dollars for higher education was over.

However, university administrators and professors had fallen in love with their research programs, not only for the supposed prestige that the programs brought their schools. Many faculty, especially the 1960s cohort, had discovered that they much preferred teaching their specialties in graduate seminars and directing dissertations to teaching undergraduate classes and reading undergraduate papers. When money was plentiful, many universities had reduced the faculty "teaching load" (a term that implies that teaching is a burden) to two courses per semester. When I was a freshman at Purdue in 1957, faculty there, and at most universities, taught four courses a semester; when I began my teaching career at Indiana in 1971, I was assigned to teach half that many. The university expected faculty to spend the rest of their time doing research.

When state funding to public institutions declined precipitously, the logical steps would have been to cut back on research and ask faculty to teach more classes. That did not happen. Instead, most schools made classes bigger and also hired more part-timers and graduate students to teach them. Small classes of fifteen to twenty students taught by a full faculty member not only occupy a large amount of the professor's time—line-editing every paper and long office hours are extremely labor intensive—but such classes also create red ink: too few tuition dollars for too much salary and other expenses. However, classes with 150 or more students generate enough tuition dollars to cover the salaries of the professor and the teaching assistants as well as some departmental expenses.

Lecture classes are far less labor intensive. The irony of lecture courses—and why they are so appealing to many research-oriented faculty members—is that they are much easier to teach than small classes: The professor can give the same set of lectures year after year and does not have to read a single word of student writing. All tests and exams are corrected by machines and/or assistants—and the faculty member can choose to have minimal contact with students.

Similarly, in this period, schools force-marched undergraduates from small classes into huge lecture courses, along with some reasonable-size classes sprinkled into their schedules. However, for an increasing number of classes with fewer than twenty-five students—money losers when taught by faculty—schools began hiring lowly paid non-tenure track faculty or grad students to teach them and to generate a small profit. In the 1970s, the expression "Follow the money trail" became popular; it also applied to university life, particularly class size and professorial salaries.

Until the 1960s, most university departments had a uniform—and low—salary scale, with increases tied to years in service. The flood of research money and the "Academic Arms Race" changed that. As part of the massive hiring of the 1960s, schools went headhunting: They offered senior researchers and junior faculty with research potential bags of money to join their departments. Some universities practically "bought" illustrious departments almost overnight. Rarely, if ever, was teaching part of the conversation—unless it had to do with negotiating how *little* the new hires would have to do. In the late 1960s, English at the State University of New York at Buffalo went from obscurity to fame in this manner.

The bottom line was obvious to everyone—particularly PhD candidates and young faculty: Universities reward research fame and potential with promotion, ever-increasing salaries, and other incentives (e.g., special labs for scientists, even lighter teaching loads—one course per semester, no courses at all, etc.), and they do not reward teaching, particularly teaching undergraduates. Universities do not hire away outstanding teachers from other institutions, nor do they offer jobs to new PhDs on the basis of their potential as teachers.

In the 1960s, I did not find any of this remarkable. Graduate school at Berkeley required me to spend countless hours on research in courses, seminars, tutorials with faculty, and my dissertation. But I do not recall Berkeley spending any time teaching me to teach, even when, as an advanced graduate student, I was assigned my own courses. All of this was a very clear signal that research mattered enormously, whereas the instruction of undergraduates did not count for much at all. According to our training, the only teaching of any importance occurred in graduate courses. Never forget that we teach the way we were taught, and so my contemporaries and I imitated the research seminar model. I know that I bewildered undergraduates in my classes with my research concerns, and I doubt if much learning took place. That is still happening on campuses everywhere.

Berkeley became a kind of national research model, and even colleges with historic commitments to teaching undergraduates gravitated to its single-minded emphasis on research. As Berkeley sent out hundreds of PhDs in all fields, those young professors (including me) helped steer our new institutions closer to the Berkeley model.

The Great—and Permanent—Academic Depression

In the 1970s, young faculty were no more prepared for the totally changed economic reality in academia than were the administrators who ran America's universities. We could not believe that the post-Sputnik era of lavish public spending on higher education actually had ended. We went from the academic equivalent of the Roaring Twenties to the Great Depression without realizing it. We sensed that times had changed—newspapers carried articles about the mammoth cutbacks in state funding to universities—but we absolutely believed that the research imperative should and would prevail. We totally endorsed the emphasis on graduate education and large graduate programs, as well as the two-course load and the ever-increasing size of undergraduate classes. In fact, so committed was I to this new model that I invented a huge introductory lecture course for my department's creative writing program: My premise was that a class with 150 students could generate enough tuition revenue so that the department could enlarge its graduate program in creative writing and employ many of the new graduate students as teaching assistants in the introductory lecture course. To implement the plan, I convinced the department to abolish all of the small freshman sections of creative writing (taught by faculty members) and only offer the large lecture class at that level—and to make the lecture course a prerequisite for all other creative writing courses. With no alternative, students interested in creative writing took the lecture course; faculty seemed happy to get out of a time-consuming freshman course and on with their research, and the graduate program in creative writing expanded exponentially. At the time, I joked, "The department should make me supermarket manager of the year."

After a few years of teaching this lecture course, I came to my senses and recognized that creative writing, like most freshman courses, should not be taught in classes of 150 students. I managed to extricate myself from teaching the mass course, although it continues to this day, a cornerstone of the department's creative writing program. Frankly, I regret its existence: I not only regret that it trapped many undergraduates in negative experiences but also that it enlarged my department's graduate program in creative writing and spawned many unemployed—and unemployable—MFAs.

In the 1970s, however, at Indiana and many other universities, programs like creative writing were sideshows to the main events: the ever-expanding graduate programs and ever-enlarging undergraduate classes across the curriculum. Psychology departments, as part of a national trend in the field, greatly expanded their research and graduate programs, and began to teach their introductory courses in lecture classes of four and five hundred students. Again, I remember my own undergraduate days when psychology, a subject of intrinsic interest to postadolescent undergraduates, was taught by full faculty members in small classes. We could actually talk about all the fascinating stuff that was rolling around in our heads, instead of just taking notes and parroting back the material on exams!

Fast-forward to the present day, the huge lecture classes in psychology, political science, English, and many other fields are even more prevalent than they were in the 1970s. Why would these departments believe that their introductory courses should be taught in this way, particularly to freshmen—the cohort of students least able to benefit from lectures? In political science, for example, wouldn't students like to argue with the professor about political concepts? When I have asked faculty in psychology, political science, and other departments this question, some respondents have frankly stated that these courses are a positive for the department because the tuition revenue they generate help fund graduate students and research projects.

In the 1970s, the rules for faculty promotion and tenure changed, thus reinforcing the importance of research and graduate programs at the expense of undergraduate education. The research imperative was metastasizing. Up to the beginning of the decade, most universities awarded tenure to assistant professors who published a number of articles in good journals, had good teaching records, and performed some service to their departments and schools. But in the 1970s, the research imperative took hold, and the new rules required an assistant professor in the humanities to have published a book to gain tenure and candidates in other areas to have accomplished equivalent feats. The specific rules called for the tenure candidate to be deemed "outstanding" in one of the three traditional areas: research, teaching, and service. However, as the decade went on, fewer and fewer candidates achieved tenure who were not "outstanding in research," and this trend accelerated in subsequent decades. Indeed, during the last generation, the famous tenure battles reported in periodicals like the *Chronicle of Higher Education* usually have centered on young faculty members, outstanding in teaching, particularly in undergraduate courses, but not in research, and the candidates' departments and/or the deans denying them tenure. Sometimes undergrads became involved in the disputes and lobbied for the candidate's tenure: they almost never won but came to understand how little their schools valued the teaching of undergraduates.

Fast-forward to the present day: At many schools, young PhDs in humanities need to have published a book just to be hired; for tenure, they must have a number of books. Obviously, the name of the game is research and the supposed prestige that it produces for a school, which forces participants to spend the vast majority of their time on research. Lip service is paid to undergraduate education, but the unavoidable fact remains that teaching undergraduates in a conscientious manner is very labor-intensive. How can a young faculty member or a PhD candidate working as a part-time instructor square this circle? How can these men and women spend the necessary amount of time on research and still spend many hours on undergraduate teaching? The answer is obvious, or as one young faculty member recently told me, "Forget about sleeping." In the real world of academia, the circle cannot be squared, nor can the necessity of spending all those hours on research be ignored. Obviously, undergraduate teaching is neglected; indeed, the current system institutionalizes its neglect.

This faculty situation—and it also applies to tenured faculty, most of whom want the promotions and salary increases that come only from research success—is the main cause of the rampant grade inflation that has afflicted the academy since the research imperative took hold. A nonaggression pact exists between many faculty members and students: Because the former believe that they must spend most of their time doing research, and the latter often prefer to pass their time having fun, a mutual nonaggression pact occurs with each side agreeing not to impinge on the other. The glue that keeps the pact intact is grade inflation: easy As for merely acceptable work and Bs for mediocre work.

A faculty member does not have to justify giving a high grade to a student, and few students will complain about a high grade, earned or not. But a faculty member who gives a student a C or less has to expect complaints—and has to spend a fair amount of time justifying the grade with detailed written comments on the test or exam and meeting with an upset student. Not surprisingly, many faculty choose the nonaggression pact.

Research Prestige and Poll Mania

Despite the economic hardships of inflation and recession in the 1980s, the research imperative controlled the academy. Early in that decade a new phenomenon mightily reinforced it: *U.S. News & World Report* began publishing its annual rankings of American colleges and universities. Its poll imitated the popular college football and basketball polls that asked sportswriters and/or coaches to rank teams. The *U.S. News* academic one was and still is highly subjective and fallible. From its inception, the basic flaw in the *News* poll was its bias toward university research. But in the early years of the poll, rather than condemn the methodology, schools began striving for as high a position as possible.

Americans love polls, love the illusion that there really is a "number-one" college football team or car or school, and that the world can be reduced to simple rankings. From its inception, the annual college rankings edition of *U.S. News* sold more copies than any other edition and continues to do so to this day. Indeed, the poll has become so important that schools spend large sums of money on various programs in order to score higher in specific *U.S. News* categories and improve their overall poll positions.

The most significant factor in a school's *U.S. News* ranking has always been the most subjective, its "academic reputation." Unlike an institution's graduation rate, which can be measured mathematically and counts for 5 percent of a school's *U.S. News* score, "academic reputation" is based on the magazine's survey of college and university administrators throughout the country. It counts for 25 percent of the total score.

The panel of *U.S. News* voters offer their opinions about schools similar to theirs. But unlike the sportswriters and coaches, the *U.S. News* voters cannot see the academic equivalent of games on TV—actual classroom situations at other schools—and instead they base much of their vote on gossip heard about other schools, such as "At lunch one day, someone was saying that Northern State is really improving, they have some hotshot young profs who are doing interesting research." So the voter gives Northern extra points on the questionnaire and helps raise its "academic reputation" score and ranking.

Again, because research gives the illusion of tangibility, whereas teaching is elusive, research always trumps teaching in academic reputation. Indeed, by definition, *U.S. News* voters at a specific school know very little about the quality of teaching at another school—except if they happened to have attended or worked at the other school; however, this fragment of knowledge is negated by the fact that *U.S. News* asks them to vote on many schools.

To its credit, in the last decade *U.S. News* has increasingly tried to measure the caliber of undergraduate education at America's colleges and universities. It also recognizes the difficulty of that task and has lobbied for "outcomes tests," measurements such as the Graduate Record Exam that test what students have learned in their undergraduate careers. Not surprisingly, the vast majority of schools resist *U.S. News'* request for such tests—I suspect that they do not want the world to discover that their undergraduate education programs have no clothes and that most of their seniors would not score well on "outcomes tests."

The *U.S. News* rankings, for all of their admitted and real fallibility, remain a driving force in American higher education, and because of the importance of the "academic reputation" score, they are a force that perpetuates the privileging of research and graduate programs over undergraduate education.

Another national publication that tries to measure the quality of undergraduate education as well as student life is the *Princeton Review*. Most famous for its annual list of "Party Schools," the publication also ranks colleges and universities in such categories as "Professors Bring Material to Life," "Professors Make Themselves Accessible," "Class Discussions Encouraged," "Teaching Assistants Teach Too Many Upper Level Courses," and "Best Overall Academic Experience for Undergraduates."

Critics, particularly administrators at schools that rank high on *Princeton Review's* negative lists, detest the publication and condemn its methodology. (It casually polls about 50,000 students a year at the colleges and universities on its lists—357 schools in 2004.) Like *U.S. News* and the sports rankings, there is no pretense of "hard science" in this poll. But *Princeton Review* does seek a very large sample and appears to offer a good insight into its schools. For example, an in-depth study of the actual percentage of teaching assistants doing upper-level courses at the 357 schools probably would produce a list very similar to the one in *Princeton Review*.

Similarly, in the "Professors Bring Material to Life" category, no one should be surprised that small Marlboro College in Vermont comes first, followed by Reed, Carleton, Davidson, and Wabash colleges. None of these institutions ever gave in to the research imperative, and, over the last few decades, they have not wavered in their commitment to undergraduate education. They hire and promote faculty on the basis of their teaching, and although they expect some research from them, they do not want it to interfere with teaching.

These schools and ones like them—St. John's College in Maryland and its campus in New Mexico, Swarthmore, Sarah Lawrence, and Eugene Lang—scored in the top cohort of schools where "Professors Make Themselves Accessible," "Class Discussions Encouraged," and "Best Overall Academic Experience." Quality undergraduate education is alive and well in the United States—it just does not exist for most students at public universities. Unfortunately, all of the schools on these lists are private and very expensive. Thus, only a tiny percentage of all American college students receive a high-quality undergraduate education—as opposed to the much higher percentage that received it when I was an undergraduate in the 1950s.

It is true that honors programs at public universities provide a quality undergraduate education. But honors programs are a form of triage, placing a tiny percentage of students at public schools into educational lifeboats while the institution allows the rest of the student body to drown in huge lecture courses and other academic oceans. Thus, contrary to honors program advocates, they are not a solution to the ills of contemporary undergraduate education—merely lifeboats for the lucky few who are pulled into them.

Solutions exist. Here I list a number of proposals that would, I believe, reform the current problems our universities, particularly public ones, face and place in remission the cancer that afflicts undergraduate education. Without radical solutions, the patient will die.

1. Establish research institutes for "pure" research. In many western countries, separate research institutes—sometimes funded by the government, sometimes by private industry—exist. In America for many

decades, Bell Labs produced some of the best scientific research in the country. The workers at the institutes are professional researchers and devote their time and energy to their research work—they do not spend part of it teaching undergraduates.

With this model in mind, universities should divide their graduate programs into research training and undergraduate teaching tracks. In other words, some PhD candidates would focus on research and others on undergraduate teaching. Both groups would learn about past and current research in the field; however, the researchers would then concentrate their graduate work on research and would strive for a career in research, whereas the graduate work of the students on the teaching track would focus more on pedagogy.

This model would cut the costs of graduate programs enormously: Schools would admit fewer graduate students and have fewer graduate courses and classes. Most likely a return to teaching three or even four courses a semester would result. Just as pilots in the airline industry have learned to give up very cushy jobs for reasonable work at decent pay, faculty members might do the same. We might be pleasantly surprised to find that quite a few professors would gladly cut back on research in order to be real teachers.

2. Hire, promote, and reward faculty *either* for research *or* for teaching. In hiring, promoting, and rewarding for research, universities should use all of the criteria now in place; for teaching, they should emphasize the teaching of undergraduates. In a technological age, evaluating teaching is much easier than ever before. Unobtrusive video cameras can record classes, transcripts of tutorials can be provided on the web, and, also electronically, students can supply feedback and evaluations of every class during the semester. When candidates on the proposed teaching track apply for jobs or promotion, they can submit very complete teaching portfolios to highlight their strengths. Indeed, these days, universities could *require* applicants for faculty positions to submit teaching portfolios. Schools rarely ask candidates to do this; however, they usually require candidates to give a public lecture on their research during on-campus job interviews.

At this point, teaching faculty will no longer have to do much research, and many academic research projects done for promotion and tenure will no longer appear. But the research that the teaching faculty will produce probably will be of higher quality than previously—true labors of love rather than make-work.

3. Abolish teaching methods that turn undergraduates into passive receptacles; emphasize interactive, inquiry-based learning. Before the twentieth century, the justification for lectures in higher education was transmission of information. Books were expensive and relatively scarce, and so professors transmitted knowledge of a subject to students orally, who wrote it down in note form. Today books are ubiquitous, and the retrieval of information has never been easier: Rather than laboriously taking notes on the Plantagenet kings of England, a student can turn to Google and instantly have a list of Plantagenet kings and a great deal of information about them.

However, students need to learn how to make sense of all the entries that bombard them during a database search. Which entries are useful, which are garbage, and, most difficult of all, which are partially useful and partially garbage? In my final years at Indiana, I found that I was mainly teaching critical skills—how to make sense of databases and how to order and use the material from them. This strategy is "process learning," whereas lecturing usually ends up as "product learning." Students produce lists of Plantagenet monarchs or genotypes but cannot evaluate the information or use it. A college education in the twenty-first century should center on process learning, and not on product acquisition and regurgitation.

Even with the incredible technological advances of the last half century, education is still rather simple. My main regret is that a freshman at Purdue or Indiana or any similar school today has a much more difficult time obtaining the quality education that I received as an undergraduate.

In my own small way, I contributed to that difficulty by ingesting the research model at Berkeley and then living so many years of my faculty life in its thrall. Mea culpa. I hope that the story of my academic journey can bring a little enlightenment to the current debate on undergraduate education and that the next fifty years will not be as destructive to that enterprise as the last fifty have been.

10

America's Modern Peculiar Institution

Frank Deford

GROUCHO (Dean Quincy Adams Wagstaff): Have we got a stadium?
FACULTY: Yes.
GROUCHO: Have we got a college?
FACULTY: Yes.
GROUCHO: Well, we can't support both. Tomorrow we start tearing down the college.

—From *Horse Feathers*, 1932, starring the Marx Brothers

The first thing to understand about big-time sports and academia is that they simply cannot work together. Never have and never will. Big-time sports, or "B-TS," will always win, and they will always adversely affect education.

The first intercollegiate American competition was a crew race between Harvard and Yale in 1851. It might surprise you, though, to learn that the race was not held on the Charles River or the Connecticut River. Rather, it was held way up in New Hampshire, on Lake Winnipesaukee. Why? Well, a man owned a railroad that went from Boston to Lake Winnipesaukee, and there he also happened to own some choice vacation lots that he had up for sale. What better way to market his wares than to have the wealthy friends and family of the Yale and Harvard rowers ride up on his railroad?

So, as you can see, the very first American intercollegiate athletic competition was a bowl game. The institution is cursed with original sin.

The first college baseball game was between Amherst and Williams in 1859. Amherst won. Williams immediately protested that Amherst had used a ringer, the hefty town blacksmith.

The first college football game was held in 1869 between Princeton, my alma mater, and Rutgers. Later that very fall, the Princeton faculty demanded that the third game must be cancelled because football was already diverting the student body from scholarship and religion. It was, however, only a brief setback in the ascent of the charm of college sports. Soon the annual Princeton-Yale football game, held in New York over the new Thanksgiving holiday, was such a smash that the whores in town wore orange-and-black or blue-and-white garments to best attract their gridiron clientele.

But then, more recently the National Collegiate Athletic Association (NCAA) has taught us, with its television contracts, that prostitution comes in many guises.

Of course, sport is good for you and not necessarily antithetical to learning. Hey, Plato wrestled. And, like the ancient Greeks, many distinguished Americans have been successful at athletic and academic pursuits alike. It is certainly not an either/or proposition. But whereas sport-as-exercise has every right to exist in education—especially at a time when so many of our children are growing up overweight—sport-as-entertainment only creates problems for the institutions whose names are appropriated for use on the fronts of uniforms.

It is fashionable, of course, to defend college sports by suggesting that they are a healthy outlet, both for those who play and those who watch. School spirit! Among other things, this rationale allows many universities to levy, in effect, a sports tax on the whole student body. These fees, which bring in hundreds of thousands of dollars to the university, essentially subsidize sports. In a very real sense, lowly students are obliged to directly underwrite the scholarships of the so-called student athletes.

Athletic directors also always argue that by having those great modern American cathedrals—stadiums and arenas—on campus, the box office receipts and complementary television payouts not only support what are known so candidly as revenue sports—usually just men's basketball and football—but also pay the bills for all other intercollegiate sports. In fact, while nobody really knows how many colleges actually profit on sports, it is probably no more than a handful. The other forty or so colleges that claim that they break even or make a slight profit apparently only do so on account of the compulsory student taxes and other sleight-of-hand bookkeeping. If English departments received the kinds of subsidies and indulgences that athletic departments do, they could be listed on the Nasdaq exchange. Whatever the numbers, it is simply impossible to argue that big-time college sports are a financial boon for their universities.

Ironically, when carping educators actually had the nerve to suggest that campus athletic spectacles ate up money that would be better spent on (unfashionable) education, that contention produced an even worse situation. In response to this criticism, many athletic departments volunteered to break away from college control and raise their own funds. This seemed to be a very fair proposal, but it resulted in a classic case of the law of unintended consequences. Now that the athletic departments were essentially freed of financial oversight, they could take on even more power of the purse and exert even more control over their own entertaining way of life.

This athletic hegemony has resulted in several problems, the first of which is celebrity coaches getting sky-high salaries. It is interesting to note that whereas college coaches have always been stars, even idols, multimillion-dollar contracts that compete with those in the professional arena are a recent phenomenon. When Johnny Wooden, the most successful college coach of the twentieth century, retired from UCLA in 1975, his salary was a mere $42,000. Yet now that athletic departments are their own fiefdoms and can easily raise money from gung-ho supporters who care nothing for real education, we are treated to incredible examples of athletic indulgence. Nothing illustrates this better than the recent case at Auburn. In this instance, a booster provided a jet to take Auburn officials—including the school president himself—on a secret trip to Kentucky to try to seduce the University of Louisville football coach into breaking his contract and taking the Auburn job. Had the clandestine deal not been revealed in the press and created such a stink, the new hire would have cost the athletic department an additional $4 million to buy out the current coach's contract on top of the huge contract that would have been paid out to the new coach. So Auburn would have been paying several millions of dollars a year to two football coaches at a time when all colleges are facing budget cuts.

As disheartening as it must be to most professors to see the great, disproportionate sums paid to coaches, the athletic scholarship remains the most indefensible element in college sports. Not only are these scholarships awarded without considering need, they are virtually the only scholarships granted to students because of their extracurricular talent. How can anyone rationally argue that a baseball player should get a college scholarship, but a piano player should not? What does it say about a college's regard for art, literature, drama, and music if the finest young painters, writers, actors, and musicians are not eligible for the same rewards as are athletes? (When I mentioned this in a speech once, I was called to account by an offended college president, who told me that his university most certainly did award other extracurricular scholarships . . . to prominent members of the band that entertained at the halftime of football games.)

The athletic scholarship not only means extracurricular discrimination, but it gives the athletic department a power over its players that no academic department enjoys. Cross us, and we'll take away your scholarship. Keep in mind, too, that athletes today have no limited "season," the way they used to. Once the scheduled games end, athletes are expected to work out with weights the rest of the year and to engage in "informal" practices.

(An heretical aside: Given current reality, when such sums of money are earned for the school by the student-entertainers, football and basketball players, and given the gigantic salaries that coaches are paid, it seems only fair to me that college football and basketball players should be paid a salary for their efforts. It strikes me as just as hypocritical to award a scholarship to a lacrosse player or a golfer as it is to employ football and basketball players as indentured servants.)

All these excesses aside, I would suggest that the lure of the athletic scholarship is more damaging even than the reality. Entirely too many parents today urge their children to concentrate on sports, so that they might eventually gain an athletic scholarship. Just as too many inner-city kids ignore their secondary education, holding out for the possibility of a professional sports career, so do too many middle-class kids devote themselves to a sport in the false hope that they will get athletic scholarships. It is well known that parents will not only press their young children to concentrate on athletics, but they will even steer them into particular sports where they feel there will be less competition for scholarships.

Of course, inasmuch as not all colleges award athletic scholarships, it has generally been the comfortable sense—especially enjoyed by us Ivy League elitists, looking down our noses at the barnyard institutions in the hinterlands—that it is only the big-time sports schools that have blown athletics out of perspective. The book *The Game of Life*, by James L. Shulman and William G. Bowen, the former president of Princeton, has blasted that delusion to smithereens. No colleges, it seems, escape the siren call of sports. Specifically, what Shulman and Bowen showed is that, in many respects, the small, highly regarded private universities are caught up more in the thrall of athletics than are the B-TS universities.

At least in the B-TS schools, athletes constitute only a small proportion of the student body, and are more or less quarantined, loosed from their special dormitories only now and again to entertain the levy-paying students and the red-meat alumni. They do not infect the student body. But at smaller private schools, athletes proliferate throughout. For example, 40 percent of Williams's students are varsity athletes. Only children of faculty get better admission consideration at the best private schools than do athletes. Moreover, whether at large B-TS public universities where athletic scholarships are granted, or at elite private colleges, the apparatus for searching out and proselytizing athletes is firmly in place. By contrast, there are virtually no institutional or volunteer programs that seek to recruit equally qualified writers, actors, musicians, or artists. Thus, scholarships notwithstanding, the double standard in favor of athletes everywhere exists, serving to disproportionately admit jocks instead of aesthetes.

Having said that, those same small private schools that do so highly value athletes also offer more athletic opportunities for all students than the B-TS universities. The athletic ideal in education should be to provide every student with a chance for healthy exercise to complement book-learning rather than devoting the lions' share of athletic opportunity to a few superior talents. In many respects, though, the larger the university, the fewer resources are provided for athletic participation.

We talk about the *over*emphasis of sports as being so dreadful, but the irony is that participatory athletics are, on so many of our campuses, *under*emphasized. Often it is the case that larger universities offer only a few varsity sports, and students even lack much opportunity for organized intramural games.

The bald fact is that all types of our colleges attach too high a value to athletic success. Whatever the type of school, we are really all sinners. A couple of years ago, I received a long, plaintive letter from a young college art professor, who seems to have written to me simply out of despair with the athletic situation at his school. *What is particularly interesting is that the scandalous goings-on he describes occur at one of the lesser Division One athletic programs—what are referred to, euphemistically, as "mid-majors."* Yet even here, what Don King calls "trickeration" thrives, with student-athletes posing as students. The professor writes:

> In the art department we got quite a few student athletes needing fluff classes that didn't require much of them. . . . *it was clear that all the prominent players had their papers written for them* [italics mine]—even Volleyball and Field Hockey [players], not just Football. I was told to suck it up and forget it.

To be sure, this is but one anecdotal account that will allow all presidents and coaches and co-opted professors to claim that no such thing would ever happen at their college. In fact, though, it seems to be a fairly typical assessment of the way student athletes are understood to be greased along. They do, after all, have to spend some time in class with real students; the tales of their failings and favors leak out and become a cynical part of the everyday college culture throughout the country. Apparently, too, it is a natural way of life that has existed as long as college athletics have mattered. Listen to Amory Blaine, F. Scott Fitzgerald's alter ego in *This Side of Paradise*, grouse about the way we were at Princeton before World War I: "I was probably one of the two dozen men in my class at college who got a decent education; still, they'd let any well-tutored flathead play football."

So, let's face it: All types of colleges sell themselves out in one way or another. And who is guiltier: the lower-academic colleges where occasionally we even hear tales about how functional illiterates are allowed to stay eligible for games? Or the very finest repositories of learning, where athletes' SAT scores are twisted so far off the curve they turn into curly-cues? "If I woulda went to college I woulda went to Duke," Kobe Bryant has informed us. Assuming Duke woulda took him, which I am sure we can assume, do you think any other undergraduate not on the basketball team could have been admitted there with that deficient command of basic grammar? But Duke is an honorable school; so are we all honorable schools when it comes to getting players to win games for dear old alma mater.

The point is this: No one really rises out of the swamps of victory. One of the more depressing analyses that Bowen and Shulman display is that as women's sports become more competitive, female athletes succumb to the same athletic viruses as do their male brethren. Not so long ago, members of college women's teams tended to be better students who were active in other campus activities. Female athletes now exhibit declining grades and live insular campus lives, keeping company, for the most part, with other jocks. As they fall under the spell of the athletic culture, even the brightest young sportswomen begin to post grades below what had been predicted for them or what they are capable of.

Efforts to upgrade the requirements for college athletics invariably fail because the wistful idealists are invariably outmuscled by the athletic juggernaut. If I had a nickel for every suggested college athletic reform that has died aborning, I would have enough money to donate to some B-TS athletic department so that I would be allowed to pay more to buy a good seat in the football stadium. How will anything ever really change? After all, for all that it postures, the governing intercollegiate sports body, the NCAA, is not about education; it is about eligibility. At its heart, it is a Chamber of Commerce for college sports.

Hope is thereby always invested in the Knight Commission, which is peopled by educators and other notables with the best of intentions. Knight is supposed to be some sort of self-appointed watchguard of college sports, that can at least point the NCAA in the right direction. And sure enough, the Knight Commission regularly issues high-falutin' statements and suggestions, advising us that, yes, the sky is still falling. Then the members hie back to their campuses, secure in the delusion that they have done good and that it's just a damn shame that everybody is cheating except my school.

It is especially difficult to seriously upgrade the eligibility rules, too, because so many of the most visible student-athletes are indigent African Americans, so that cries for reform invariably get tangled up in charges of racism. Arthur Ashe, who was, in fact, the very model of a student-athlete, spoke out boldly a few years before his death, arguing that lower academic standards for athletes actually hurt blacks in the long run, and he was promptly lacerated by the athletic establishment for being insensitive, for cozying up to the white man. There has not been much of a peep out of anybody on this subject since then. Yet as distinguished Harvard professor Henry Louis Gates Jr. points out in a *New York Times* op-ed article, there are about 70,000 black doctors and lawyers in this country and only 1,400 professional black athletes, but altogether too many black boys continue to hold to the belief that their best career path lies with sports. A Harris Poll reported that an incredible 43 percent of high school African American athletes still believe they will make the pros. How many of them are nurtured to think this way because all they hear and see about black collegians is associated with athletics?

Insofar as my own profession is concerned, it would be fascinating to know what percentage of journalists who cover college affairs are sports writers. I would imagine that the figure is well over 90 percent. In the American media, college pretty much *is* sports; education is red-shirted.

Of course, we are always encouraged to believe that the situation will soon be corrected. In fact, though, there happen to be two annual lies in American sport: Next year soccer will become popular in the United States, and next year college presidents will reform college athletics. (Well, like flowers, maybe these lies are more perennial than annual.) I happen to admire college presidents very much. I think they have an incredibly difficult job, and almost all I have met really do want college sports reformed. I believe most of them would agree with what their colleague James J. Duderstadt, who was the president of the University of Michigan, baldly told the Knight Commission: "Big-time college sports do far more damage to the university, to its students and faculty, its leadership, its reputation and credibility, than most realize—or at least are willing to admit."[1]

After President Duderstadt stepped down to return to teaching, he wrote a brave little book, *Intercollegiate Athletics and the American University*, which was really something of a mea culpa, in which he admitted that he had basically turned a blind eye to sports when he was president. Instead, President Duderstadt wrote that he merely said a silent prayer that nothing too scandalous in Michigan sports would erupt on his watch.[2] The fact is that all college presidents simply have too much to do to spend their time fighting the powerful and rich athletic department, the alumni-cum-fans and all the others—including the media—who care more for a school's playing fields than its classrooms. It is a losing proposition—and, indeed, a risky one. As Shulman and Bowen advise us: "Courage among presidents on questions of athletics rarely portends a long tenure."[3] B-TS is our modern peculiar institution, and it is simply too entrenched in Americana for us to ever rearrange it, let alone to diminish it.

Perhaps, though, if we awake to the new challenge, we can save high schools from the same fate that has befallen colleges. Unfortunately, already now some high school teams play schedules like a road show *Les Miserables*, ESPN televises high school games to a national audience, *USA Today* ranks high school teams nationally in a variety of girls' and boys' sports, and scouting services can pinpoint *eighth*-grade prospects. So probably that cause is already lost, too, as more and more high schools give in to athletic demands.

More than forty years ago, C. S. Lewis wrote: "In my view there is a sense in which education ought to be democratic and another sense in which it ought not. It ought to be democratic in the sense of being available, without distinction of sex, colour, class, race, or religion, to all who can—and will—diligently accept it. But once the young people are inside the school there must be no attempt to establish a factitious egalitarianism between the idlers and dunces on the one hand and the clever and the industrious on the other."[4]

Indisputably, sport is the finest, purest meritocracy, where performance is genuinely rewarded, fairly, at face value. The irony is that in college in America, sport is not fair, not democratic. Athletics is privileged, and athletes have come to form a mandarin class, where they play by different rules and thereby diminish the substance and the honor of education. That is the real March Madness, all year long.

Notes

1. Speech made to the Knight Commission, Washington, D.C., October 18, 2000.
2. James J. Duderstadt, *Intercollegiate Athletics and the American University: A University President's Perspective* (Ann Arbor: University of Michigan Press, 2000).
3. James L. Shulman and William G. Bowen, *The Game of Life: College Sports and Educational Values* (Princeton, NJ: Princeton University Press, 2000), p. 10.
4. C. S. Lewis, *The Screwtape Letters* (New York: HarperCollins, 1970), p. 15.

11

Worlds Apart: Disconnects Between Students and Their Colleges

Arthur Levine

Students come to higher education with particular needs, abilities, and wants, only to find a gap between what they are seeking and what colleges are offering. Today, five such mismatches stand out. Let me first identify them in shorthand as "money, convenience, teaching and learning, free time, and priorities," and then explain them in some detail. Finally, I will suggest a solution, one that also can be expressed in shorthand: Colleges and universities will have to change because students are unlikely to do so.

The Money Mismatch

Forty years ago, the federal government and the higher education community made a commitment to the twin policies of universal access to college and choice among institutions of higher education for all qualified Americans. The goal was to ensure that income, gender, race, religion, and geography were not bars to college attendance or a student's ability to attend the most appropriate college. Today that promise is fading.

One of the reasons for this unfortunate change is that the price of college is rising far more quickly than family incomes in the United States and financial aid is not keeping pace. During the 1980s and 1990s, college tuition rose at more than twice the rate of inflation but family income increased only 27 percent. This means a higher proportion of family income is required to pay for a college education than in the past, and the burden falls largely on low-income families and to a lesser degree on middle-class families. In 2001–2002, college tuition represented an alarming 60 percent of a low-income family's paycheck versus 42 percent thirty years earlier. For middle-income families, the comparable figures were 16 percent in 2001–2002 and 13 percent in 1970–1971. And for high-income families, the numbers actually dropped from 6 to 5 percent.[1]

College attendance rates match these numbers. Eighty-six percent of those from families with incomes in the top quartile attend some form of postsecondary education versus 57 percent from the bottom quartile. Adding academic ability into the equation, a student from the highest income quartile and the lowest aptitude quartile is as likely to attend college as a student from the lowest income quartile and the highest aptitude quartile.[2] What does this mean? That the least able affluent children have as good a chance of attending college as the poor kids with the highest marks.

Where students attend college follows the same pattern. Seventy-four percent of the students attending the 146 most selective colleges in the United States are from the highest income quartile versus 3 percent from the lowest. Indeed, almost half of low-income students attend two-year colleges versus a tenth of their high-income peers. And less than one in five low-income students will enroll in a four-year college within two years of high school graduation in contrast to two out of three high-income families.[3]

The bottom line is that family income significantly influences access to college, and rising tuition levels are increasing the chances that Americans will not be able to go. Interviews I conducted in the 1990s with low-income and middle-class families indicate that college choice is declining as the cost of college increases.[4] Families are increasingly being forced to send their children to the colleges they can *afford* rather than the schools that will best serve their educational needs.

Both college and government policy contribute to this situation. During the Reagan administration, the federal government shifted financial aid policy from an emphasis on grants to loans and began extending financial aid without increasing the total amount to include higher and higher income level families. Lawrence E. Gladieux, a leading financial aid researcher, described the change this way. "Twenty years ago, grants accounted for 55 percent and loans 41 percent of available aid (with work study making up the rest). Ten years ago, the proportions of grant and loan aid were about even. Today loans account for almost 60 percent of the total."[5] Loans, according to my research, discourage the poor from attending college, for many loans are an insurmountable barrier.

In addition, in order to keep talented students in state, states began adopting scholarship programs for high-achieving students without reference to need. Georgia was the first state to do this with its well-known Hope Scholarship program in 1993. The effect was to move away from financial aid based on need to financial aid based on merit.

Institutions of higher education have shifted in the same direction in order to raise their ratings in national rankings, such as *U.S. News & World Report*. Today 61 percent of U.S. colleges and universities—two year and four year, public and private—report having no need-based financial aid—a nearly 20 percent increase since 1979.[6]

These state and institutional policies reduce the amount of financial aid available to needy students in favor of those most likely to attend college already. They also represent a dramatic change in the country's financial aid philosophy and practice. Since the earliest colleges scholarship support has been reserved for the "poore, but hopeful scholare."[7] This change seems particularly unfortunate at a time when the fastest-growing populations in the United States are low-income minorities with the lowest rates of college attendance.

The Convenience Mismatch

Today fewer than one in five college students meet the traditional undergraduate stereotype: eighteen to twenty-two years of age, full time, and living in a dormitory.[8] The new majority is older, part time, working, and living off-campus. For many of these students, college is not as central to their lives as it was to their predecessors. It is just one of many activities they engage in every day. Often it is not even the most important of these activities. Work and family overshadow college.

I conducted a study of America's college students via surveys and focus group interviews during the 1990s, resulting in the book *When Hope and Fear Collide*.[9] Among other questions, I asked what kind of relationship they wanted with their colleges. They preferred relationships like those they already had with their bank, utility company, and supermarket.

To understand what this means, think about the relationship you want from your bank. I would like an ATM on every corner. I would like to know that when I arrive at the ATM, no one else will be in line. I want deposits entered into my account the moment they arrive. And I want no mistakes—unless they are in my favor. There are also things I do not want from my bank, such as softball leagues, psychological counseling, or religious services. If I desire these things, I can arrange them myself.

The new majority of college students is asking for roughly the same things from their colleges. They want their colleges nearby and offering classes during the most convenient times for them, preferably twenty-four hours a day. They want easy accessible parking, no lines, and a helpful, polite, and efficient staff. They want accessible, high-quality instruction by professors who are up to date in their fields, who return assignments quickly, who offer useful evaluation of student work, and who are expert at teaching. They want all of these things at low cost. In short, they are asking for convenience, service, quality, and low cost.

They do not want to pay for the activities and programs they do not use or can get elsewhere, such as the cornucopia of elective courses they will not take, a fitness center they will not use, or a bulging menu of extracurricular activities they will not attend.

The new majority is bringing to higher education exactly the same consumer demands they have for every other commercial enterprise with which they do business. They believe that since they are paying for college, their schools and their professors should give them what they want. And what they want is a stripped-down version of higher education. If traditional colleges are unable to provide this, they are quite willing to seek alternatives. They are very willing to consider non-traditional institutions, located in the suburbs where most live or the urban business districts where they work. They are seeking institutions that offer low-cost instruction; faculties with day jobs in the professions who teach without the distraction of research expectations; limited numbers of majors; few electives; and a commitment to quality teaching. Distance learning is another possibility, offering the appeal of instruction at home or in the office at any time they wish.

The University of Phoenix has capitalized on this need, and combines both approaches—physical campuses in 150 locations and a worldwide online degree program. This for-profit college, enrolling more than 200,000 students, is regionally accredited and traded on Nasdaq. Phoenix offers students three out of four of the features they are asking for: service, convenience, and quality instruction. I know of no other college in this country as committed to continuing evaluation of instructional quality.

However, Phoenix does not offer students low tuition. In fact, it is more expensive than competing schools. Its strength is that it is meeting the needs of the new majority of college students better than traditional higher education. It is building its student body on higher education's weaknesses. When a potential student calls a college admission office to ask for an application and it fails to arrive, Phoenix gets a new student. When a student calls to find out about her financial aid package and is told "Mary is on vacation, call back in two weeks," Phoenix gets another student.

Indeed, the business community is watching the enormous success of Phoenix and increasingly seeing higher education as the next healthcare industry in need of a private sector remake. During a conversation, one entrepreneur highlighted the point perfectly: "Your business is out of touch with its customers, low in productivity, high in cost, weak in leadership, and low in technology use. We are going to eat your lunch." The appeal for the business community is that higher education is a growth industry—it has expanded every year for the past century except for two years of the Depression and during the world wars. There is a dependable cash flow, and customers make long-term purchases varying from one term to four years. It is government subsidized, and it is a rare countercyclical business: Enrollments increase when the economy is bad and decline when it is good.

The competition to traditional higher education is on the rise. How these institutions teach students will also be important.

The Teaching and Learning Mismatch

Charles Schroeder, professor of higher education at the University of Missouri, describes learning in terms of two polarities: active or passive.[10] One can learn best about coal mines by reading a book on the subject, by actually working in a coal mine, or some combination of these activities. Learning also can be described as abstract or concrete. That is, one can learn best about coal mines by studying the theory underlying them, by studying the specifics of their operation, or again by studying some mix of the two.

Here is the problem. More than half of college students learn best by means of "direct, concrete experience, moderate-to-high degrees of structure and a linear approach to learning. They value the practical and the immediate and the focus of their perception is primarily on the physical world." In contrast, three-quarters of the faculty "prefer the global to the particular, are stimulated by the realm of concepts, ideas, and abstractions, and assume that students, like themselves, need a high degree of autonomy in their work."[11]

In short, we have a student body favoring active, concrete learning being taught by a faculty predisposed to abstract, passive learning. This divergence may help to explain why faculty are critical of the quality of the students in their classes and students find their classes abstruse and inaccessible.

This mismatch extends beyond faculty and students to the curriculum. Determined by the professoriate, the undergraduate program begins with general education, which is the most abstract of subject matters and generally depends on passive learning materials, such as "The Great Books." The majority of students, who concentrate in professional fields, would do better starting with a major and concluding with general education. They would have greater success with active and concrete pedagogies such as case studies, internships, and field-based learning. This disparity in teaching and curriculum promises to grow as the percentage of high school graduates entering postsecondary education continues to increase. Most Americans are concrete, active learners.

In order to bridge the gap, colleges will have to change their curricula to match the way students learn and professors will have to change their teaching styles to fit the way students learn. Students cannot transform themselves to fit the current model; this is not the way they learn. *It is the mission of the university to teach its students, not the other way around.*

The Extracurricular Mismatch

When asked to describe the ideal college, U.S. President James Garfield said it was Mark Hopkins, the nineteenth-century president of Williams College, on one end of a log and a student on the other. Similarly, nineteenth-century philosopher of education John Henry Cardinal Newman thought of the college as a community or family committed to learning for its own sake. This college never existed, but the notion of an academic community remains the ideal among academics. It is a vision faculties regularly trot out to describe what they believe the university once was or wish it would become.

But the fact is that student life is moving in the opposite direction, growing more divided and atomistic. This dispersion is being fueled in part by the increasing numbers of students attending college part time, working longer hours at off-campus jobs, and living in nonuniversity housing. But it is being exacerbated by four main changes in the beliefs and behaviors of today's college students.[12]

The first change that I see is that current students are more concerned with their differences than their commonalities. In a study I conducted in the late 1970s, I asked college students to describe themselves. They focused on common generational characteristics: being career oriented, wanting material success, being politically disinterested, and so on. When students were asked the same question in the late 1990s, they emphasized the characteristics that made them unique or different: race, gender, geography, sexual orientation, ethnicity, and religion. For example, one student said he grew up in a small town in which he was one of a handful of Asian Americans in school. He said he never thought of his Asian roots as being important until he got to college. By the end of his freshman year, he realized it was the most important aspect of his being. That was until his junior year, when he decided being Korean was even more important. When asked to describe himself, he told me that he was Korean American. Many additional questions were required to get him to talk about any of his other characteristics and interests.[13]

A second important change is student life is experiencing an increasing level of mitosis as differences within groups are magnified and intensified. By way of example, on one campus I visited in the course of my research, the college business club divided into thirteen different clubs: the women's, black, Asian, Latin, gay, and a variety of others. The differences among the members of each business club overshadowed their common interest in business. This example may be extreme, but this kind of division is quite common on many campuses.

Third, in addition to growing divisions among students, campuses also are growing more segregated, voluntarily. Even by generous standards, less than a handful of campuses visited in the course of twenty-eight college site visits that were part of my national college student research could be described in any other way. Walk into most college and university cafeterias, and the tables are separated by ethnicity. The larger the campus, the sharper the divisions. At small colleges, there are likely to be Hispanic and Black tables. At bigger colleges, this becomes Puerto Rican, Dominican, Chicano, Colombian, Panamanian, and Jamaican tables. Students describe the situation:

> In the cafeteria, sides are literally assigned—one side white, one black, one Asian.
>
> In the dining room, if you see one person you know the rest of the table.
>
> I think the races are pretty much separate and happy about it.
>
> There is separation in the dining room. Different places on campus are claimed by different groups. The lower lounge is black. The other lounge is Hispanic. The engineering lounge is Asian.

Forty-one percent of four-year colleges in a 586-campus study reported locations on campus that belong to particular groups by virtue of "squatter's rights."[14]

What is particularly troubling is that students overestimate the degree of segregation. In the course of the 28-campus study, social events promoted by different campus groups were visited and interviewers took attendance. When Asian students were questioned about how many whites attended a speech they sponsored, they said whites never attended their events. However, a count of the audience revealed that at least a third of the audience was white. After a dance, when white students were asked how many blacks attended, they said maybe twenty. In reality there had been over fifty. This raises two possibilities. Either students are so convinced of campus segregation that they do not perceive integration even when it occurs, or worse, even when diverse students are in close proximity, they are so isolated that they do not interact.

The fourth change seen is a growing sense of victimization among college students. Students often expressed a feeling that they are being disadvantaged and that others are profiting at their expense. Men and women point fingers at each other. Racial majorities and minorities each believe the other is benefiting at their expense. International and domestic students make charges about one another. And religious groups claim preferential treatment for other religious groups.

The result of these four conditions? America's colleges are *deeply* divided. Attendance at major campus events is down while the number of activities sponsored by the multiplying number of clubs representing particular affinity groups is mushrooming. Social life is also moving from the campus to the local community, student apartments, and local bars, where students say they feel more comfortable.

Beyond signaling the disparity between the ideal of community on campus and the reality of division, the current situation raises the prospect of our campuses becoming Hobbesian worlds.[15] In a time of shrinking resources and space shortages at many colleges, the danger is that campuses will become battlegrounds for growing numbers of groups to compete with each other for resources, places in the curriculum, and physical space on campus.

The Priorities Mismatch

If someone from the business world were to look at the way colleges and universities operate, she would likely conclude they have two customers, their students and their faculties. Students are an obvious choice. But many in the academy would be surprised at the notion of faculty as customers. The fact is that professors are independent professionals that universities, particularly the most selective and research oriented, hire and retain—and compete with each other to do so. The quality of a university is dependent on the excellence of both their students and their faculties. Certainly in graduate school rankings, research money and faculty productivity are critical elements, and student quality follows faculty excellence.

Universities treat students and faculty members as customers whom they must satisfy, but their interests are not always the same. Student desires go beyond the convenience, service, quality, and low cost mentioned earlier. While new majority students ask for a stripped-down version of higher education, traditional students want the reverse, a full-service institution with all the bells and whistles, ranging from psychological counseling to vegan cuisine in the dining room. Both also want financial aid, small classes, adequate numbers of courses so they are not closed out, and sufficient numbers of classes in the appropriate time slots that will allow them to graduate in four years. They want courses taught by professors rather graduate students, top-of-the-line facilities, and the latest technology.

This list is at odds with the things faculty want. High on their lists are small numbers of advisees, light dissertation loads, and classes. They also want to be able to offer courses in their specialty areas, to offer classes at times that are convenient for them, and to avoid offering required and introductory courses outside their field. In addition, faculty would like to be able to take time off from classes to attend professional meetings and to have graduate students to assist them with their teaching and research. Time and support for research are essential, particularly at research universities and the most selective colleges.

The differences in the two lists are striking. One seeks greater professorial contact with students, and the other tries to limit that contact. There is a split between offering courses students want and classes professors want to teach. Students put an emphasis on teaching; faculty at research universities and selective colleges are more concerned with research itself. Additional funds would be used either to augment student services or to strengthen faculty support.

For the most part, colleges and universities have resolved these differences in favor of their faculty. This is less true at low-selectivity private colleges with small endowments because they are highly enrollment dependent. But at other four-year schools, classes tend to be scheduled at the convenience of the faculty member and not the student. There is an imbalance of elective courses in faculty specialty areas over classes students are required to take to graduate. Leaves and research buyouts complicate course sequencing and student graduation plans. Bread-and-butter courses often are relegated to graduate students and adjunct professors. Student course evaluations have more impact on choosing the teacher of the year than in improving the quality of senior faculty teaching or in denying tenure to poor teachers with excellent research credentials.

How will students react to all of these disparities? They are more consumer-oriented than their predecessors and more likely to believe that the principle of caveat emptor applies to university attendance. With rising numbers of students spending less and less time on campus owing to part-time attendance and work, it has become easier for them to see themselves as consumers rather than members of a community. As the media and government raise questions regarding rising tuition costs, faculty workloads, program and teaching quality, admission standards, and graduation rates, it is also easier for them to see the university as just another business. One can expect rising activism both on campus and in the courts. Additionally, they are being presented with alternatives to traditional higher education, where they are likely to be treated as valued customers.

Conclusion

Mismatches between colleges and their students are by no means new. They have existed since the earliest colleges. However, the world of higher education itself has changed. The United States government, which in the decades following World War II asked only that colleges increase their capacity by hiring more faculty and enrolling more students, is now demanding accountability from higher education. It is deeply concerned with the efficiency and effectiveness of the postsecondary enterprise. It is probing issues such as tuition costs, faculty workloads, the balance of research and teaching, financial aid, diversity, admission requirements, and graduation rates. Government is willing to regulate higher education to a far greater degree than in the past to achieve increased effectiveness and efficiency, particularly when colleges and universities are perceived to be dragging their feet in responding to problems.

Students are more consumer-oriented than in the past and are asking more from colleges than their predecessors. They are willing to press complaints on campus or seek solutions off-campus. At the same time, the range of alternatives to traditional higher education is expanding. More and more for-profit colleges like the University of Phoenix are springing up. New noncampus, online colleges are developing both within higher education and without, nationally and internationally.

More than ever before in history, these changes put pressure on colleges to redress the mismatches with their students. The risk higher education faces, if it fails to act voluntarily, is that government will impose remedies. The marketplace of new higher education providers may respond to the mismatches first. And students may show their displeasure with their feet, choosing alternatives to traditional higher education.

To a greater degree than ever before, the future of higher education is in jeopardy. Highly selective, well-endowed universities and colleges are certainly not in danger of closing. But they could easily become dated and marginal. As my Teachers College colleague Jim Borland reminds me, *Tyrannosaurus Rex* was once an outstanding brand name.

Notes

1. Lawrence E. Gladieux, "Low-Income Students and the Affordability of Higher Education," in Richard D. Kahlenberg, ed., *America's Untapped Resource: Low-Income Students in Higher Education* (New York: Century Foundation Press, 2004), p. 26.
2. Ibid., pp. 21, 24.
3. Richard Kahlenberg, "Introduction," in Kahlenberg, ed., *America's Untapped Resource*, p. 2.
4. Arthur Levine and Jeanette Cureton, *When Hope and Fear Collide: A Portrait of Today's College Students* (San Francisco: Jossey-Bass, 1998), p. 49.
5. Gladieux, "Low-Income Students," p. 28.
6. Anthony P. Carnevale and Stephen J. Rose, "Socioeconomic Status, Race/ Ethnicity, and Selective College Admissions," in Kahlenberg, ed., *America's Untapped Resource*, p. 121.
7. This was the language Harvard College used to establish the first scholarship endowment raised by any college in America.

8. Levine and Cureton, *When Hope and Fear Collide*, p. 49.
9. Ibid.
10. Charles C. Schroeder, "New Students—New Learning Styles," *Change*, vol. 25, no. 4 (September–October 1993): 21–26.
11. Ibid., p. 25.
12. The section is based on a study of America's undergraduates, including a survey of a representative sample of undergraduates and student affairs officers on 586 college and university campuses, as well as focus group interviews at 28 diverse institutions conducted by Arthur Levine and Jeanette Cureton, published in *When Hope and Fear Collide*.
13. Ibid., pp. 79–85.
14. Ibid., p. 86.
15. This refers to a divided world of each against all, described by Thomas Hobbes in his book *Leviathan*.

12

Leaving the Newcomers Behind

Roberto Suro and Richard Fry

"Only Asian American high school graduates are more likely to enroll in higher education than Latino high school graduates."

Is that statement true or false? Our guess is that you answered false, because, after all, everyone knows that whites go on to higher education in a greater percentage that Latinos and that Latinos lag in educational achievement. But you would be wrong: In fact, Latinos who finish high school go on to college in the same percentage (82 percent) as their white counterparts. Only Asian Americans, at 95 percent, surpass that rate.[1]

But that is about the best news we can report. By almost every other measure, America has a serious problem on its hands: Hispanics are more likely than their white peers to attend community colleges instead of four-year institutions, to attend nonselective four-year institutions if they make it that far, to be working full time while attending, to be enrolled in nondegree programs, and to drop out before graduation.[2]

That is the bad news. The good news is that America has met such challenges before. We have shown that our education system can help newcomers find their place in this country, and now we face that test again.

From 1900 to 1950, the share of American youths enrolled in college increased sevenfold, an extraordinary achievement that, among other things, helped complete the incorporation of a great wave of immigrants.[3] Opening up and expanding the system of higher education gave the newcomers' children the chance to achieve a full measure of social, economic, and civic enfranchisement.

At the beginning of the twenty-first century, the United States is again undertaking the business of immigration. Much has changed, but the measures of success are the same. When a nation expands its population by taking in newcomers, the important results become evident only after a generation or two. It is often an immigrant's fate to struggle and adapt but still lag behind the native born. The nation's goal should be to ensure that the immigrant's children and grandchildren join the mainstream. The success of the Ellis Island enterprise became apparent in the middle of the twentieth century, when the immigrants' children helped establish the United States as a world power, and helped build a colossal industrial economy. By the 1950s, children of immigrants were moving into a new suburban middle class. Small wonder that "the Melting Pot" has achieved iconic status. Whether we can repeat that success with the new wave of Asian and Latino immigrants remains to be seen. We are still closer to the start of the process than to the end, but now is the right time to take stock because much can be done to shape the final outcome. Today, however, a great many newcomers are being left behind.

A New Wave of Immigration

Ever since the current era of immigration began in the 1970s, the number of foreign-born persons in the United States has tripled to more than 33 million people, or about 12 percent of the total population. Two streams have dominated the flow, one from Asia, which has produced about a quarter of the current foreign-born population, and the other from Latin America, which is responsible for more than half. The educational attainment of these streams differs drastically. Census Bureau data for 2003 shows that Asian immigrants actually reach higher levels of education overall than the host population and thus represent an extraordinary chapter in the history of migration to the United States. Half of the Asian immigrant population in the United States holds a bachelor's degree or more compared to a bit more than a quarter (27 percent) of the native-born population. By contrast,

Latin American immigrants attain lower levels of education; just 49 percent graduated from high school compared to 88 percent of the native-born population. In this regard, today's newcomers from Latin America more nearly fit the mold of the transatlantic wave of a century ago. Once again, as was the case one hundred years ago, the process of incorporation for Latino immigrants, if successful, will involve substantial gains in educational achievement from the first generation, the immigrants, to the second, their U.S-born children.[4]

A historical coincidence greatly magnifies the nation's stake in educating Latino youths: Over the next couple of decades, as the Baby Boom generation moves on to old age, the children of Latino immigrants will reach working age in ever greater numbers. Latino immigrants and their offspring will, in effect, serve both as the replacements for the departing boomers and as the major source of growth in the labor force. The intersection of these two trends—the boomers' passing and the Latino influx—soon will bring about a profound change in the content of the U.S. population, and especially its workforce. According to projections by the Pew Hispanic Center, the non-Hispanic school-age population will shrink slightly between 2000 and 2020, while the number of Hispanics aged five to nineteen years old will increase by nearly 6 million people, a growth rate of nearly 60 percent. More than 4.5 million of the new Latino school-goers will be the U.S.-born children of immigrants. Over those two decades, the second-generation Latinos of school age will double in actual numbers and as a share of the total. Between 2010 and 2030, as the boomers head to their retirement years, the non-Hispanic population of working age will shrink slightly as well. Meanwhile, the number of Latino workers will increase by 55 percent, and the second generation will account for the lion's share of that growth.[5]

The Educational Challenge

Given these irreversible demographic realities, it should be self-evident that the nation has a sizable stake in ensuring the best possible outcomes for the children of today's Latino immigrants. These children will be added to the U.S. population at a rate of more than a half a million a year in the next decade. They will be native-born U.S. citizens, and they will be the products of our institutions, our schools, and our economy. Most of their parents are already here, and even if their parents were born somewhere else, these are our kids now. The United States has again embarked on the great national enterprise of incorporating immigrants, but this time it is doing so when the host population is aging and barely growing, if at all. The outcome of this extraordinary demographic change depends largely on how well Latino youths are educated.

For many years, the high school dropout rate has received considerable attention as a measure of Hispanic educational achievement, and deservedly so. Unfortunately, the dropout rate for Hispanics who do finish high school and then go on to college has received much less attention. These students, who have met society's key expectations by enrolling in postsecondary studies, should be the key target of any effort to ensure that young Latinos are properly trained to fill their role in the U.S. labor market. As mentioned, Latinos who finish high school pursue postsecondary studies at the same rate as whites (82 percent by age 26); only Asian Americans enroll at a higher rate (95 percent).[6] Clearly, the desire to continue schooling among Latinos who graduate from high school is prevalent and powerful. Undoubtedly, this second generation is motivated. Among Latinos and among Asians, college enrollment is higher for the children of immigrants than for either foreign-born young people or those whose parents were born in the United States, the third generation and higher.[7]

Consider the case of Hugo Vasquez. Chicago born and raised, Hugo is the child of immigrants from Guatemala and the first in his family to finish high school. "I knew from the time I was little that I wanted to be educated," Hugo said, "and it wasn't because anyone told me so or was pushing me. I just knew that I wanted to go to college."[8]

But that ambition has long competed with the need to work. His parents are divorced. Hugo and a younger sister live with their mother, who cleans houses for a living. When he was a senior in high school, Hugo worked twenty hours a week as a busboy and still managed to graduate on time. The demands did not stop when he enrolled in college. Financial aid covered his tuition costs at Northern Illinois University, but he had to work as a hotel housekeeper to cover his living expenses. He found himself struggling with academic work that was harder than he expected and a schedule that left him insufficient time to study. Most of his fellow students seemed to have such carefree lives that in Hugo's eyes they might as well have come from another planet. "They had a lot of apathy because they took it all for granted," he said.

Before the end of freshmen year, Hugo was falling behind. He could not afford to stop working, but he could drop courses. Doing so, however, imperiled his financial aid. Eventually he decided that living away from home was economically unfeasible. At the end of the academic year, he returned to Chicago and immediately enrolled at community college, intent on making up lost ground.

It took him a year and a half to earn enough credits and improve his skills sufficiently to apply for admission at DePaul University and gain acceptance.

"This was the dream come true to me, living with my family, going to a great school," he said. "I was sure I was going to make it." DePaul provided financial aid that covered tuition as well as a mailroom job. He declared majors in philosophy and economics and came achingly close to completing the requirements for finishing junior year. But a familiar dynamic set in.

Economic problems at home caused him to take a second job. His grades began to slip. He dropped classes. He again recognized weaknesses in his academic preparation, especially in writing skills, that meant he needed more time for schoolwork when he steadily had less. Once again his academic status was imperiled, and he interrupted his studies. Hugo is now working full time as a waiter and taking a single course through an adult education program at Northwestern University. He fully intends to return to DePaul and finish his degree, but realizes it may be a long haul.

"I am not only going to get college; I'm going to law school or graduate school," he said confidently. "I do not question that, it is going to happen. But for right now I am concentrating on getting a job that pays better."

As Hugo's case demonstrates, enrollment is not the same as completion, and his experience is unfortunately all too common. Among high school graduates who enroll in some kind of postsecondary studies, whites are twice as likely as Hispanics to finish with a baccalaureate degree (47 percent vs. 23 percent). This gap constitutes the greatest disparity in educational outcomes between the nation's largest minority group and the white majority. And, given the importance of college completion, especially the acquisition of a four-year degree, to occupational options, future earnings, and the likelihood that the next generation of children will go to college, this disparity also creates the potential for long-lasting differences in socioeconomic status between Latinos and whites. It also raises questions as to whether these young Latinos will be sufficiently trained to take their place in the U.S. labor force when they begin to fill in for the retiring Baby Boomers.[9] There is no simple fix to this problem because it is the product of several different factors. Some of the causes lie in the K–12 system. Some are due to the characteristics of the Hispanic population. Other causes can be found in America's colleges and universities. Solutions are much harder to find because the plight of students like Hugo Vasquez gets very little attention from educators and policymakers. This nation's demographic realities, however, argue for a change in that situation.

All High School Diplomas are Not Equal

Not all high school diplomas are equal in value, and part of the achievement gap between white and Hispanic college students results from the fact that many Hispanics do not start out as well prepared. For example, nearly half (46 percent) of Hispanic high school graduates do not complete Algebra II (a course most frequently taken in eleventh grade) or any more advanced math, compared to about a quarter (28 percent) of white high school graduates.[10] If the huge differences in college completion rates were completely the result of poorer preparation, then the problem could be fixed entirely in the nation's high schools. But preparation alone does not explain the gap between whites and Hispanics in postsecondary education. In fact, several studies have indicated that a majority of the roughly 200,000 Latinos beginning college each fall are adequately prepared academically to succeed in a four-year college.[11] The sad fact is that Latinos do not achieve the same results in college even when they are equally well prepared as other students. In fact, much of the gap in college completion is purely a product of what occurs after students finish high school.

The first step toward understanding the disparity in attainment levels for whites and Latinos is to examine the kinds of colleges that they attend. According to a 2003 Department of Education study, 44 percent of Hispanic undergraduates ages eighteen to twenty-four attend community colleges in comparison to 30 percent of white undergraduates. Community colleges provide a great many services, such as adult basic education or employment training, that are not aimed at producing a degree. However, the distribution of Latinos across different kinds of programs is very similar to that of other students at two-year campuses: All but 10 percent enroll in hopes of finishing with a credential.[12] So, by several measures, community colleges play a disproportionately large role in determining how many Latinos and which Latinos end their postsecondary education with a credential.

Community colleges and other two-year institutions typically appeal to Latino students on a number of grounds. For one thing, tuition is far lower than at most four-year colleges. Degree programs often are designed to accommodate part-time students, and classes are scheduled in the evenings to accommodate students with full-time jobs. All this is obviously attractive to students from low-income families and those who need to earn a living even as they are studying. Although many Hispanic undergraduates fit that description, economic necessity alone does not explain their higher rates of enrollment in community colleges. If it was all just a matter of money, then we would expect African Americans, who are as poor as Latinos if not poorer, to rely on two-year institutions as well. But, in fact, African Americans attend two-year institutions at a much lower rate than Latinos, indeed a rate similar to that of whites. So we have to look beyond the money issues.

Another part of the appeal is that community colleges usually are located near residential areas and rarely feature dormitories. An emphasis on close family ties is one characteristic shared by most Latinos regardless of national origin or income, and among Latino immigrants this often translates into an expectation that children will live with their parents until they marry. Moreover, many community colleges welcome students with low levels of academic achievement or aptitude, and many also offer classes in English as a second language. Community colleges often have transfer agreements with baccalaureate institutions so that credits earned at a two-year institution can be applied toward a four-year degree, thus providing a cheaper and more accessible way to make a start toward a bachelor's diploma.

Despite these benefits, however, two-year schools may adversely affect Latinos' chances of finishing with a degree. Recent U.S. Department of Education tabulations of student persistence rates suggest that Latino students are more likely to drop out if they begin their college studies at two-year colleges.[13] Starting at a community college decreases the odds of finishing with any kind of degree. More than half of the students who initially enroll at two-year colleges never complete a postsecondary degree, whereas almost six out of ten of those who begin at a four-year college end up completing at least a bachelor's degree.[14]

The low rate of bachelor's degree completion for Hispanics who begin at two-year colleges is also a product of what happens when they try to transfer to a four-year college. Transfer rates are fairly low. Less than 45 percent of Hispanic two-year college entrants who want a bachelor's degree succeed in transferring to a four-year college within six years of initial entry. And successful transfer is not a silver bullet anyway. Fewer than half of all community college students who transfer to a four-year institution complete a bachelor's degree, a completion rate significantly below that of those who start at a four-year school. So, all students desiring a bachelor's degree face an uphill climb if they start at a community college. But again, Hispanics fare worse than others. Among those seeking a bachelor's degree, 18 percent of Hispanic two-year students will succeed versus 26 percent of whites.[15]

All College Degrees are Not Equal

Latinos' propensity to enroll in community colleges, however, does not fully explain their much lower levels of degree completion compared to whites. A much broader pattern that extends to four-year schools became apparent when we analyzed newly available data from the National Educational Longitudinal Survey (NELS). This major U.S. Department of Education survey tracked a nationally representative sample of some 25,000 young adults from the time they were in the eighth grade in 1988 until 2000, when most were twenty-six years old. The NELS provides detailed information on high school preparation as well as the course of an individual's postsecondary studies. With these data, we were able to compare Latino and white students who started out on the same academic footing when they graduated from high school, and we could see what kinds of colleges they attended and how they fared. Two important results emerged from this study: Latinos go to less selective institutions than their white peers, and even when they do enroll at the same kinds of schools as white youths, they are less likely than their white peers to graduate. The results are depressingly the same for all types of students: The best-prepared Latinos fare worse than whites of equal preparation, and the least-prepared Hispanics fare worse than their least-prepared white peers.

The first step in this analysis was to sort out whites and Latinos who had the same quality of preparation in high school. The second step was to look at the colleges they attended based on admissions selectivity. The nation's colleges and universities use a variety of criteria (some academic, some not) to choose among applicants and each college admissions office weighs the criteria differently. But colleges can be, and often are, ranked on the basis of their admissions selectivity (i.e., the proportion of their applicants accepted for admissions). Highly selective colleges accept less than half their applicants. The least selective four-year colleges accept more than 85 percent of their applicants.

Selectivity matters because college selectivity and college completion go hand in hand. Students who enroll at highly selective colleges are more likely to finish a bachelor's degree than those at less selective institutions. This is not just because the kids who get into more selective colleges tend to be smarter or better prepared and are therefore more likely to complete no matter where they go. More selective schools often have more generous financial aid programs, place greater emphasis on graduation within four years, and make special efforts to retain minority students. Regardless of the causes, the data are clear in showing that selectivity is especially important for Latinos. Between two equally prepared Hispanic students coming out of high school, the one who goes to the more selective college is more likely to graduate.

The trouble is that equally well-prepared white and Latino college-bound youths do not go to the same kinds of colleges and universities—as mentioned, Latinos enroll in less selective institutions. Among the best-prepared young college students, nearly 60 percent of Latinos attend nonselective colleges and universities, compared to 52 percent of white students. The same holds for those who are not so well prepared. Among students with average levels of high school academic preparation (the majority of both Hispanic and white students), nearly 66 percent of Latinos initially enroll in "open-door" institutions. Less than 45 percent of similarly prepared white college students initially enroll at open-door institutions.[16]

Those who aim for the top—and are very well qualified—achieve considerable success, and they are the exception to the rule that Latinos are less likely to enroll in more selective institutions than their white peers. Hispanic undergraduates with the strongest preparation do enter the nation's highly selective colleges and universities at similar rates as whites. Latinos who do very well on the SATs (1300+) have their scores sent to top schools at the same rate as their white peers. And the NELS data reveal that 9 percent of both Hispanic and white undergraduates from the highest quintile of academic intensity enroll in highly selective colleges and universities. Once they make it to the best schools, Latinos graduate in large numbers (83 percent gain a bachelor's degree in four years), although they still trail behind whites (90 percent).

Without minimizing their accomplishments, the impact of these stellar students on overall outcomes has to be kept in proportion. The nation's highly selective colleges educate only 3 percent of the nation's entering undergraduates and an even smaller percentage (2 percent) of the nation's Latino undergraduates. Success at this level is a very poor measure of overall educational progress. It is, however, a measure of what is possible. When institutions dedicate resources to recruiting qualified Latino students, they enroll at the same rate as their white peers. When financial aid programs and other resources are directed at retaining these students, they do well enough to make up some of the gap in degree completion. It is simply unrealistic, however, to expect that the bulk of the nation's colleges will ever be able to match the kinds of funds and personnel that are available at elite institutions.

Nor is it realistic to expect that all students can be instilled with the same motivation and purposefulness displayed by the most stellar undergraduates. At the top, both the students and the institutions are instructive exceptions at best.

Unfortunately, the difference in the pathways that Latino and white youths take to college is not the only factor producing the achievement gap. The NELS data show that even when Latino and white youths of equal preparation go to the same kinds of schools, the Latinos do not perform as well.

A Different Starting Line

The headwinds confronting Latino college students also involve a constellation of factors related to economic status, family structure, and cultural dynamics. In short, Hispanic students are much more likely than any others to be working full time while studying, going to college part time, and contending with family responsibilities while they strive to attain a postsecondary degree. No one of these factors explains the whole college achievement gap, but each adds to the likelihood that a student will fail to graduate. As we considered each factor, it became increasingly apparent that there are many Latinos like Hugo Vasquez, struggling against the odds to get that credential.

Among eighteen- to twenty-four-year-old students enrolled at four-year colleges, relatively small shares of whites (14 percent) and blacks (16 percent) and even fewer Asians (9 percent) are working full time. By contrast, 19 percent of all Latino undergraduates are putting a whole day at work five days a week even as they pursue a bachelor's degree. That average disguises major differences among Hispanic national origin groups. Although students of Cuban origins and some South American nationalities work at rates as low as whites, 26 percent of those of Mexican origins, a less economically advantaged group, are working full time. Even looking at lower levels of work commitments, the impacts are disproportionate. More than a third (37 percent) of Latino undergraduates at four-year colleges report limiting their class loads because of work responsibilities compared to about a quarter (27 percent) of whites and blacks.[17]

Another factor that puts a baccalaureate degree at risk is delaying entry to college. The U.S. Department of Education unequivocally asserts that "the odds of earning a bachelor's degree or higher change when entry into postsecondary education is delayed. . . . Furthermore, the longer students delayed their entry into postsecondary education, the lower their average levels of educational attainment."[18] Among young four-year college students, 19 percent of Hispanics waited more than a year after high school graduation to start college, compared to 12 percent of white four-year undergraduates. Delayed enrollment is even more pervasive among Latinos going to two-year institutions. Having financial dependents or being a single parent are two more widely recognized risk factors for college completion.[19] And again, Hispanic undergraduates are worse off. Indeed, they are nearly twice as likely as whites to have children or elderly dependents. Research on college persistence consistently has found that residing on campus enhances the probability of completion.[20] This fact may be because students who live on campus are more socially engaged and integrated into college life, fostering a sense of belonging. Almost half of Hispanic four-year students reside with their parents, compared to less than one-fifth of their white peers.

Contending with all of these risk factors would seem to require a massive undertaking, but in fact the challenge is not so overwhelming. We've already seen that there are plenty of Latinos enrolling in college with adequate preparation to seek a bachelor's degree. What would happen if they attended the same kinds of colleges as whites who finished high school with the same level of preparation? We estimated the potential by running some statistical simulations, and the problem starts to seem a bit more manageable. Census Bureau figures indicate that there are now an about 689,000 Hispanics in the eighth grade.[21] If they perform similarly to the Hispanics studied in the NELS, about 450,000 of them will attend postsecondary education and roughly 125,000 will attain bachelor's degrees. Now, just suppose that those 450,000 Hispanic undergraduates attend the same kinds of colleges that similarly prepared white undergraduates attend. This scenario would yield 150,000 Hispanics with bachelor's degrees, a 20 percent improvement, and that is without doing anything about graduation rates.

Alternatively, say those 450,000 Hispanic undergraduates will go to the same kinds of schools as the Hispanics in the NELS sample, but let us assume that they complete college at the same rates as white undergraduates. In this second scenario, our calculations show that 177,000 Hispanics would attain bachelor's degrees, a 42 percent improvement. Either way there is clearly the potential to increase significantly the number of Latinos with four-year degrees. And it is equally clear that both the pathways Hispanics take into undergraduate education and the disparities in college completion rates among students on the same pathway need to be considered.

The Challenge of Equity

Addressing these issues need not require massive reforms in educational structures or prolonged interventions to change the course of individual lives. The target population here is a relatively small number of teens who have graduated from high school with the preparation necessary to get a postsecondary degree and who have applied, been accepted, and enrolled in college. It is just a matter of getting them to the same quality of schools as their white peers and then working with them for a few years to help them finish with a degree. All of this is within the ambit of our higher education system. We are not trying to minimize the challenge, but it is important to realize that compared to other social undertakings—consider welfare reform, controlling healthcare costs, or ensuring the solvency of the social security system—increasing the number of Latinos with bachelor's degrees seems a modest goal. The potential benefits and the downside risks, however, are of historic proportions.

During the last transatlantic immigration wave, the newcomers and their offspring benefited from a series of initiatives that broadened access to an educational establishment that was continuously expanding decade after decade. From the extension of mandatory public education to secondary school to the creation of the land-grant colleges and finally the GI Bill, the United States created the conditions that allowed the children and grandchildren of European immigrants to become fully enfranchised members of a robust industrial democracy. Since that time, the stakes have only gotten higher, as have the challenges.

Just as it was a century ago, the United States is engaged in the dual processes of demographic change through immigration and economic transformation. Just as industrial economy of the twentieth century required a better-educated labor force than the agrarian economy of the nineteenth century, the knowledge-based information economy of the twenty-first century places higher educational demands on its workers than its predecessor. A baccalaureate degree has become the credential necessary for admission to the American middle class while high school graduation was enough a generation ago. Meanwhile, the economic and social rewards for acquisition of such credentials have grown in a manner that has expanded the gap between those who have the necessary credentials and those who do not.

If current trends continue, a disproportionately large number of Latinos will be left behind, particularly in the large and growing group of children born in immigrant households. Rather than serve as an engine of economic mobility and a crucible of social stability, our institutions of higher education would become the great barriers in our social structure. Rather than serve as a point of entry for a new wave of newcomers, the college campus could become the point of exclusion.

Notes

1. National Center for Education Statistics, *Racial/Ethnic Differences in the Path to a Postsecondary Credential,* NCES 2003-005 (Washington, D.C.: NCES, 2003).
2. In the text, the terms "Hispanic" and "Latino" are used interchangeably.
3. In 1900, 238,000 people were enrolled in college, comprising 2.3 percent of the population aged eighteen to twenty-four years old. By 1950, 2,659,000 were enrolled, or 16.5 percent of the age group. U.S. Bureau of the Census, *Historical Statistics of the United States, Colonial Times to 1970*, Bicentennial Edition, Part 1 (Washington, D.C.: 1975).
4. Luke J. Larsen, *The Foreign-Born Population in the United States: 2003*, Current Population Reports, P20-551 (Washington, D.C.: U.S. Census Bureau, 2004).
5. Roberto Suro and Jeffrey S. Passel, "The Rise of the Second Generation: Changing Patterns in Hispanic Population Growth," Pew Hispanic Center report, Washington, D.C., 2003.
6. NCES, *Racial/Ethnic Differences in the Path to a Postsecondary Credential.*
7. Richard Fry, "Latinos in Higher Education: Many Enroll, Too Few Graduate," Pew Hispanic Center report, Washington, D.C., 2002.
8. Hugo Vasquez, interview with the authors.

9. Richard Fry, "Latino Youth Finishing College: The Role of Selective Pathways," Pew Hispanic Center report, Washington, D.C., 2004.
10. National Center for Education Statistics, *The Condition of Education 2002*, NCES 2002-025 (Washington, D.C.: NCES, 2002).
11. The Department of Education constructed a composite measure of academic qualification for four-year college work based on high school grade point average (GPA), senior class rank, Scholastic Achievement Test (SAT) and American College Test (ACT) scores, academic coursework, and aptitude test scores. According to that measure, 53 percent of Hispanics who graduated high school in 1992 were at least minimally qualified to do four-year college work. See National Center for Education Statistics, *Access to Postsecondary Education for the 1992 High School Graduates*, NCES 98-105 (Washington, D.C.: NCES, 1997). An analysis of data from the National Educational Longitudinal Survey suggests that 57 percent of young Hispanic postsecondary entrants are at least minimally qualified using the same college qualification index. See Watson Scott Swail, Alberto F. Cabrera, and Chul Lee, "Latino Youth and the Pathway to College," Pew Hispanic Center report, Washington, D.C., 2004.
12. National Center for Education Statistics, *Community College Students: Goals, Academic Preparation, and Outcomes*, NCES 2003-164 (Washington, D.C.: NCES, 2003).
13. National Center for Education Statistics, *Descriptive Summary of 1995–96 Beginning Postsecondary Students: 3 Years Later*, NCES 2000-154 (Washington, D.C.: NCES, 2000).
14. Thomas J. Kane and Cecilia Elena Rouse, "The Community College: Educating Students at the Margin Between College and Work," *Journal of Economic Perspectives* (Winter 1999): 63–84.
15. Authors' tabulations of data from: *1996/01 Beginning Postsecondary Students Longitudinal Study*, National Center for Education Statistics.
16. Of all high school graduates going on to college, these fall in the second to fourth quintile in the origin of their high school curriculum, meaning that 20 percent had worse preparation and 20 percent had better preparation.
17. Pew Hispanic Center tabulations from the U.S. Department of Education's 1999–2000 National Postsecondary Student Aid Study.
18. National Center for Education Statistics, *Educational Attainment of 1980 High School Sophomores by 1992*, NCES 95-304 (Washington, D.C.: NCES, 1995).
19. National Center for Education Statistics, *Profile of Undergraduates in U.S. Postsecondary Education Institutions: 1992–93, with an Essay on Undergraduates at Risk*, NCES 96-237 (Washington, D.C.: NCES, 1995).
20. Alexander W. Astin, *What Matters in College? Four Critical Years Revisited* (San Francisco, CA: Jossey-Bass, 1993).
21. Authors' calculations from October 2001 Current Population Survey, School Enrollment Supplement.

13

Talking the Talk: Rhetoric and Reality for Students of Color

Heather D. Wathington

> Despite our limited educational victories over the years, the chasm between America's democratic rhetoric and unequal reality still seems as vast as the Grand Canyon for black, brown, and poor people.
>
> —Manning Marable, *Great Wells of Democracy*

Colleges use all the right words. The University of Georgia says it "seeks to foster the understanding of and respect for cultural differences necessary for an enlightened and educated citizenry. It further provides for cultural, ethnic, gender and racial diversity in the faculty, staff, and student body."

The University of Nebraska at Lincoln claims that it "promotes respect for and understanding of cultural diversity in all aspects of society. It strives for a culturally diverse student body, faculty, and staff reflecting the multicultural nature of Nebraska and the nation."

A small liberal arts college in New York City makes similar pronouncements. "Committed to the achievement of a pluralistic community, Hunter College offers a curriculum designed to meet the highest standards while also fostering understanding among groups from different racial, cultural, and ethnic backgrounds."[1]

I do not intend to single out Hunter, Georgia, or Nebraska. The fact is, the mission statements of at least one-third of all institutions of higher education make similarly bold statements about their commitment to diversity. Unfortunately, the gap between rhetoric—what we all say about our educational aspirations for all students—and reality—limited, even declining, opportunity for students of color—has never been wider. Certainly, this hypocrisy has been pointed out many times by renowned contemporary scholars, such as Manning Marable and Cornel West, and even going as far back as W. E. B. DuBois. The rhetoric masks the plight of students of color and hampers our ability to act to achieve equity and reach American democratic ideals. Whether higher education can go beyond talking the talk and actually start *walking the walk* is the great unanswered question of our time.

Conversations about the civic purpose of higher education have always reflected our high aspirations. Thomas Jefferson believed that the virtues of higher learning were vital to the preservation of a free and democratic society. Today's educators echo Jefferson in their mission statements and public pronouncements, emphasizing the vital link between higher learning and democracy. Yet, most of higher education has lost touch with the mobilizing power of Jefferson's values. As they respond to the challenges they face—the revolution in technology, the transnational dynamics of globalization, escalating costs—too many campus officials have ignored or abandoned the larger democratic purposes of higher education, especially its role in building pluralistic communities.

Inequality of educational opportunity continues to affect students of color profoundly; it always has done devastating economic and social damage to communities of color. Mired in racial discrimination and fear for much of the twentieth century, colleges have neglected or underserved racial and ethnic minorities, contributing to the stark underrepresentation and dramatic underperformance of people of color in higher education. On any list of the populations that higher education has historically served and educated, students of color are at or near the bottom. According to the U.S. Census Bureau, only 17.4 percent of African Americans and 11.1 percent of Latinos hold bachelor's degrees, compared to 21.5 percent of the White population.[2] We hear their plaintive voices through revealing stories and statistics, but most acutely, we hear the collective voices of communities of color who bear witness to higher education's shortcomings. The stark realities facing residents in many of these communities—poorly funded, underperforming schools; inadequate health care; chronic unemployment and poverty—all represent a missed opportunity, an unfulfilled promise of higher education. Ironically, the unmet needs of communities of color also raise the question of whether higher education has even done right by the students it has served. After all, if advantaged students and graduates can remain indifferent to the struggles of the poor and people of color, can higher education really claim to foster ethical and democratic values—or has it failed to serve us all?

The Story of Unequal Access

Although society proclaims educational progress for all students, history belies this claim. A decade after World War I, college enrollments grew at unprecedented rates, while selective colleges further constricted the access of Jewish students and other ethnic minorities. We see a similar pattern today, except the public also has played a key role in undermining access for students of color. Public support for affirmative action and race-based scholarships has declined, and this demonstrates a reconfigured racial reality within higher education. Over the last four decades, colleges and universities made significant progress in their attempts to diversify their student bodies. But a series of court decisions, public voter referenda, and institutional policy shifts in the late 1990s altered the racial/ethnic representation of students at these institutions. Enrollment gains among students of color in the 1980s and early 1990s at state flagship campuses fell dramatically in Texas, Florida, Washington, California, and Maryland, even as the minority populations in these states steadily increased.[3] And at the same time that universities in these states began to look for new ways to prepare and recruit undergraduate students of color, the number of students of color at graduate and professional schools declined precipitously. In 2003, the Supreme Court determined in *Grutter v. Bollinger* that race could be considered in college admissions, settling many contentious admissions debates. But, the recovery of minority enrollments in most places has been slow and incomplete.

Even post-*Grutter*, many universities still struggle to enroll students of color in the new legal context. The University of Michigan has seen black enrollment drop significantly since it successfully defended legal challenges to its race-conscious admissions policies in 2003. Since the highly publicized Supreme Court ruling (and the university's decision to adapt its admission application to conform to that ruling), there was a 28 percent drop in the number of black applicants and 14.6 percent decline in the number of black students in the entering class of 2004. Ohio State University experienced a similar phenomenon, with a 25 percent drop in the number of black applicants and a 25 percent drop in black enrollments. Other selective institutions across the nation including Penn State University, University of North Carolina at Chapel Hill, and University of Georgia report similar "declining interest" among black applicants.[4]

In today's highly charged legal and political atmosphere, many colleges and universities are blowing with the winds. Some have altered or eliminated special programs for underrepresented students of color. Colleges once created thoughtful outreach, orientation, and/or academic support programs to ease the college transition for students of color or to introduce them to key fields such as science and mathematics. Other programs focused on public health, academic careers, and business to stir interest in fields where students of color are underrepresented. However, in today's harsh climate, some colleges are now inviting all students to participate in these special programs, originally designed for those whom the academy served least well. The impact of this change isn't yet clear, but it seems unlikely that underserved minorities will benefit.

If institutional leaders feel it necessary to expand these programs to all students, one possible positive outcome of program expansion would be to educate participants about the underrepresentation of blacks, Latinos, and Native Americans in higher education and in certain professional fields. Such an education could prove invaluable to compel social action and change. The Meyerhoff Scholars Program, an undergraduate science and math honors program open to students of any race or ethnicity at the University of Maryland (Baltimore County), subscribes to this pedagogy and requires all students to enroll in a black studies course and participate in two cultural events yearly. The goal is to ensure that all Meyerhoff Scholars have a better understanding of the issues that particularly affect minority communities.

Regardless of enrollment declines among students of color at the nation's elite institutions and despite changes in pre-college outreach programs, many point to record college enrollments among students of color over the last two decades as an indicator of progress. However, much of the enrollment growth among blacks, Latinos, and Native Americans has occurred at the nation's two-year colleges, where entering students are less likely to complete a baccalaureate degree. In fact, a recent report by Education Commission of the States and the League for Innovation in the Community College suggests that only 26 percent of blacks and 28 percent of Latinos who began at community college earned an associate's degree or certificate within six years. And fewer than 20 percent go on to complete a baccalaureate degree.[5] Subsequently, since so few go on to complete a baccalaureate degree, the numbers of students of color in graduate and professional schools are unsurprisingly low. Students of color miss additional opportunities, since studies show that advanced degree recipients—whether it be an MBA or a PhD—enjoy higher earnings and more influential careers than baccalaureate degree holders. According to a recent study by Pew Hispanic Center, in the 25- to 34-year-old age bracket (the typical age for graduate school attendance), 3.8 percent of white high school graduates are enrolled in graduate school compared to 3.0 percent of African American high school graduates and only 1.9 percent of similarly aged Latino high school graduates.

The apparent growth in college enrollments fails to translate into equitable representation across postsecondary sectors. Can we truly say that we have achieved equitable access to higher education in America? Whom are we educating and graduating, and whom are we leaving behind?

Unequal Educational Outcomes

Our professed democratic commitments ring hollow when we witness the low baccalaureate attainment rates among students of color. Although the number of minorities entering college and earning degrees has increased considerably over the last 20 years, black, Latino and Native American students still lag behind whites in college participation, retention, attainment, and graduation. In fact, the gaps in college participation and attainment levels among white, black, and Latino students have actually widened over the last two decades.[6]

Although many factors outside the academy continue to shape opportunities for college access (K–12 schools, family situations, finances, etc.), the challenge of recruiting, retaining and empowering an increasingly diverse student population rests squarely with higher education.

Right now, higher education isn't meeting that challenge. For example, the academy must seriously respond to the declining rates of Latino and black male enrollment and attainment. Since 1976, the percentage of black high school graduates, especially males, who enroll in higher education has steadily declined; Latino males are experiencing similar declines.[7] Currently, college graduation rates for black and Latino men hover near 18 percent. In 2002, 57 percent of earned Bachelors Degrees were awarded to women. Among Latinos, three degrees were awarded to women for every two awarded to men. And for African-Americans, women outnumbered men as recipients by two to one.[8] Admittedly, the challenge of access and success for black and Latino males is much larger than higher education can address alone. It's really a pre-K–16 crisis, one that begins in preschool and extends through college. The elementary and secondary sectors have considerable work to do, as dropout rates for these men persist. White males average 13.3 years of schooling, black males average 12.2 years of schooling while Latino males lag behind at 10.6 years of schooling.[9]

Still, higher education cannot ignore its responsibility to vastly improve its response to the needs of these students. Few programs on college campuses provide additional outreach and support to minority males. And even fewer programs exist in university schools of education to show teachers how to educate black and Latino male children. Higher education should be working from both ends of the educational spectrum to make headway toward equitable outcomes for many vulnerable male students of color. Yet we see very few comprehensive attempts to address the problem.

In addition, many college campuses continue to be haunted by inhospitable racial climates—a fact often cited by students of color as a reason for departure. Gaps in achievement relate directly to disparate student experiences on college campuses. Minority students' expressions of alienation, exclusion, and discrimination on predominantly white campuses remain an issue.[10] A perceived lack of support by administration, faculty, and staff; stereotyping by faculty and peers; social segregation—all have contributed to such feelings. Black, Latino, and Native American students have repeatedly reported that they feel excluded from campus activities and student organizations. In addition, they report that they are more likely to experience difficulty in getting acquainted with other racial and ethnic groups because of their racial and ethnic background. Colleges and universities must take greater measures to build inclusive campuses that value individuals and individual difference.

In addition to campus climates, disparate educational outcomes also require attention. One of the key variables necessary to retain and graduate students is regular examination of students' educational outcomes. All too often, institutions are oblivious to disparate rates of attainment among student groups. Stratification within the institution goes largely unnoticed because equity in educational outcomes is rarely tracked. For instance, institutions do not monitor the grade point averages or course completion rates of minority students who intend to attend graduate or professional school. We have no way of knowing how well or how poorly these students are doing relative to their White and Asian peers.

There is one hopeful sign. Over the last few years, some institutions have begun to disaggregate their institutional data by race and ethnicity in order to understand differential student outcomes. This practice must be adopted more widely for it to be truly useful. Merely understanding the data isn't enough to close gaps between groups, but it serves as a beginning point to address disparities. The low status of students of color in today's colleges and universities calls for higher education's serious attention and commitment.

A Recommitment to Service

American institutions of higher education have always engaged in egalitarian rhetoric, but their performance has fallen far short of American ideals, particularly for students of color. Nearly two hundred years ago, educators established colleges such as Oberlin and Bowdoin with the belief that such institutions could become catalysts for building a more racially just society. Not only were blacks welcomed as students, but all students who attended these institutions were educated in praxis—reasoned theory with principled action to compel social change for racial justice. The founders wanted all students to be liberally educated to create pluralistic democracy, so that blacks and others would have equal opportunity and equal citizenship. Today, can higher education say that it confers on its beneficiaries a status that imposes social obligations? Can higher education show how aspirations of equity translate into true equitable outcomes for students of color?

I would argue that higher education confers rhetoric without social responsibility on its beneficiaries. Its commitment to furthering the advancement of students of color and pluralistic communities is questionable at best. Philosopher and former president of Amherst College, Alexander Meiklejohn said sixty years ago that, to whittle away at our racial aristocracy, "democracy must have a dwelling place in our colleges." Today, rhetoric and good intentions overshadow democratic practice on our campuses. Moreover, the failure is not measured solely or even primarily in the diminished educational achievements of poor and minority students. Rather, it is most obviously demonstrated in the apparent indifference of educated, advantaged Americans. The message from those served least well is that, despite the world's urgent need for enlightened, democratic actors, those who have graduated from our colleges and universities have not been served well either.

Notes

1. Jack Meacham, a professor at SUNY Buffalo, recently examined mention of diversity in institutional mission statements. Not surprisingly, nearly a third of all institutional mission statements he studied held valuing diversity as an integral part of the educational charge. *Diversity Digest* vol. 7, no. 3 (2003).
2. U.S. Census Bureau Statistics, 2002.
3. J. Chapa, "Hopwood Effects and Responses: The Search for Race-Blind Means of Improving Minority Access to Higher Education," presented at a research conference sponsored by the American Council on Education, January, Washington, D.C., 1999. B. Pusser, "The Contemporary Politics of Access Policy: California After Proposition 209," in D. E. Heller, ed., *The States and Public Higher Education: Affordability, Access, and Accountability* (Baltimore, MD: Johns Hopkins University Press, 2001). S. Hurtado and H. Wathington Cade, " 'Time for Retreat' or Renewal? The Impact of Hopwood on Campus," in D. E. Heller, ed., *The States and Public Higher Education*.
4. Universities Record Drop in Black Admissions, *Washington Post*, November 21, 2004.

5. Joint Report of Education Commission of the States and The League for Innovation in the Community College, *Keeping America's Promise*, Boulder, Colorado, 2004.
6. American Council on Education, *Minorities in Higher Education 2002–2003*, Twentieth Annual Status Report, Washington, D.C.
7. R. Coley, *Gender Differences in Educational Achievement within Racial and Ethnic Groups*, Educational Testing Service Report, Princeton, New Jersey, 2001.
8. U.S. Census Bureau Statistics, 2002.
9. Richard Fry, "Latinos in Higher Education: Many Enroll, Too Few Graduate," Pew Hispanic Center report, Washington, D.C., 2002
10. S. Hurtado, J. Milem, A. Clayton-Pedersen, and W. Allen, *Enacting Diverse Learning Environments. Improving the Climate for Racial/Ethnic Diversity in Higher Education* vol. 26, no. 8 (Washington, D.C.: The George Washington University, 1999).

14

It is Only a Port of Call: Reflections on the State of Higher Education

Julie Johnson Kidd

For twenty-five years I have served at the helm of the Christian A. Johnson Endeavor Foundation, a family foundation that has contributed over $65 million to almost one hundred institutions of higher learning during that period alone. Over the course of my tenure I have met presidents, deans, and faculty from colleges in every region of the United States. Many of the foundation's grantees have been liberal arts colleges in the East. They are strong now, but were weaker institutions when the foundation first initiated its support. Additionally, the foundation has supported historically black colleges, Appalachian colleges, and American Indian higher education, as well as pioneering colleges in other parts of the United States and, most recently, in Europe.

As I reflect on this quarter century of involvement with higher education, I feel compelled to express my belief that American higher education has lost its bearings and is falling short in its vital educational mission. Although many generations have had the good fortune to participate in our system of higher learning and have benefited in many important ways, I believe that our system has developed serious flaws that interfere with its ability to develop in our young people the depth of critical thinking, intellectual curiosity, and human understanding so essential for dealing with the problems in our world today.

Most critics blame our educators for the shortcomings they see. I believe that the fault lies with a far broader set of constituencies, not only educators, but trustees, parents, and society at large. In my view, higher education can be no better than our collective expectations of its power to change lives. It can be no better than the readiness of students to make the most of what it offers. It can be no better than the level of financial support that we are willing to provide to meet our expectations, and no better than the philosophy we hold in establishing appropriate financial priorities. Finally, higher education can be no better than the imagination and vision we bring to it, coupled with our willingness to challenge traditional ways of thinking and acting.

I will argue that as a society we lack a clear, universally agreed on understanding of the place of higher education in young people's lives. We fail to nurture in students the emotional and intellectual characteristics necessary to gain from higher education its grandest lessons. We misunderstand and do not provide the financial and philosophical support necessary for students to achieve excellence. Finally, we lack vision, imagination, and boldness in thinking of ways to improve our institutions of higher learning.

For a vast majority of our eighteen- to twenty-four-year-olds, life at college or university may become little more than a four-year frolic through late adolescence with a little learning thrown in along the way. Pockets of excellence do exist, particularly amongst the small liberal arts colleges, where some students are transformed and broadened in thrilling ways. Yet even those students could benefit more if the college environment encouraged their development as whole persons.

The Meaning of Higher Education

I believe that various educational constituencies frequently distort the place of higher education in the lives of young people. We understand fully the *practical* benefits of higher education but little about the intangible, deeper, and more far-reaching benefits. Parents often see going to college as an opportunity to build a peer network that can be helpful in the future or as the perfect arena for finding a mate. They may see college as a safe place to park young people until they are needed in the workforce; or attendance may be an unconscious means for insecure adults to gain prestige from their children's accomplishments. Too often, college becomes a way for students to make up what they should have learned in high school but did not. Thus we push our young people into an increasingly frenzied race for admission to our colleges and universities but often for reasons of secondary importance. Attendance at the "best" possible college or university becomes a necessary part of a "credentialing process," a sorting mechanism indicating levels of achievement that will become relevant in the workplace. These demands on higher education bear little relationship to education at all.

Pressuring our young people to attend college for such reasons addresses only the fringe benefits of education, fringe benefits that can be delivered as easily by mediocrity as by excellence. In light of such misplaced objectives for higher education for our children, is excellence even needed or relevant? What difference does it make if classes are large and lectures are dull? Does it matter that many graduates remain largely untouched intellectually or emotionally? Are our children truly "set for life" just because they weathered the storms of late adolescence, received the desired diploma, and established a network to help them find a job? Could this really be all that matters?

Excellence in higher education, however, can take a young person far beyond the practical benefits just enumerated. Excellence in education has the power to enrich and deepen the life experience, to open new vistas for consideration, and to develop critical thinking as a habit of mind. It helps students to develop ethical and moral principles by which to live, engendering compassion and open-mindedness and igniting the ability to see connections between diverse issues and ideas. Students learn to find inspiration and solace in the arts and to make the life of the mind and the heart the central features of a meaningful life. In an uncertain world in which challenges to our physical and economic well-being are many, qualities of mind and spirit may be the life force that sustains us.

We live in a world of far greater complexity than that of fifty years ago, and we cannot make sufficient sense of those complexities by the age of eighteen, even with the very best high school education. Our institutions of higher learning must prepare young people to deal with the challenges posed by cultural conflict, globalization, technological innovation, and environmental change, among other things. Consequently, we must rethink how the undergraduate experience can broaden the perspectives, understanding, and abilities of students to meet the challenges they will face throughout their lives. We must recognize the need to update our educational models so that our children will have the perspective and skills necessary to find ways to protect and nurture our planet and all its living beings into the future.

If these become our aspirations and goals for higher education, if we replace our currently more limited agenda with such a mission, we are bound to make a profound difference in the significance and quality of higher education. Such a mission would provide a framework for action, suggesting the measures and guideposts we need to make the changes that will inspire and transform. If higher education could approach this level of excellence, the fringe benefits would fall into place automatically.

Emotional and Intellectual Readiness for Education

If we really want excellence from our institutions of higher learning—that is, excellence in the intellectual, moral, and emotional development of our students as whole persons—then we must send them to college ready to learn and grow. They cannot be tired, burned out, confused, and alienated, whether as a result of overdetermination by their parents or as a function of the pressures of society as a whole.

Unfortunately, many of our students are lacking in sufficient emotional and intellectual preparation. They arrive at college carting their prescription medications, their refrigerators and microwaves, their depressions, their cynicisms, their well-honed abilities to cut corners, to game the system, to promote themselves, and with their underlying desires to escape it all at the next party, through binge drinking or worse. A conversation I recently had with a young exchange student from Germany, who is studying at one of our most prestigious universities, illustrates this point. He said that he was "shocked and horrified" by the life of the American undergraduate, citing, for example, his observation that the only thing on students' minds seems to be where to get the next beer or find the next party.

It is the hunch of many of us that today's students are really too exhausted to learn, too programmed to have any idea who they are, too depressed by this fact to be enthusiastic, and too tired to do anything about it but escape. There is already evidence that even less-pressured school environments gradually will be swept up in the powerful pull of this pulsating drive. Young people everywhere feel the pressure to have a piece of the materialistic American dream, whether through competition for admission to our most prestigious universities, through athletic prowess or through some other avenue to "success." Others may reject this notion of the American dream but then become consumed and distracted with the overwhelming task of creating something meaningful with which to replace it.

What are the causes of this sad state of affairs among our young people? I believe they arise from the driving forces behind our culture, the driving forces behind almost everything we do—materialism and consumerism—and from the power of the mass media to shape what we think and desire. We have come to assume that the ultimate value in life is the marble bathroom equipped with a Jacuzzi as large as the average living room. Thus we ask only how to ensure that our children will be able to participate in this orgy of consumption and how to prove our own worth in this world of intense competition.

We as parents have a tendency to think of college as the last destination to which we must bring our children. If they attend college, preferably a prestigious one, they will be "set for life." There will be nothing further that we must do for them. We do not send the message that college is a very important port of call, one in which students can fuel their minds and hearts for the lifetime of endeavor that lies ahead. But college is just that—only a port of call. It does not provide inoculation against the need to deal with problems of all sorts in later life. It is not the ultimate destination that makes or breaks you.

By making college the destination, the be-all and end-all of life, the ultimate statement of success for a young person and for his or her parents as well, we thwart the normal developmental process of childhood and adolescence. Young people cannot be prepared by overscheduling; they must be allowed the space to grow. Childhood should be a time of experimentation and self-discovery. By shifting the whole focus of those years onto résumé building in preparation for the college admissions race, we inadvertently turn this vital time into a pressure cooker devoid of meaning. We rob young people of the opportunity to make their own decisions and thus come to know themselves. We do not teach them that it is aiming low, not failure, that they should avoid. We often protect them from the consequences of their actions and from taking responsibility for those actions.

Consider, for example, today's overscheduled, overachieving young person. Out of the home at age two, enrolled in an afterschool squash program by age eight (proficiency in squash might be his or her "ticket to the Ivies"), taking PSAT prep courses by grade nine at the latest, and from there on filling every moment with accomplishment, risk-taking, community service, experiences abroad, extracurricular activities, all in order to be acceptable to the college of one's choice. For others different pressures may predominate, such as the need for a twenty-hour workweek in addition to school to augment the family's income or to have the resources to keep up with peers with cars and credit cards. Although many of these activities are beneficial, when they are undertaken for the wrong reasons or under pressure, their essential value is negated. At any rate, for most, life means no time for slacking—*get going, keep up, outdo, get all As, make sure you win the game. No time for pleasure reading, no time for a crossword puzzle, no time for a walk in the woods, unless it is part of an accredited course that will look good on your résumé. A little cheating here and there—well, there is so much pressure on our kids that it is understandable that they'd have to cut corners somewhere. Don't dwell on it. Hurry on, get going, don't miss the deadline because it will all be worth it in the end. You'll be in college and you'll be set for life. No more worries, no more hurdles. The hardest part of college is getting there. Then you can relax. Then you can have fun. Then we won't have to worry about you anymore.* Given this context, is it any wonder that these students are emotionally disadvantaged when they arrive at college?

The Christian A. Johnson Endeavor Foundation has spent the last twenty-five years of its existence providing funding to help create the most imaginative, relevant, stimulating, and enthralling academic experiences possible for young people. Yet all the most compelling and broadening programs in the world, such as those at many of our small liberal arts colleges, will make little if any difference if students are not ready to reap the rewards of exposure to them or are too emotionally stunted to learn.

Providing the Necessary Financial and Philosophical Support for Higher Education

> As a senior at Middlebury College, one of the nation's most expensive private colleges, I have seen the comprehensive fee increase nearly $10,000 in four years to reach its current level of $40,400. If the rise in tuition was correlated with a rise in academic vigor, most students would accept the additional cost. This, unfortunately, is not the case. Indeed, many colleges like Middlebury have used excess revenue to finance vast building projects, which, while aesthetically pleasing, do little to enhance the quality of a student's education.
>
> —Amichai Kilchevsky, letter to the *New York Times*, October 22, 2004

Much is made of the exorbitant costs of higher education today. It is of course true, and much to be lamented, that a middle-class family in this country can no longer afford to provide a college education for one, much less two, children as they would have been able to do, albeit with difficulty, in the middle of the last century. The reasons for these high costs, however, do not lie primarily in low professorial productivity, as many have cited, but rather, once again, in our own expectations of the services and environment that should be provided.

First, the elegance and plethora of facilities of all kinds, often designed by iconic architects and often including grandiose rotunda-like entry courts unnecessary for study, are a heavy drain on facilities maintenance and energy costs and require substantial numbers of personnel to oversee their operation. Particularly egregious are the outsized expenditures for impressive athletic facilities with their accompanying vast number of coaches. The large sums spent on elaborate student centers are rarely justified; although impressive on admissions tours, students often do not make full use of them. Basic infrastructure costs are also elevated by the need for additional electrical wiring in dorms for luxuries and distractions such as refrigerators, microwaves, televisions, and stereo equipment, accoutrements that have come to be perceived as essentials. I have spoken with many a college president who has affirmed with regret that in order to attract the students the college wants, it is imperative that the college be able to compete on a facilities level with its peer institutions. Such facilities are a source of pride for alumni, attracting alumni dollars, in that they are a visual testament, supposedly, to the quality of their alma maters.

The costs mentioned so far bear only a marginal relationship to the quality of the educational process, which is presumably the reason for attending college to begin with. Unfortunately, our society gives little thought to the appropriateness and effect of such lavishness on the worldview of our young people and how living in such an environment can accustom them to feel entitled to a life of privileges. An environment with the nonstop provision of services does not equip them for life after college. The tension between what they learn theoretically in the classroom and the luxury that surrounds them can be a source of alienation. Students, insulated at college from a world in which poverty is so often the norm, are ill prepared to take their place in a globalized world.

Marketing efforts made to attract "the best" student body possible also drive up tuition charges significantly. These efforts are not aimed only at enrolling a class of "quality," but also are aimed at attracting as many applicants as possible so that a college can then reject a high number of students to enhance their selectivity rating in the college rankings of *U.S. News & World Report.* Some estimates have indicated that these marketing efforts cost a college on average about $5,000 per student enrolled.[1] In reality, when indirect costs are included, this number is significantly higher, amounting nationally to hundreds of millions of dollars per year, spent almost solely in the hunt for prestige. The trustees and alumni of our colleges and universities expect ever more successful marketing efforts and thus have unwittingly "corporatized" our institutions of higher learning and converted them into service providers. Student applicants do not immediately understand that they have become pawns in a larger competitive game and often become disillusioned when they come to this realization.

Other significant nonacademic costs are incurred in both the legal and counseling areas. Parents who make unreasonable demands on institutions of higher learning in holding them accountable for their children's behavior often initiate expensive lawsuits. Likewise, the spiraling costs of counseling for the growing numbers of students with emotional problems of varying sorts resulting from influences that shaped them before they even arrived at college absorb large sums.

Most of these costs have little if anything to do with the missions of our institutions of higher learning, little to do with the intellectual and emotional development of our young people, little to do with developing critical thinking, a broad worldview, and the other elements that characterize all that liberal education can be. If we lament the costs of higher education and are reluctant to pay the price, we have only ourselves to thank for the situation. We must recognize that quality higher education *is* a costly proposition if it is to fulfill its potential. Redirecting the way our colleges and universities spend their money from the purposes just mentioned into fulfilling their core academic missions would provide a sound foundation for change. It also would send a different message to young people about the priorities in which we believe. I submit that despite the efforts of faculty to counteract some of our cultural malaise, what young people see in the world around them before college is largely reinforced by the institutional behavior of our colleges and universities. Rather than being an antidote to the materialism that surrounds young people, colleges and universities have been drawn into and infected by that materialism as well. To many of our students, the philosophy of materialism is the underlying philosophical principle of higher education. This materialism, which has seeped into all parts of our culture, keeps higher education from truly fulfilling its mission.

The Need for Vision, Imagination, and Boldness

There is an ongoing failure of vision, imagination, and boldness when we evaluate ways to improve our institutions of higher learning. Before proceeding further, however, I would like to exempt the presidents of many of our small liberal arts colleges from this charge. I have met with many who do possess the passion, sensitivity, and imagination necessary for this task. They are, however, shackled to principles and actions in which they do not believe by the dominant expectations of the public at large, who, directly or indirectly, provide the funding for higher education. With respect to the leaders of our public and private research universities, I am personally acquainted with only a small number of those, some of whom are also able, at least in vision, to rise above societal expectations although they too are constrained by society's pressures.

There are many examples, both small and large, of higher education's failure in vision and boldness. For example, the Mellon Foundation has provided extensive research demonstrating that the commitment of our colleges and universities to a near-professional level of athletics is not only unconscionably costly but also weakens the very fabric of our institutions of higher learning.[2] Yet trustees and alumni have shown virtually no willingness to allow their presidents to attack this sacred cow. On another matter, Dr. Richard Levin, president of Yale University, in responding to his serious concerns about the pressures on our young people before coming to college, has called for the elimination of the early decision system and its replacement with a new admissions process.[3] Similar pleas have come from other quarters, such as the National Association of Independent Schools, but precious little real willingness to engage the subject deeply and seriously has been forthcoming.[4] Issues such as class size, overemphasis on faculty research at the expense of teaching, and the tenure system are perennially on the table but never really addressed. It is also widely understood that standardized tests and rankings are, on the whole, of little value, yet we continue to warp our system by using these tools. It has long been recognized that our state governments place a relatively low priority on higher education, resulting in university program and financial aid budget cuts as soon as legislators see a need for belt-tightening. These political decisions undermine quality and consistency, yet the public has never called our legislators to task on readdressing priorities. Our state systems need much more money, not less, to improve the core elements of the teaching–learning process.

I would like to make two suggestions for change. The first is that private donors, whether individuals or foundations, begin to think more creatively about their contributions to higher education and to consider distributing their contributions differently. Our richest private institutions keep getting richer while other schools with worthy ambitions and important roles to play struggle. Do our richest institutions really need to widen that gap? Do our young undergraduate students really need to study in environments so luxurious that life will almost never again be as sweet? As alumni we may like to think of our alma maters almost as shrines to which we contribute ever more splendid buildings to glorify our own pasts and as generous expressions of our own devotion and thanks. In the interests of our nation as a whole, however, should we not consider spreading donations over a broader range of institutions? This would promote a more level playing field, one in which young people live in more modest circumstances, more in keeping with what they might expect after college. To confer great privilege on a small number of our young people before they have earned it is a recipe for unrealistic expectations, misunderstanding, and a sense of entitlement. Further, an even spreading of resources and a reduction in spending for frills would allow more institutions to provide financial aid for international students so that all Americans can learn to respect other cultures and what other cultures can teach us. For every dollar we contribute to our wealthiest institutions, I suggest contributing another dollar to a financially weaker institution.

Second, I would like to suggest that we rethink what we mean when we speak of "the best" students. Are "the best" students necessarily the ones with the highest scores on standardized tests, the highest grades, and the most extracurricular activities, or are they the students with the most to gain, with the greatest thirst for change, with the emotional maturity to ingest what is around them? Or should "the best" student body be one in which we have a mix of students that involves all these definitions, which mirrors the complexity of the world around us? Can we ever really know what "the best" means? If we were to cease worrying about attracting "the best" by recognizing that we cannot ever truly know its meaning, we then could redeploy our resources in more fruitful ways, ways not dictated by the marketplace mentality that now dominates our decisions and choices.

Conclusion

I would like to return to a theme raised at the beginning of my essay: Higher education will not improve until our own understanding of its potential in relation to the needs of our children broadens and deepens. Higher education should not be about prestige, credentialing, competition, ego gratification, escaping, killing time, or positioning oneself for a contract with the Los Angeles Lakers. It should be about the development of the whole person, and it should be only one port of call along the lifelong voyage of self-discovery and self-realization. Until we, as parents, let go of our extraneous notions and focus on the growth of our children and the development of their ability to find life rewarding no matter what may come their way, we will not be able to improve our system of higher learning. Until our boards of trustees focus their attention away from rankings and onto what is taking place in the college community and the classroom, we will not be able to improve our system of higher learning. Faculties must realize that their first responsibility is to their students and that they must make the classroom experience more relevant to the "outside world," as is increasingly the case at our small liberal arts colleges through their "engaged learning" courses. Until faculties are given the freedom to address that responsibility, many students will continue to be disinterested in the intellectual life of their colleges or universities and half-hearted in their commitment to learning. We must emphasize that a rewarding, satisfying life bears little necessary relationship to material wealth. We must also emphasize that the proper stewardship of financial resources can be beneficial in addressing global problems but that wealth is not an end in itself. This concept is little stressed in our national rhetoric or by our institutions of higher learning. Overall, our institutions must play a far more substantive role in fostering the ascendancy of profound values as the essence of human existence.

This review is by no means a comprehensive list of all the issues, but rather is a sampling of some of them. Without deep consideration with fresh and open minds, we will continue only to nibble around the edges of change rather than to develop a head-on challenge to the status quo. Without the changes that such a challenge can bring, we will relegate our young people to the role of commodities in a huge game of marketplace economics. The healthy emotional, ethical, and intellectual development of our young people should be our first priority. Failure to focus on these key issues obviously does not emanate from venal motives, but rather, I believe, from a lack of recognition of the seriousness and depth of the ever-growing malaise around us. If we do not take the time to address these issues collectively, we will be jeopardizing not only the well-being of our nation but also the future of our children and, indeed, of our planet.

Notes

1. Private conversations with college presidents.
2. James L. Shulman and William G. Bowen, *The Game of Life: College Sports and Educational Values* (Princeton, NJ: Princeton University Press, 2001).
3. Karen W. Arenson, "Yale President Wants to End Early Decisions for Admissions," *New York Times*, December 13, 2001.
4. "In the Grip of the University," *Independent School*, Winter 2003.

15

The Curriculum and College Life: Confronting Unfulfilled Promises

Leon Botstein

Undergraduate life on the residential American campus, whether at freestanding liberal arts colleges or in private and public university settings, has been marked by a persistent and radical discontinuity. A basic tension, or rather contradiction, exists between the principles and standards of the curriculum on one hand and the culture and conduct of everyday life on campus outside the classroom on the other. Campus life, even at the most selective and prestigious institutions, reveals a Jekyll and Hyde–like paradox and dichotomy. We encourage idealism, ambition, seriousness of purpose, and hard work in our students in the classroom. Yet the demands on students to do well, however time-consuming, leave more than ample downtime, hours if not days in which nothing is required—no labs, lectures, or deadlines—even for the most ambitious and talented. In the vacuum of time, passivity, convention, and vulgarity in behavior are all too pervasive.

The problem could reasonably be identified as one of thwarted expectations. The underlying and optimistic belief behind the effort to make access to higher education as universal as possible is a traditional conviction that there must be a causal link between education and human progress. The notion of progress can be understood in various ways, in terms of civility, understanding, tolerance, ethics, aesthetic judgment, or citizen participation. One of the sharp ironies of contemporary life is that although more Americans are completing more years of formal schooling than ever before, including time in college, we find ourselves confronted, it seems, despite more exposure to learning, with an absence of progress in these arenas. One needs only to cite the declining quality of public political debate, lapses in integrity and standards in professional and business practices, public entertainment (e.g., reality television), precollege school achievement, and what the eighteenth century called civic virtue.

Of Those to Whom Much Is Given, Little Is Asked

College is a unique opportunity. Young adults are given the possibility of devoting an expanse of time during four years of their lives to learn not only how to prepare for a career, but to satisfy their curiosity over a wide range of subject matters as well. They are spared, for the most part, extensive direct responsibilities for others. This applies even to the least economically privileged students, for whom paid employment during college is a necessity. Explicit in the American ideology of undergraduate liberal learning and general education, two distinct but related curricular entities, is the notion that the kind of study possible in the undergraduate curriculum, even within preprofessional bachelor degree programs, offers a potential link between learning and life, broadly defined. Even the way the college major is organized goes beyond the strictly utilitarian. Undergraduate specialization is defended as providing the first adult opportunity to accumulate, with a particular focus, knowledge, and skills of interpretation. The objective is in-depth learning in a manner that is transferable. Hence English majors become lawyers, sociology majors become doctors, biology majors become investment bankers, and theater majors become members of the clergy. Although undergraduate majors may not determine specific careers, we believe that the habits and interests cultivated in college can influence the conduct of life after graduation; the patterns of activity from the college experience, we claim, are maintained throughout adulthood.

The habits of mind that colleges purport to disseminate in the classroom—often described as critical thinking (the demand for careful analysis; the examination of intuitive and counterintuitive hypotheses; the raising of questions; the tolerance of ambiguity, uncertainty, and fallibility; and the pursuit of curiosity)—are deemed not only useful but also desirable for the duration of one's life. Utility and virtue are not understood as being in conflict. Explicit in the ideals articulated in every undergraduate catalog is the conviction that graduates will become engaged and therefore better citizens, neighbors, and professionals. If one follows the standard rhetoric put forth by colleges, a better-educated citizenry increases society's capacity to fashion a stronger participatory democracy committed to freedom and reason.

Furthermore, in the context of contemporary politics and economics, the best informed of our future citizens—those with a college education—ought to be better prepared to deal with the world beyond North America and Europe. Indeed, during the post–Cold War years, most campuses have reported an increase in student interest in courses on the history, languages, and cultures of Asia, the Middle East, and Africa. This increase confirms the notion that many students in college study what they think will be vital in the future. They take responsibility for calculating possible connections between their course of study and their lives after college. In this ongoing shift within and between generations, trends emerge to which colleges, in their curricular arrangements and investments, seek to respond.[1]

But this coincidence of rhetoric and practice is limited to curricular requirements and choices. Curricular changes notwithstanding, what has remained frighteningly consistent despite nearly a half century of increased access to college is that the encounter with the primary purpose of being in college—learning—seems not to have left many traces on our lives after college. The presumed civic and cultural benefits of going to college continue to elude us. The experience of classroom learning (writing papers, tackling problem sets, completing laboratory assignments, taking examinations) has not influenced college graduates, as adults, to live their lives differently or, one might suggest, better. Classroom learning seems to have had little effect on the manner in which students conduct their daily lives or graduates pursue vocations and careers, if one believes the critics of the contemporary practice of medicine and law. There is little empirical justification for the conceit of influence embedded in the rhetoric of liberal learning and general education.

Locating Causes

Does the fault lie with students for their failure to seize opportunities offered to them? Or are subtle but significant changes in the essence of the collegiate experience we provide the cause?

The old tend to blame the young, of course. At the height of the so-called culture wars, alumni of many institutions bemoaned changes in the undergraduate curriculum, claiming a lowering of standards, notably the loss of a core curriculum based in a tradition labeled Western Civilization. One could reasonably have asked, had there actually been a golden age of education in Western Civilization and a higher level of discipline, idealism, and standards, why it was that the generations of graduates from that golden age presided over the very cultural decline that so alarmed them. The evils that the neoconservative critique of culture and values in society sought to bemoan beginning in the late 1970s, whether about politics, ethics, literature, music, or public mores, were not the consequence of student behavior and so-called radical faculty but the culture of adults. The elite among these adults were themselves college graduates from those allegedly better days with higher standards. The past they invoked was at best a distortion masquerading as nostalgia. There was never a golden age in which intellectual idealism flourished on the college campus, as Robert M. Hutchins observed in the 1930s. [2] Allan Bloom's legendary paean to the era of the 1950s, *The Closing of the American Mind*, was his particular personal fantasy.[3] American adults beyond college age, today's parents, not recent college students, are responsible for the alleged decline in reading literature, the low rates of political participation, the deterioration in public schooling, and the so-called degraded standards in cultural taste.

The plain fact is that in modern history, from the early twentieth century on, life on the American campus has not been defined by the ideals of the curriculum. With few exceptions, learning and that noble phrase, the life of the mind, have not lent institutions their distinctive characters, their identities; dimensions of extracurricular life—the rituals and patterns of life in college—entirely separate from the classroom have consistently overwhelmed the curricular experience for most students. And that extracurricular life has displayed aspects of anti-intellectualism that directly contradict and undermine the stated academic ideals and intentions. Complicit in this state of affairs are not only alumni, who seem at many institutions to care most for sports and fraternities, but the faculty and college administrators as well.

Residency Matters

Residency, and all residency entails, is the heart of the matter. The rationale for a residential campus in the United States, one in which students do not commute from home, one with dormitories and dining facilities, has its roots in the English model of Oxford and Cambridge. Even the great land-grant colleges and research universities designed more along German lines adopted the notion that a residential campus was desirable. Living on campus was more than a necessity; it was deemed a virtue. The argument for the residential campus in some cases relied heavily on the English conceit regarding the formation of a governing elite. But as Jefferson predicted, American institutions developed a special rationale for campus life that was specific to the requirements of our democracy. We continue to assume that a residential campus offers the chance to build a community, to teach public service, tolerance, civic participation, and empathy, goals that are particularly useful in a pluralistic democratic culture. To this end, common dining and dormitory life are justified because they bring together individuals without previous connections, with different talents and interests, and from diverse regions, ethnic and religious backgrounds, and social classes.

This ingathering of young adults of the same age to take up residency within the geographical confines of an institution of higher learning continues to be attractive in terms that are neither financial nor practical. Such an assemblage would seem to be promising because each student has one crucial attribute in common: Each has come to college, presumably, in order to learn. Learning and living together with colleagues spanning an age range of about six years, particularly at four-year colleges dominated by students of traditional college age, seem to offer an extracurricular experience designed to assist learning. By being together outside of class, students might reinforce their one common bond, learning, and help each other. And they might find ways to cope with a diverse, mobile, and dynamic social order in which merit and achievement can prevail over wealth and inherited social status.

What actually occurs is that the social life on campus, the "living" part, bears little connection to the unique experience of a sustained concentration on learning, the students' common bond. No doubt there are extracurricular activities that bring together like-minded undergraduates with shared interests—college newspapers, community service initiatives, student governments, choruses, theaters, orchestras, religious organizations, and interest-based clubs, political and nonpolitical. But these activities often engage only a minority of students. For the majority of students, however, daily life is defined by patterns in social behavior that are unexceptional and ordinary, entirely unaffected by the supposed centrality of learning.[4]

Despite the extraordinary context of dormitory life and common dining, campus life turns into a more convenient, if slightly less comfortable, version of ordinary communal life outside of the family. For most students, what distinguishes campus life is the experience, for the first extended period of time in their lives, of living as an independent adult, free of parental or guardian supervision. What comes to dominate are the making and breaking of friendships and relationships and the partying that have always been (and will always be) part of student life. Before 1960, because of the novelty of personal freedom at an early stage of adulthood, the private life of students was more rigidly regulated by institutions than it is now. But in the two decades between 1945 and 1965, institutions, willingly and unwillingly, stepped back from both the notion of in loco parentis and the vestiges of a nineteenth-century sectarian construct of the college experience as intentionally character building. These goals have become obsolete.

Nonetheless, institutional rules of student conduct and behavior still differ from the code of law that applies to adult citizens in civil society. Although all institutions take care to develop cooperative relationships with local police and courts, what is left of the premodern autonomy of the university from civil authority is the voluntary delegation to colleges of the routine maintenance of order on the part of local authorities. In turn, colleges maintain security personnel and in some circumstances professional law enforcement staff.

However, in the wake of concerns over racism and sexual violence during the last quarter of the twentieth century, institutions have had to reassert their authority over not only campus life in general but the personal behavior of students as well. Contemporary codes of conduct and expectations articulated in college rulebooks regarding membership in the college community reflect this development. Each institution has an elaborate system of standards and disciplinary procedures that must survive procedural scrutiny in the courts. Penalties imposed by colleges can be enforced, including expulsion for nonacademic reasons. Regulations of recent vintage concerning so-called hate speech and sexual harassment remain the most controversial and debated grounds.[5]

The Gradual Disappearance of the Faculty from the Campus

If at one time the faculty members were the dominant adult figures in residential campus life, that is no longer the case. First, the tradition of on-campus housing has slowly vanished. Compensation has reached monetary levels that render the in-kind supplement no longer necessary or desirable. At some campuses, even the president no longer lives on campus. This pattern began in the late 1960s, when presidents and their families felt uncomfortable in the midst of campuses marked by protest and turmoil. In retrospect, this trend was unfortunate, particularly for institutions with strong residential traditions. As in any organization, the leader of a college or university must send a positive signal about the character of a campus. For an undergraduate institution, the home of the president should be a place where students and faculty are welcome, to which they have ready access, and where events, formal and informal, can be held. Second, even a pattern of the faculty living close to or within walking distance of a campus has become less common than it used to be, particularly in urban and suburban institutions. Third, the frequency of two-career households in the faculty has helped eliminate the last vestiges of a tradition in which a male faculty member invited students to his home where his wife poured tea. Multiple career demands also have led to residency at commuting distances from the campus far greater than were customary a half century ago.

But these developments are less significant than a far more fundamental and influential shift in the self-definition of undergraduate faculty. With the consent of their institutions, faculty members define themselves today in terms of their disciplines first and their institutional affiliations second. A much higher level of scholarly professionalism is now generally presumed. Service to an institution beyond the carefully defined boundaries of the academic is no longer a key factor in a teaching career. However, current professional standards for faculty, even at exclusively undergraduate campuses, are not so onerous as to demand a mythic choice between publishing or perishing. Rather, since World War II colleges have taken proper advantage of an extraordinary advance in higher education in the quality and extent of disciplinary training and standards among faculty. For most if not all fields of study, institutions have realized that a high level of teaching excellence is nearly impossible to maintain without active involvement in one's field.

Undergraduate institutions now expect faculty to sustain some minimal amount of scholarly work (or its equivalent) in the chosen arena of specialization, which understandably takes them beyond the confines of any single institution. Maintaining a professional life with colleagues outside of the home institution among contemporaries in the same field has become a nearly universal and welcome expectation. To remain a fine teacher at the college level requires more than contact with students. But encouraging faculty to venture professionally beyond the home institution has had the unfortunate effect of leading them away from close engagement with campus life outside the classroom. It has also fueled a dream of upward career mobility—moving from one institution to another as one's status in a field increases—that is more powerful and prevalent as fantasy than reality, except for the most distinguished scholars and scientists.

A fourth factor, a shift in mores during the last quarter of the twentieth century, has further encouraged the faculty to define their roles quite narrowly in terms of classroom instruction and the assumption of academic tasks strictly outlined by a curriculum (e.g., periodic tutorial instruction, and thesis advising). Although it has been the policy of colleges in the post–1960s era to presume that undergraduates are adults, informalities in student-faculty contact have come under extreme scrutiny. Given the near universality of the minimum legal drinking age at twenty-one, the proverbial sherry with the Oxford don depicted in popular films, notably *Chariots of Fire*, and any comparable socializing with or without alcohol is not only frowned on and forbidden, but it can lead to dire consequences. Faculty members and their institutions can and have been sued; they risk the allegation of unprofessional behavior for behaving in too convivial a manner. The distinctions in age and power have come to the fore sufficiently to discourage strongly social informality. The era of tacit acceptance of the occurrence of sexual relations between teachers and students, a pattern that has persisted literally throughout history, has passed. The same-sex relations reminiscent of early twentieth-century Oxford and Cambridge as well as the more talked about heterosexual relations that apparently went on before the mid-1970s are no longer tolerated. A permanent precedent has been established that in the event of a relationship, the faculty member and the institution are culpable for violating professional standards. The presumption of adulthood for students ironically but appropriately has been circumscribed. Student status is understood to create a structural vulnerability comparable to that shared by subordinates in the workplace. It must not be exploited. The argument of adult consent does not apply.

The Perils of Informality

Teaching has properly been defined as analogous to professional medical care. Professional standards delimit behavior and can be construed to discourage a range of personal interaction with students that might in fact be benign. Furthermore, institutions have become sensitive to the allegation that the temptation to breach the boundaries of professional behavior and to exploit the vulnerability of students may be fueled by an institutional culture that appears to encourage informal contact between students and teachers. Therefore, faculty wisely adhere to common rules of decorum: holding defined office hours, keeping distance from anything personal. There is even some reluctance to meet with students one on one. Administrators, responding to the public debate and legal vulnerability, take care to remind the faculty of proper standards. In short, whatever relaxed atmosphere of informality and privacy that once existed with institutional sanction has been supplanted by the trend toward formality and public transparency.

These are not unwelcome changes. There are only rationalizations, not justifications, for the abuses of a culture of campus informality. A relaxed atmosphere in which students can get to know members of the faculty remains nonetheless one of the key benefits of a residential campus. There has been an understandable reaction to the emergence of a climate of structured distance. In recent years one hears more and more about mentoring. Mentoring students has become the current, albeit infelicitous, euphemism that seeks to describe a virtue critical to good teaching that occurred more spontaneously on undergraduate campuses in earlier eras. As adults, students are entitled to be the objects of special personal interest on the part of teachers; students deserve attention beyond the grading of their work, the marking of their tests, and the answering of their questions.

The benefits of informality include the increased probability that some admirable adult who is not a relative might take an active role in the life and career of a young adult. The interest shown by faculty has accounted for a good deal of the positive and confidence-building learning experiences of undergraduate life. The practice of mentoring attempts to make informal encounters more structural and professional (and thus more acceptable) and to eliminate the inherent vulnerability of personal attachments. Unfortunately, the moment an informal pattern is managed, labeled, and rendered official, it can lose its power and become construed as a routine professional obligation, intertwined with contractual issues, such as course loads and professional expectations.

As a practical matter and as a criterion of self-definition, faculty involvement in campus life beyond the classroom has become marginal. The undergraduate campus, therefore, has become distinctly age-segregated. Faculty rarely eat with students at lunchtime and certainly not at dinner. At lunch, colleagues who often live at significant distances from one another take the time to transact business. At dinner and in the evening, faculty are not present in the dormitories and dining areas. On weekends, matters are worse. Because large numbers of faculty live off-campus and work at home, they have little reason to come to campus on the weekend or even in the evening. The exceptions are faculty in the sciences and the arts who require campus facilities and equipment. And those in the arts and the experimental sciences frequently are involved in collaborative ventures that include undergraduate students. Modern Internet technology has further reduced the necessity for faculty in many fields to come to the campus to use, for example, the library. For most of the day and week, students have little routine or spontaneous interaction with the faculty outside of the defined moments of instruction.

The Stopgap Strategy Goes Nowhere

These changes have taken place over decades. In response, colleges and universities have greatly expanded the numbers of professional, non-faculty staff who are required to be on campus. These individuals hold administrative appointments and are usually classed as student life professionals. Campuses have sought to fill the absence of faculty by supplying residence life staff, counseling staff, a separate advising staff, deans of students, and directors of student activities. These individuals range from very young adults, straight out of college with minimal training, to doctoral graduates from programs in psychology, social work, and counseling. In institutions with graduate programs, graduate students make up for the lack of an adult presence on campus; they are paid to live in dormitories or take on extra work in areas of student life. These incipient professionals, owing to the contractual definition of their function, rarely achieve something significant in their contact with students.

The problem with this solution is that although it protects the institution from potential accusations of negligence in the oversight of campus life, the adult staff hired to manage and enrich campus life, no matter how idealistic and qualified, are second-class citizens. The hierarchy in an institution of higher education is traditional and logical. The faculty—those who are hired for their expertise and talent as teachers and scholars—mirror the essential purpose of the institution. They create the reasons why students enroll. Student life professionals are by comparison marginal; they are viewed by students and faculty as peripheral. They possess neither the status nor the tools needed to forge a substantive link between the curriculum and campus life. It is one thing for a faculty member, a teacher—whether of physics or music—to have a cup of coffee with a student, sit together with students at a lecture or concert, invite students to his or her home, speak with a student's parents, give advice, eat dinner in the dining hall, or maintain a residence in a student housing facility. In that case, contact with students is powerful because it is entirely voluntary and supplemental to a primary teaching function.

This informal contact derives from the institution's central intellectual and pedagogical function. The authority and impact of extracurricular contact gains from the respect accorded faculty status, which in turn signals accomplishment within fields of study that students pursue. A professor of physics is perhaps no wiser or better company than the average citizen. But for most undergraduates, the only time in their lives they will ever get to consider shared aspects of the world (not issues requiring expertise) from the trivial to the cosmic with scholars, writers, artists, and scientists is in college.

The college years may be the only ones during which young adults can spend time with and come to know, as human beings, those few who have chosen research and teaching at the university level as vocations. The exposure to those for whom the life of the mind and the pursuit of inquiry are—noncommercial ambitions—at the center of a life and career may be a crucial component of the potential benefits of campus life. That experience can have the constructive consequence of creating a citizenry that celebrates and protects those who make that choice, thereby helping to secure, as a matter of public policy, the support of individuals and institutions devoted to the pursuit of inquiry and the arts for their own sakes.

Student life professionals, no matter how good, are permanently crippled by disadvantages. At worst they are akin to paid camp counselors, watchdogs, and professional companions—the moral equivalent of the professional staff in a nursing home. Through no fault of their own, their influence on the intellectual character of student life and campus life is limited. However, what they achieve is essential and indispensable: an adult presence, the protection of students, and the care of those in distress and difficulty. They spend most of their time at the margins of the student population: with the highly self-motivated leaders and those in difficulty. Because the consciousness of status and rank permeates campuses, it is unlikely that those to whom the care of students and campus life is entrusted will receive the due they deserve. Varsity sports coaches and financial officers are more likely to win more institutional recognition and respect.

What Has Been Lost

Without the participation of the faculty in campus life beyond the classroom, it is unlikely that a culture that encourages intellectual pursuits and civic activities as part of daily life on the part of students will flourish. What may be lost, for example, is the goal that colleges should challenge among young adults the popular definitions of leisure, entertainment, and fun. The residential college campus can be an ideal setting for redefining the distinction between what we consider work and play. Insofar as boredom is a source of resentment, patterns established during the college years can help individuals use their imaginations—their minds—in ways that for the rest of their lives can avert the sense of boredom. Key to this objective is the capacity to think counterintuitively about matters that seem straightforward. So too is the joy of finding complexity and beauty not only in the ordinary but in forms of expression that are not commercial or dimensions of popular culture. Campus life ought to encourage students to resist mere fashion and clichés, to gain the capacity to listen and observe, and to debate and discuss. To make these habits active requires translating skills honed within the confines of disciplines, courses, classes, and assignments into an engagement with the ordinary and routine conduct of daily life.

The college years are a time when new tastes and pleasures can be cultivated. Colleges and universities have an obligation to encourage participation in ongoing traditions of human expression that are not dependent on being profitable or pleasing millions. These forms include dance, experimental film, the making of visual art, music (e.g., jazz and classical), theater (beyond Broadway), and writing that is not routine best-seller material, notably poetry. These categories cross all cultural boundaries. At stake here is not an outdated distinction between the elite and the egalitarian or the high and the low.

By suggesting that we open students' eyes and ears to artwork that is not directed at a mass audience, no implied or explicit critique of popular culture is intended. Rather, a campus can offer an antidote to the limited aesthetic experience that most entering college students bring with them.

If the engagement of the faculty in campus life is indispensable to achieving this goal—without placing on them the nonsensical burden of being regarded as authorities beyond their fields or as role models—then the structure of the curriculum and the allocation of resources must change. With respect to the undergraduate curriculum, there must be, particularly in the first year, but preferably throughout the four years, dimensions of a common ground. Whether this involves core courses with common syllabi and shared issues or rites of passage toward degree completion such as comprehensive written or oral examinations and senior theses, a curricular structure beyond the major that engages all students and spans disciplinary divisions is essential for three reasons. First, such a structure forces faculty from different areas to work cooperatively and form connections outside structural enclaves such as departments. In colleges, faculty are usually organized in imitation of the bureaucratic and professional definition of traditional disciplines. These enclaves are derived from established schemes of graduate training. However, undergraduates think not in terms of disciplines but of issues, questions, and problems. They are driven by a need to know how to do something, understand something, or create something. Their path to specialization cannot always be charted along lines formulated for graduate students. The questions undergraduates are likely to ask are large, and the strategies for the clarification of these questions derive from many disciplines.

Second, faculty members should be seen in the classroom and outside of it as articulating views and interpreting materials in arenas beyond their specialization. In a democracy, we are obliged to formulate judgments and views as observers and recipients of expertise and testimony. The critical evaluation of circumstances and issues ranging from war and peace to the directions of scientific research (e.g., stem cell research and biotechnology) and from the nature of domestic politics to the exercise of aesthetic judgment can be learned from observation. Members of a college faculty can demonstrate how critical inquiry can be applied to issues that concern us all. They may be the first individuals students encounter who declare the fallibility of views, the plausibility of varied interpretations, the limits of a field of expertise, and the complexity of the ways language is and can be used. A curriculum must be organized so that the relationship between teacher and student is not exclusively limited to that of expert and novice within a very narrow range of questions, skills, and information. General education curricula offer an opportunity for students to encounter authority defined not as superior knowledge but as greater experience in how to interpret and judge in matters where there may be no reductive definition of right and wrong.

Third, programs of general education generate a common ground among students, whose only link to one another is their status as young adults and as students. One of the singular advantages of teaching the so-called Great Books is that, for generations, readers have used them to illuminate urgent matters of daily life. This is particularly the case for classic works of philosophy and political and social theory. For conversation and socializing among students to develop into serious debate and dialogue, reference points beyond subjective and personal experience on the crucial issues of the day are helpful.

But the task of lifting the level and range of discussion among students cannot be left only to programs of general education. In defining so-called majors or fields of concentration, colleges should put into place routine opportunities for students to present their work in public, not only to fellow students in the same field but to the lay population within the student body. Because courses in the major usually account for most of an undergraduate's academic program, we must build connections between and among disciplines for undergraduates that touch on common themes. We also must enlarge the impact of focused and dedicated undergraduate study in a discipline. Just as music majors perform for the general public, so too should science majors present their work to a general audience, as should majors in, for example, English, history, and foreign languages, where, for example, the teaching and publication of translations are extremely useful. This can be done through lectures, presentations, and publications that involve undergraduates.

Designing a curriculum that can influence the conduct of daily life, not in accordance with a sectarian doctrine but with rigorous and open habits of inquiry, analysis, and interpretation, does not necessarily force the faculty to do battle with the tiresome issues regarding priorities in the choice of content.[6]

To achieve this curriculum, colleges and universities must reconsider the allocation of resources. Incentives to create programs of general education and integrate and connect curricular life and extracurricular life require human and financial capital. The successful reconfiguration of a campus culture may demand more faculty with differing sets of obligations. The character of campus events and their frequency must be reconfigured. Theater, dance, concerts, exhibits, screenings, lectures, debates, and panels need to be regularly scheduled events that students and faculty attend and in which they can participate, not only as spectators. Public events that have an integral connection to the curriculum and the cultural eye beyond the campus should use the spaces on campus and assume a centrality in the academic calendar. Strategies must be found to lend them prestige and status. Within the confines of the campus, the use of old technologies (e.g., radio and television) as well as the Internet can be helpful as well. The placement of some public forums within the dormitory and dining areas, in the midst of student life, also can be beneficial.

Last but not least, an entire campus, including faculty, administrators, and students, should interact with the communities surrounding them in ways that reflect the privileges and resources unique to universities and colleges. These interactions can include educational services for primary- and secondary-school students and for men and women incarcerated in our prisons; programs for teachers in precollege institutions; collaborations with libraries, arts organizations, museums, nongovernmental entities, government services, and private enterprises whose activities intersect with courses of study on the campus. The undergraduate campus should be a destination point for the larger community, a welcome public arena.

The candid fact is that our colleges and universities have never successfully focused on making the life of the mind and the love of learning the centerpiece of campus culture. The continuing expansion of access to higher education, the remote probability that the standards of precollege instruction will rise, the acceleration in intellectual and economic competition in the years ahead, particularly from China,

India, and Eastern Europe, and ideological intolerance and religious fundamentalism all make it imperative that we deliver now on the promises of undergraduate education. For more than half a century the United States has maintained a preeminence in higher education and in science and scholarship, largely as a result of the quality of our graduate and professional schools. If we are to maintain that achievement, we need to radically improve what happens in our undergraduate colleges. Perhaps more vital than preserving the comparative excellence of the American university in the world is the goal of sustaining an active democracy here at home, a public life marked by liberty and dissent. The overdue reform of college and campus life has no more noble purpose.

The leaderships in our colleges, from trustees to faculty, needs to make this effort with more than some routine attempt at eloquence. We must highlight the urgency we face. The elections of 2000 and 2004 may be the strongest evidence we have that American democracy faces a challenge that can be met only by universal undergraduate education of real quality. What these elections suggest is that there is a growing epistemological divide in the country between those who accept the premises of rationality shared by the Enlightenment and the Founding Fathers and those who have put their faith in a religious piety that they presume should govern our daily lives. That use of piety was foreign to the framers and founders of American democracy. It is also fundamentally at odds with the premises of the modern university. It very well may be that a deepening of the connection between learning and life for a young American is a crucial strategy in confronting and overcoming this epistemological divide.

As our Founding Fathers, particularly Thomas Jefferson (despite the damage to his reputation from recent scholarship), realized, neither democracy nor the university is compatible with the sort of theology that has experienced a dramatic revival all over the world and in the United States. The claims of liberty and civic quality presume, as John Locke understood, a capacity for morality and ethics linked directly to the universal possession of language and instrumental reason. The conduct of modern science and inquiry and the fate of the progress of civilization may all hinge, particularly in the United States, on our capacity to persuade future generations of citizens of the rightness of the fundamental epistemological and therefore political claims on which this republic and its institutions of learning were founded. To achieve this goal we need to go beyond the classroom and the narrow framework of our degree requirements during the undergraduate years. There is no time to lose.

Notes

This essay is a reflection based on thirty-five years as a college president between the years 1970 and 2005. The argument I make applies to all institutions with an undergraduate student body in residence, to so-called selective institutions and those that are not. It assumes that the problems of campus life exist throughout the wide spectrum of undergraduate programs. This discussion assumes no elite exceptions. It takes as a premise the notion that a broad range of faculty and students exists in each institution. No limited set of institutions has a monopoly on faculty or students in terms of academic motivation, capacity, and ambition. The observations therefore apply to institutions of varying demographic distributions in terms of size, class, ethnicity, location, religion, and gender.

1. Among such positive, predictable, and benign trends (e.g., increased interest in film studies), one disturbing pattern has attracted wide interest only recently: the steep decline since the 1960s in the proportion of American undergraduates choosing science and mathematics as primary objects of study. Our citizens in the years ahead must possess a high standard of scientific literacy. It is therefore encouraging that many institutions are now trying to respond, despite the poor standards of secondary science education. Indeed, new ways to inspire college students without extensive backgrounds to study and major in science need to be designed.
2. Robert M. Hutchins, *The Higher Learning in America* (New Haven, CT: Yale University Press, 1936).
3. Allan David Bloom, *The Closing of the American Mind: How Education Has Failed Democracy and Impoverished the Souls of Today's Students* (New York: Simon and Schuster, 1987).
4. Students gravitate to like-minded fellow students and those from similar backgrounds. Colleges exploit the residential aspect of college to reinforce their own self-interest. Institutions seek to cultivate a pseudo-Masonic loyalty to the alma mater, exploiting local traditions that do not derive from the academic experience itself. Each institution has its own nearly feudal rituals and, often, organizations such as fraternities, sororities, eating clubs and secret societies. The college calendar reveals consistent efforts to generate a sense of club identification with the institution. Institutions cultivate symbols of membership, including school songs, colors, and rivalries that are often linked to intercollegiate sports.

5. It is crucial to remember that, since the late 1960s, two factors have come to influence the way in which institutions manage the noncurricular aspects of campus life: publicity and legal vulnerability. Campus life has become, unfortunately, a routine subject of undisciplined journalistic scrutiny. And colleges and universities have not remained immune from a broader societal trend toward the use of the law and the courts to redress grievances and complaints. Beyond the issue of institutional liability for matters of physical safety, colleges and universities find themselves sued as the result of events that occur in the lives of students, particularly on campus, that are not connected to the curriculum.
6. In science, many of these issues are less contentious. In the social sciences—the humanities, history, and the arts—the criteria of which issues and materials to teach should be strategic and instrumental. Which have the greatest probability of enlarging the perspectives of students, the skills of analysis, motivation, curiosity, and the will to study and learn? Which materials and issues can most rapidly form a sense of enjoyment and ambition and the will to allocate time to inquiry? Which materials and issues can help diverse individuals within a single generation form criteria of judgment, enjoy learning, inspire confidence and ambition, and embrace excellence? The answers to these questions will remain unstable. Texts and issues will change. Some will resurface. No curriculum, either general or particular, can be permanently effective and normative. Some traditions must be altered since one cannot merely add on the new to the old. Areas of inquiry will experience erosion; in their absence will come novel strategies that too will experience strategic obsolescence. The study of Asia and its languages may push aside the priority once assigned to the study of Europe and its languages. But there is also the possibility of finding ways around some boundaries, as the comparative study of antiquity suggests. Likewise, the study of human rights is now enjoying what may turn out to be a temporary popularity as a beginning point for the study of politics. It may be supplanted in the future by some other construct that raises fundamental issues of social and political organization.

Afterword
What Difference Does a College Make?

Richard H. Hersh

When I was president of private liberal arts colleges, traveling the usual admissions and fund-raising circuits, I often encountered the following paired questions: "What difference do small liberal arts colleges make and are you really worth the thousands of extra dollars?" I earnestly gave affirmative answers to these questions: higher graduation rates, smaller classes, professors who actually taught and advised, greater alumni satisfaction, greater proportion of graduates going on to graduate school, and the inspiring anecdotes about lives transformed. But as salutary as my answers were to my audiences, they rang increasingly hollow to me. The *difference* in education one college or university makes compared to another after admissions selectivity is taken into account is not well documented.

Do *more* good things happen at colleges where students have high SAT scores, or where the graduation rate is over 95 percent? Do students learn more when classes are smaller, faculty salaries higher, and libraries bigger? Is a college or university better because it turns down most applicants? How much does where you go to college really matter?

The media make it sound so simple. To guarantee your children's future, enroll them in the best preschools and follow that with the best of elementary and secondary schools. They must earn good grades in advanced placement classes, participate in tons of extra-curricular activities, get into a prestigious college or university, obtain that degree, and, *Voila!:* money, prestige and the good life are sure to follow.

In truth, however, most Americans follow a very different path to campus and attend colleges and universities most reporters ignore.

And reporters rarely ask the key question that Tom Wolfe asks in his Foreword: Wherever they happen to go, "does anybody have any idea what happens to them in college?"

Surely whether one goes to Harvard and other "elites" must matter. Otherwise, the anxiety-driven college application process would be an exercise in masochism, the *U.S. News & World Report* rankings a sham, and all of the money spent on athletic teams, hotel-like residence halls, wireless campuses, and famous faculty would be a terrible waste.

Harvard, Yale, Stanford, Amherst: those names open doors in the real world because, until now, no one has been able to measure with any accuracy what students actually learn during their four years on a campus. No one has been able to answer Tom Wolfe's important question. But that is changing.

In the name of "accountability" the public has been assessing institutions once assumed on faith to be satisfactory. We have learned that hospitals and doctors with equivalent facilities and prestigious reputations vary widely in their success rates. We know that the school a child attends makes a difference and therefore we demand that schools Leave No Child Behind. Grade inflation, widespread cheating, and complaints about college students being unable to read or write adequately at graduation have garnered much attention. The accountability spotlight now shines on higher education. Are its sharply rising costs worth the value received?

The essayists in this volume properly question the current quality of American undergraduate education, adding their voices to those calling for greater transparency and candor. The most direct way to assess higher education quality is to measure student learning and not rely on student opinion surveys or "reputation" rankings by academic leaders. Tests and papers, of course, are used in individual courses, but to date we have no measures of the cumulative result of an undergraduate education.

The academy has resisted this assessment challenge claiming it is impossible to measure the important learning that happens in college and/or to do so is time consuming and expensive. Campuses and others use selectivity in admissions and graduation rates as surrogate measures of quality. Yet these merely reflect a "diamonds in, diamonds out, garbage in, garbage out" perspective on quality. Ideally, excellence and quality should be determined by the degree to which an institution develops the abilities of its students. It's what economists call "value added." Several colleagues[1] and I have spent the last few years developing a way to determine the "value-added" of a college education—a way of measuring what students learn over the entirety of their undergraduate programs. So too have other researchers.[2]

"Value-added" measures the contribution to students' capabilities and knowledge as a consequence of attending a particular college or university. Measuring such added value requires pre-testing—assessing what students know and can do as they begin college—and post-testing—assessing them again during the college years and after they have had the full benefit of their college education. Value-added is the difference a college makes in their education. What we have learned with data from campuses across the nation is that different institutions create greater or lesser value-added, even if the campuses look equivalent in all other respects. *What college or university one attends does make a difference in what and how a student learns!* As it turns out, one may garner greater value-added in places other than Harvard!

Higher education at its best is, as they say, "priceless," but the research suggests that relatively few students graduate with more than degrees in mediocrity. But if colleges and universities get serious about adding greater value to the experience of their students, we could be on the verge of a new day. How might that worthy goal be achieved?

Government cannot reform higher education; legislators will demand blunt measures like graduation rates, which will only lead to a weakening of requirements and grade inflation. I believe the public must assert pressure on academia by asking the question, "What difference are you making?" And now that we have begun to develop sophisticated learning measures there is a way for each campus to answer the question.

Left alone, higher education has never demonstrated an ability or willingness to be transparent with regard to what students are learning and so, in a very real sense, this book, *Declining by Degrees*, is our individual and collective lament over the gulf that now exists between the promise of American undergraduate education, and the reality.

For each of us, higher education should seek and demand excellence. It should inspire. It should liberate the imaginations and intellectual energies of those enrolled. That some campuses add value to a significant degree is the good news, evidence that it can happen on your campus, or on your child's campus. We should be satisfied with nothing less.

Notes

1. Roger Benjamin, President, Council for the Aid to Education; Stephen Klein, Senior Research Scientist, RAND Corporation; Richard Shavelson, Professor of Education, Stanford University.
2. Charles Blaich and his colleagues have undertaken the same task at the Center of Inquiry in the Liberal Arts at Wabash College.

Afterword

John Merrow

Of all the students I met during nearly two years of working on our PBS documentary and this book, I continue to be intrigued by a sophomore named Nate. After proudly proclaiming that he was maintaining a 3.4 GPA despite studying less than an hour a night, he wondered aloud, "It's not supposed to be this easy, is it? Shouldn't college be challenging?"

He described his "boring" classes, including an English class he described as "a brain dump." But we found it stimulating. The teacher had assigned students to write parodies of *The Road Not Taken*, knowing that, to do the assignment well, they would have to read and understand Frost's poem. She was meeting students at their level . . . and trying to push them to go beyond it.

She was trying to move them out of their "intellectual comfort zone" and lead them in new directions.

Tough job, because Nate (and undoubtedly most of his classmates) had succeeded in high school by figuring out what was going to be on his tests. That approach also got him into college and was now earning him a solid B average. Ask him the purpose of college, and he would probably say something about "getting a good job."

I spent my first 25 years as a reporter immersed in the world of K–12 schools, and, in the end, I could not escape my past. That is, I ended up seeing higher education's many problems through the lens of K–12 schooling. To improve the quality of learning on *college* campuses, I believe K–12 must be radically changed. I have also become convinced that higher education may be its own worst enemy, but more about that later.

American high schools are, for the most part, rigidly authoritarian institutions that are also so large that it's difficult for students to be known by name. Seventy percent of U.S. students attend high schools with enrollments of more than 900, while hundreds of high schools have enrollments in excess of 2,500 students. Bells ring every forty-six or fifty-two minutes throughout the day. Subject matter is a hodge-podge of factoids, and teachers are told what to cover, when to cover it, and how much time to devote to it. One period for the Magna Carta, one period for the Slave Trade, one period for penicillin and the polio vaccine. Almost inevitably, kids like Nate only want to know if this information will be on the final exam.

And who can blame them? Why would they want to know anything else? After all, their content-driven high school structure encourages students to "get the right answer," not to think about how they know what they know, or how answers are arrived at. It's a perverse reward structure that discourages curiosity, and may even penalize those who display it.

Is it any wonder that, in some communities, one out of three eighth graders fails to finish high school? Moreover, ACT reported in late 2004 that only 23 percent of high school graduates are academically prepared to do college work.

What sort of preparation is high school for the nearly total freedom that awaits college freshmen? Young people like Nate must get used to exploration, to asking questions and searching for answers, in science and math of course—but also in every other class. It's simply too much to expect this to suddenly and miraculously happen when students arrive on campus. This means that it never happens for most kids, but only for the lucky few who have skilled teachers and are in school environments that encourage them to develop.

Smaller, more personal high schools that encourage inquiry are a step in the right direction, but America's colleges and universities also need to recognize that the post–high school education of our young is no longer a national priority. It has not been for about twenty years.

Higher education used to be a social good, and the nation willingly invested in it. We believed that communities, states, and the entire nation benefited when Johnny and Mary went to college. They were likely to become productive, contributing citizens, strengthening our national fabric. Before Ronald Reagan became president, the bulk of student aid was in the form of scholarships and grants. During his two terms, which I remember as years of national selfishness, the balance shifted, and education came to be seen as a personal good, just another item one might purchase: "Which do I want more, that BMW or a college degree?"

When we learned that college graduates made more money than high school graduates, as much as a million dollars more over their working lives, the mantra became, "If you want an education, then you pay for it." Unfortunately, higher education swallowed that line—hook and sinker included. "Education Pays" proclaim billboards around the state of Kentucky, encouraging kids to go to college to nail down that good job. During the past two years, I have met hundreds of kids who are going to college because they've been told that they need a diploma to get a good job. They arrive on campus determined to major in "business," and many remain impervious to the efforts of their professors to shake them out of their "comfort zone."

It's all too easy for many students to settle into a pattern of behavior that looks like an unspoken "non-aggression treaty" in which professors don't ask much of students (so they can do their research and maybe receive tenure) and most students don't expect much from their professors (as long as they get A's and B's).

The good news is that many faculty members work with energy and imagination to move their students beyond that simplistic "diploma = $$" formula. Even more heartening is the fact that many students intuitively know that they're being shortchanged.

I admire students who squeeze as much as they can from the experience, and I salute the teachers who dedicate their energies to seeing that students succeed. However, too much is left to chance, and too many lives are blighted by our national indifference to what is *actually* happening on our campuses during the years between admission and graduation.

About the Contributors

Leon Botstein has been president of Bard College since 1975, where he is the Leon Levy Professor in the Arts and Humanities. He is also the music director of the American Symphony Orchestra and the Jerusalem Symphony Orchestra, the orchestra of the Israel Broadcast Authority. President Botstein's writings about education have appeared in the *New York Times*, the *New York Times Magazine*, *Harper's Magazine*, and the *Chronicle of Higher Education*, among other publications. He is the author of *Jefferson's Children: Education and the Promise of American Culture.*

Frank Deford, the author of fifteen books, is a member of the Sportswriters and Sportscasters Hall of Fame. He has won a National Magazine Award for his work at *Sports Illustrated* and both an Emmy and George Foster Peabody Award for his work in television journalism. He is a weekly commentator for *Morning Edition* on National Public Radio.

James Fallows is national correspondent for the *Atlantic Monthly* and the author of numerous books, including *Breaking the News* and *National Defense*. He has won the American Book Award for nonfiction and the National Magazine Award for public service. He has written for the *Atlantic* and other magazines about various aspects of higher education, including an annual survey of trends in college admissions.

Richard Fry is a senior research associate at the Pew Hispanic Center. Previously he was a senior economist at the Educational Testing Service, where he focused on trends in U.S. college enrollment. His research at the U.S. Department of Labor focused on immigrants.

Howard Gardner is Hobbs Professor of Cognition and Education at the Harvard Graduate School of Education. He is author, more recently, of *Changing Minds: The Art and Science of Changing Our Own and Other People's Minds* and coauthor with Mihaly Csikszentmihalyi and William Damon of *Good Work: When Excellence and Ethics Meet.*

Vartan Gregorian is former president of Brown University and the New York Public Library and current president of Carnegie Corporation of New York. The author of *The Road to Home*, Dr. Gregorian received the Presidential Medal of Freedom, the highest honor given to civilians, in 2004.

DAVID L. KIRP is professor of public policy at the University of California at Berkeley. His most recent book, *Shakespeare, Einstein, and the Bottom Line: The Marketing of Higher Education*, traces the rise to dominance of the marketplace ethic by telling campus tales whose significance reaches far beyond their specifics.

JULIE JOHNSON KIDD has been the president of the Christian A. Johnson Endeavor Foundation for twenty-five years. She is the founding chair of the European College of Liberal Arts in Berlin and former member of the board of trustees of Middlebury College, Hamilton College, the Brearley School, and Teachers College, Columbia University.

ARTHUR LEVINE is professor and president of Teachers College, Columbia University. A prolific writer, he was previously president of Bradford College, director of the Harvard University Institute on Educational Management, and senior fellow at the Carnegie Foundation for the Advancement of Teaching.

GENE I. MAEROFF is a senior fellow at the Hechinger Institute on Education and the Media at Teachers College, Columbia University, where he was founding director. His most recent book is *A Classroom of One: How Online Learning Is Changing Our Schools and Colleges*. Earlier in his career, he was national education correspondent for the *New York Times* and, later, a senior fellow at the Carnegie Foundation for the Advancement of Teaching.

JAY MATHEWS is an education reporter and columnist for the *Washington Post*. His "Challenge Index" high school rankings appear in *Newsweek*. He has written several books, including his new college admissions guide, *Harvard Schmarvard*, which explains why famous schools are not as good as people think they are.

CAROL GEARY SCHNEIDER has been president, since 1998, of the Association of American Colleges and Universities, the leading national association devoted to advancing and strengthening undergraduate liberal education. There she has initiated several major projects, including *Greater Expectations: The Commitment to Quality as a Nation Goes to College* and *American Commitments: Diversity, Democracy and Liberal Learning*.

MURRAY SPERBER is a professor emeritus of English and American studies at Indiana University at Bloomington. He is the author of four books about college life and college sports, including *Beer & Circus: How Big-Time College Sports Is Crippling Undergraduate Education.*

ROBERTO SURO is director of the Pew Hispanic Center, a nonpartisan research institute in Washington, D.C. For nearly thirty years he worked as a journalist for the *Washington Post*, the *New York Times*, and other publications. He is the author of numerous books, articles, and papers on the Hispanic population in the United States, including *Strangers Among Us: Latino Lives in a Changing America.*

DEBORAH WADSWORTH was president of Public Agenda until her retirement in 2003. As an interpreter of public opinion research for the past eighteen years, with a particular interest in education, she currently serves on the boards of the Education Development Center, the National Center for Public Policy and Higher Education, and as chairman of the Board of Trustees of Bennington College.

HEATHER D. WATHINGTON is assistant professor in the department of leadership, foundations, and policy at the University of Virginia. She previously served as the director of programs in the office of diversity, equity, and global initiatives at the Association of American Colleges and Universities.

TOM WOLFE (Washington and Lee B.A., Yale Ph.D. in American Studies) is the author of *I am Charlotte Simmons* (2004), a novel about contemporary undergraduate life, as well as a dozen other books, among them such contemporary classics as *The Electric Kool-Aid Acid Test, The Right Stuff, The Bonfire of the Vanities,* and *A Man in Full.*

Index